People, Machines, and Politics

of the

Cyber Age Creation

Rocco Leonard Martino, Ph.D.

BLUENOSE PRESS
WWW.BLUENOSEPRESS.COM

Please visit: www.roccoleonardmartino.com

Published by:

BlueNose Press, Inc.
www.bluenosepress.com
Printed in the United States of America
Published June 2011

Portrait by Bachrach
Cover by Ron Gamble
Cover Photograph courtesy of John William Mauchly, Jr.

Novels by Dr. Rocco Leonard Martino

9-11-11: The Tenth Anniversary Attack

The Plot to Cancel Christmas

Nonfiction Books by Dr. Rocco Leonard Martino

Applied Operational Planning

Allocating and Scheduling Resources

Computer-R-Age with Webster V. Allen

Critical Path Networks

Decision Patterns

Decision Tables with Staff of MDI

Dynamic Costing

Finding the Critical Path

Heat Transfer in Slip Flow

IMPACT 70s with John Gentile

Information Management

Integrated Manufacturing Systems

Management Information Systems

MIS Methodology

Personnel Management Systems

Project Management

Resources Management

UNIVAC Operations Manual

Reviews of *The Plot to Cancel Christmas*

"Rocky Martino is like Rocky Balboa. His book is a punch in the heart and a hug at the same time. So hold on – don't just read it – pray it!"
   -Jim Murray, Co-Founder, Ronald MacDonald House

"A timeless tale that speaks volumes...a modern Christmas Carol."
   -Joe Looby, Voice Actor

"A book that gives you pause – could this really happen? An engaging story of what greed can lead you to do."
   -Patricia Parisano, Legal Secretary

"Rocky gives us a snapshot of how powerful individuals, organizations and institutions can use politicians as pawns and puppets in an attempt to enrich themselves. We are reminded that the 'Greed is Good' philosophy needs our vigilance in a world that should care for the needs and rights of the individual. He offers hope in a distressed world."
   -Jim Fitzsimmons, President, Malvern Retreat

"Reading this book is an experience in theater. Martino limns his two-dimensional characters with the skill of an artisan bringing them to the third dimension with extraordinary color. They literally dance from the page to the stage."
   -Sister Marianne Postiglione, RSM, ITEST

"It's delightful – a modern day Dickensesque Christmas Carol!"
   -Dr. Joseph Holland, President, Pax Romana

"This book is a gift that will put your life in perspective."
   -Tim Flanagan, Founder and Chair, CLI

"A Classic Battle between might & right!"
   -Jim White, CEO, JJ White, Inc.

"Martino's story reveals the human spirit and all of its wonderful contradictions through one man's campaign to cancel Christmas. A miser who believes happiness is only found in money just might find true happiness accidentally in his quest for riches & power."
   -Joseph J. McLaughlin, Jr., President, Haverford Trust

Reviews of *9-11-11: The Tenth Anniversary Attack*

"Drawing on his vast expertise in national security, defense and the internet, Rocco Martino has done it again. 9/11/11 is a fascinating read that is a product of our time depicting the dangerous world in which we live. I foresee a future big screen Harrison Ford blockbuster!"
   -Rear Admiral Thomas Lynch, United States Navy (Retired)

"Dr Martino lays out a credible Al Qaeda sponsored plot to cripple the "American Satan" on the anniversary of 9/11... The theme of the book is apparently that cyber warfare particularly focused on finances is the way we can successfully combat terrorism."
   -Clifford Wilson, Former Member New York Assembly

"Timely plot, well-developed characters...and a truly engrossing explication of the complexities of international money laundering and the fearsome dangers facing western civilization from fanatics wielding weapons of mass destruction."
   - Dr. Rosalie Pedalino Porter, Author of "American Immigrant: My Life in Three Languages"

"The story accurately illustrates the complex and abstract world of cyber security and constant vigilance needed for tracking terrorist plots, including their planning, correspondence and financial movements."
   - Dr. James F. Peters, NASA Engineer and Vice President of Technology for Quasar Data Center.

"The man behind this political thriller is extremely knowledgeable about the world of computers. Dr. Martino wrote the fictional story to stress the need for America to stay vigilant and fight terrorism with Cyber Warfare."
   -Jean-Bernard Hyppolite, Chestnut Hill Local

DEDICATION

This book is dedicated to three great friends - pioneers and creators of the Cyber Age we are now living through. They are:

John William Mauchly, the guiding genius who conceived of the programmable general purpose electronic machine that could be used for much more than mere calculation, and who energized the team to make it happen;

his partner John Presper Eckert, the engineering genius, undoubtedly the Engineer of the Century, who made their joint dream a reality through brilliant innovation and invention;

and Kathleen (Kay) McNulty Mauchly Antonelli, John's wife in his lifetime, and one of the women behind ENIAC who gave birth to the software industry.

I am particularly and personally indebted to Kay and John Mauchly who engineered my meeting Barbara D'Iorio, who is now Barbara Martino and has been for almost fifty years.

ACKOWLEDGEMENTS

I did not write this book in a vacuum. It is a work of many people. I think that a usual statement that people say is the good points belong to them, the errors are mine.

I have lived my professional career with Giant Brains – Human and Electronic. This book is about both types of those giants. I worked with them, came to know them, fought with them, and finally, came to mutual acceptance.

I have been writing this book "all my life" – with my thoughts, words, and actions. One of the most difficult things for any of us is to objectively measure the effect of what we do and say on those around us, and those who will follow us. So I have tried hard to be fair in describing and evaluating the many experiences and personalities detailed here.

I have had a satisfying career, and in that I was most fortunate. My success, if any, must await the judgment of others. I believe I was in the right place at the right time. The only credit due me is that I saw the door in front of me and had the courage to open it and walk through. The work ethic and my own sense of fairness and moral code come from my heritage and my religious beliefs. The main source was my parents – a loving mother who died prematurely and a father who was undoubtedly the smartest and nicest man I ever knew or ever will know. I thank God for my parents, and especially for the long years of association with my father and his wise counsel.

The writing path to this book has been decades in the making. I started composing some of my reminiscences in 1981. I wrote up some drafts, and then put the work away until 1990, when I started again. During this time, I gave interviews and appeared on various radio and TV programs, which sparked the notion of writing the history of the computer. However, I kept finding my own life in the way. So many of the events and developments I wanted to write about were things I had been involved in. One editor captured it when he asked if I was writing a history of the computer or an autobiography.

In 2004, I finally decided to start my "personalized history project" in detail. To a large extent, this was triggered by my 75th birthday that year. With that milestone, I spent more and more time recalling the past, and as I did, I became angry at the injustice done to a great friend and mentor, John William Mauchly, the co-creator of the electronic computer. I dug very deeply into the history of the digital computer, searching books, archives, and my own memory regarding my long association with him. I renewed my acquaintance with his widow Kathleen, and in 2005, even completed a series of videotaped sessions with her prior to her death in April of 2006.

DR. ROCCO LEONARD MARTINO

As the book took form, I received the help of many people, most especially Joe Looby, who combed the archives at the University of Pennsylvania; Stanley Green, who was one of the patent attorneys at Mauchly's "patent trial of the century" in 1972; my sons Peter and Joseph, for their recollections on the more recent XRT and CyberFone years; John Mulqueen, who helped catalog many of the documents that went into writing this book; Amanda Tarby, who organized the citations and bibliography; and Patricia Popelak, who pulled it all together, organized the book's structure, and finalized the citations and bibliography.

I am also indebted to Bill Mauchly for writing the Foreword to this book and providing a personal perspective of his father; Gini Mauchly Calcerano for tirelessly proofreading the manuscript; and to all the members of ENIACtion, who have come together to create a viral means- via the construction of the ENIAC site (http://www.the-eniac.com), posting blogs, and other forms of social networks- of discussing all things related to the ENIAC. Thanks are due also to the University of Pennsylvania for the use of their archives.

Further, without Joe Looby, Ed Moser, and John Farina, this text may not have been available to the reader. While I pride myself on my ability to write, it was Joe who challenged my ideas, Ed who organized, edited, and word-smithed parts of the text, and John who kept prodding me. With their help, we hopefully found the right word to meet the nuances needed. Their help was invaluable too in filling in research aspects concerning many of my friends and coworkers mentioned in this text.

And, of course, without my wife Barbara's continual encouragement, this work might never have been completed. She and I lived through most of this, often laughing at ourselves and with others as we talked about being the "first computer-matched couple". Barbara is my wife of 49 years now because we were introduced by John and Kathleen Mauchly. Barbara had been a classmate of John's oldest daughter, Sidney. Hence, we have often spoken of being the first computer couple - picked not by a computer or by an Internet dating service, but rather by the inventor of the Computer Age.

TABLE OF CONTENTS

FOREWORD

My father, Dr. John W. Mauchly, with his partner J. Presper Eckert, invented ENIAC. It was the first electronic computer. There, I said it, and it is the truth. They not only designed *that* computer but a few more, an EDVAC and a BINAC and a UNIVAC, and in them developed the blueprint for all computers today. But you would be amazed to learn, if you don't know, how controversial my father's role is. He has been accused of fraud and stealing secret ideas; he was blacklisted from his own company and was even suspected of murder. After his death in 1980, books have been published painting him as an unscrupulous villain who sponged off the intellect around him. And yet at the same time the computer history community acknowledges that he is the one who started the computer revolution, and he is the one who has been robbed of the credit he deserves. What is going on here? What went on 60 years ago that still causes so much confusion, disagreement, and animosity?

This is a book concerning history, but it is not a history book. Dr. Rocco Martino is both an acute observer and a player in the story of the computer revolution. At the heart of the matter, in Chapter 7 he presents a bold new analysis of the ENIAC patent trial, the travesty of justice that started the bizarre controversy over my father. Dr. Martino knew him well and they founded a company together. He has given us a rare inside view of Mauchly, and other pioneers of the digital revolution, and vividly recounts their personalities as well as their accomplishments. Those accounts are woven into a bigger picture of the entire span of computer evolution, from the first and only computer to a world with too many billions of computers to be counted. Finally, the history is put in the context of today's world. The volume is further infused with Dr. Martino's views and convictions on the need for innovation in the global marketplace.

My mother, Kathleen McNulty Mauchly, had also been in computers; she was one of the ENIAC programmers. That in itself is a fascinating story that I will not attempt here. My father and mother were terrific parents, loved by all their children. But we weren't the only ones who thought they were great. There were seven of us kids, and we each seemed to have seven friends who thought our house was the best place to be because our parents made them feel welcome and so many interesting things were going on. And then there were the various computer professionals or luminaries that would come to visit. We would all gather around a big dinner table every night and the conversation could easily go from Abacus to Zeus in one evening. Mom and Dad were generous with their gifts, and people felt that.

One evening Rocco Martino came to dinner. He had been a friend of Dad's from their first meeting at Sperry Rand a few years earlier, in the 1950's. We all liked him immediately; he was friendly and animated and enjoyed talking to us kids. Dad had a great rapport with him. We all called him Rocky.

Those were exciting times for Dad; he and Rocky were starting a new venture to use computer software to do project scheduling. Dad was breaking away from Remington Rand, who didn't share his view that computer companies needed to be deeply involved in software as well as hardware.

So finally he was his own boss again. More importantly to him, I think, was that he had his own computer. The new company bought an IBM 1620 computer (yes, IBM had been his competitor until now, but already they were pulling ahead of Sperry Rand). The company used the computer by day, but Dad used it at night. It was his first of many "personal" computers. Sometimes he would bring my sisters and me to the office in the evening. We got to be very comfortable around computers and learned to use the key punch to enter data onto punch cards. I remember listening in as Dad was trying to teach assembly language to my older sister. The best part was playing Blackjack against the IBM mainframe. It was 1960.

Rocky co-founded the new company and coined the name: Mauchly Associates. He was the Executive Vice President and also in charge of the Canadian operations. Though I would like to say that they were friends for life, that was not the case. They worked together for a few years but there was a falling out over business issues. Rocky went his own way, which turned out to be a very successful way, much more so than Dad's. Rocky started a new company, called XRT, just as digital money transfer was starting to explode. But throughout his illustrious career in computer security and digital banking, Rocky kept his admiration for the man who not only had given him his start, but had really given the entire computer industry its start. And he watched with concern as the rather strange results of a patent trial triggered a series of attacks on John Mauchly's reputation.

In 1971 Honeywell sued Sperry Rand claiming that the patent on the ENIAC was invalid. The verdict shocked many people. In short, the trial said that Mauchly took the idea for the electronic computer from a John Atanasoff. This was clearly false to those who understood the technology, but it seemed that that judge did not. In this book Dr. Rocco Martino gives a detailed rebuttal to the verdict. He shows in several different ways that the trial was a travesty. He shows how Sperry's unprepared and overly confident defense team lost a case they could easily have won. It is important that this argument be made, for history is being slowly twisted by those who take the judge's statements at face value.

The trial's outcome was a big blow to my father. Even though many patents come and go, and patents are rarely important in the real history of technology, this one had an extra sting. None of it was economic; my father had no monetary gain or loss from the outcome—the patent belonged to a corporation. But it started a legend, really: the legend of Atanasoff and Mauchly. Judge Larson ruled that Atanasoff was the true inventor of the automatic digital computer.

The city of Ames, Iowa, where Atanasoff had made the machine, was pleasantly surprised to find that something famous had been invented there. They commissioned a book about Atanasoff, newly crowned father of the computer. The author, Clark Mollenhoff, decided to turn it into a good guy–bad guy story, and Mauchly was the bad guy. Even though the trial judge said he found no evidence of wrongful intent, Mollenhoff found lots of it. He had at his disposal the trial transcript with hours of testimony from all the parties. The book told the tale of the poor forgotten Atanasoff, brilliant and yet somehow naive, unjustly deprived of glory by the untalented but devious thief Mauchly. The author seemed to think that the story was more heroic if Mauchly was cast as an antagonist. It was filled with quotations taken out of context, surrounded by conjecture, used to "prove" downright lies about Mauchly. The book was soundly criticized by academics in computer history, but it was out there, and people read it, and some believed it.

Mollenhoff's book was followed by another, by Alice and Arthur Burks. Arthur Burks, as Mauchly told in a deposition for the trial, had wanted to get his name on the ENIAC patent. He had threatened revenge, and now he seemed to be exacting it. Their book tries to show how ideas in ENIAC came from Atanasoff. It is a textbook example of deceit by technical obfuscation. Alice Burks followed with a second book peppered with select phrases of testimony from the trial, colored in such a way as to "prove" Mauchly's guilt and deliberate bad intentions. Most recently, Jane Smiley released a biography of Atanasoff that retells Mollenhoff's distorted story, morphing the real people she writes about into fictionalized caricatures.

All of these books take the same slant in depicting Mauchly as a villain. This lingering problem pained John Mauchly until his death. It saddened us to see Dad get battered by the ugly repercussions of the patent case. He was never one to brag, and I rarely heard him talk about his many accomplishments. So it was very difficult for him to have some people claim he stole his way through life. People would wonder, "Why didn't you appeal the case?"—but it was not his case to appeal. It was between two corporations. He was a casualty.

Dad passed away in 1980 at 72. My mother took up the cause of defending his name and setting the record straight. She learned public speaking and wrote an article for the *Annals of the History of Computing.* All my life, really, I have been hearing the history and the stories that revolve around the early development of computers, firsthand. It is unjust that Dad had to suffer the slings and arrows that were aimed at him.

Today I often find myself needing to untangle the mass of misinformation that has been heaped on my father and the ENIAC. When I get on my soapbox, I find it helpful to separate out three ideas that are usually lumped together.

Who invented the computer? For a meaningful answer, one must define "computer." The term computer can be very general and has been applied to many machines and even people. The usual approach is to narrow the field down with features that are closer to a modern computer. First programmable computer? (Babbage? Zuse?) First electronic computer (Atanasoff? Colossus?) First programmable AND electronic (ENIAC). Today the popular meaning of computer is "a general-purpose electronic machine that runs programs and manipulates digital data". With such a definition, none of those older machines qualify. ENIAC was the first.

Did John Mauchly steal ideas from Atanasoff? A great many words have been spent showing that he easily could have; he had the opportunity. But opportunity is not evidence of theft. What is "the idea" that was stolen? I've read all the books and I still can't find one idea or component unique to the ABC that was used in ENIAC. The two machines are as different as a bicycle and a jet plane.

Was the ENIAC patent invalid? Probably, in my opinion; it was filed too late, and then amended much later. These were procedural mistakes that are now hard to argue, and they were reasons why Sperry did not bother to appeal the case. But are the actual claims of the ENIAC patent novel compared to prior art? Definitely.

In this book, Dr. Martino presents a new point, a fourth point that has never been raised and is crucial to understanding the trial. Was the judge acting according to the legal

DR. ROCCO LEONARD MARTINO

precedents that have been set for patents and intellectual property?   He carefully deconstructs the trial using extensive references to settled rulings. It becomes crystal clear that the judge's decision was not based on patent law.

There are so many, too many ways to describe how profoundly the computer revolution has changed the world. Do we care who really made it happen, or how they did it, or how those ideas grew and evolved and propelled us into tomorrow? Dr. Martino makes a strong case for the importance of innovation. He and I are agreed. Creativity cannot be mandated; invention does not happen on a schedule. An idea is just the smallest seed. It must find a place to grow; it must have an environment that supports it. It needs the "99% perspiration," the work to turn it into reality. It needs special people, people that are actually on the front lines, the first ones to face the really difficult problems, the innovators. As the saying goes, you can tell the pioneers by the arrows in their backs. At least that held true for John Mauchly.

It gives me great pleasure to introduce this important work. Dr. Martino has condensed a lifetime of adventure in technology to bring new insight and a promising outlook for our rapidly changing cyber world.

John William Mauchly, Jr.
Berwyn PA

PREFACE

The future is written in the present and the past.

People, Machines, and Politics of the Cyber Age Creation relates how the general purpose digital computer was invented and how it changed the world. I am fortunate to have lived through this. I saw how the work and inspiration of many transformed the computer, the first of which was a behemoth that filled a large room, into the handheld device that has changed the world; how we went from a handful of machines in the 1940s to billions today; and how this has come to be applied to practically every area of life.

The genesis of the computer is an important lesson for all of us. The great Harvard historian George Santayana[1] posited that those who ignore history are bound to relive it; one could also say that those who ignore the forces that forged the past will be unable to capture the future-or, if you do not know where you are going, it does not matter how you get there. From the lessons of the past come the trend lines. The lessons of what worked or didn't work and projections into the future are vital.

The computer is father to much, especially modern communications and electronic visualization and imaging. These three form a synergistic Cyber Triangle which has intensified the impact and the rate of acceptance over what they would have been had each acted separately. The result is the world we see changing rapidly all around us.

Its birth took eons as human beings wondered about their world and how to control it. While food, shelter, and protection from nature and predators were the first priority, innate curiosity and inventiveness led to great discoveries and developments. Making fire, the wheel, and now the computer are the results of this thirst for knowledge and control. It took centuries to develop the concept of a computer- or calculating machine. That general idea finally evolved into the general purpose electronic digital computer-computer for short- as we know it today.

There is much controversy over who invented the computer.

A series of books have appeared, prevailing even until this day, extolling the merits of various claimed inventors, painting others as plagiarists. One such example is the recent publication of the book *The Man Who Invented the Computer: The Biography of John Atanasoff, Digital Pioneer* by Jane Smiley[2], which propagates the opinion that John Atanasoff was the inventor of the computer.

Smiley's book has had mixed reviews. There are those who praise it without research or knowledge of the facts, accepting what is presented in the book as absolute truth. There are those with full knowledge of what really happened to dispute what is presented in the book as biased or fictional opinion.

In my opinion, backed by personal knowledge and extensive research, no single individual or group solely invented the computer. This was something that went on for centuries leading to a convergence in the 1930s and the 1940s with the work of numerous individuals. All of this culminated and came together in the first truly general purpose electronic computer- the ENIAC. Dr. John Mauchly[3] and John Presper Eckert[4] may not have invented the computer per se, but they did invent the Cyber Age which is what we have today. The root word "Cyber" is of Greek origin, coming from the word "Gubernetes", the helmsman, governor, or control. Hence the term "CyberNetics" - the science of control, especially of the mind. "Netics" is a suffix for "science of" and "GU" in Greek equals "CY". Hence, the "Cyber" root really is for helmsman or controller. As such, the Cyber Age extends beyond what has been termed as the Information Age, due to the control factor. The control enables the ability to provide information while obtaining information in the time frame to make its use possible and meaningful. That was Mauchly's dream. Eckert provided the tools to make the dream possible. The result was the creation of the Cyber Age.

Dr. John Atanasoff[5], Dr. Alan Turing[6], and also Dr. John Mauchly did create a work in the 1930s, but that was really an electronic extension of the work of Babbage in the early 19th century.

Turing, Atanasoff, and Mauchly in the early days were concerned with calculating. When Mauchly and Eckert teamed up, they were concerned with solving problems and not just with computation (although computation and logic were an integral part of the problem solution). For example, some of the earliest uses of UNIVAC were for insurance records stock market trends, the Bible Concordant, election returns and projections, and dating.

As this book will show, the ENIAC was the father of the computer as we know it today. The ENIAC worked productively for ten years after its unveiling in 1946.

The public birth date of ENIAC was February 14, 1946. In reality it was February 15th even though the press release was dated February 14th. ENIAC began operations that day in a ground floor laboratory at the Moore School of Electrical Engineering (now the School of Engineering and Applied Sciences) at the University of Pennsylvania in Philadelphia.

Since then, that computer has spawned a new era. The Industrial Revolution as the driving force for economic power and wealth generation was replaced by the Cyber Age, where products of and for the mind dominate the economy. The Cyber Triangle of computers (digesting data into instant information), immediate global communication, and multimedia visualization techniques already provide instant connection with anyone, anywhere, at any time. Science, entertainment, information, work, and messages are provided instantly on demand or pushed to anyone who has Internet access (often wireless) or a cell phone. The Global Village, as conceived by Marshall McLuhan[7] in the 1960s, has progressed to the Flat World where distance, language, and national industrial base are no longer major barriers to progress, affluence, and power for any nation with a national communications infrastructure that links individuals, businesses, and institutions to the Internet. While armed conflict is still a factor in global politics, by and large the power struggles of the future will be heavily economic in nature.

The nature of work itself has changed significantly. In the Flat World of the Cyber Age, work comes to us no matter where we are, or where the work originates; a major shift from the Industrial Age, when work was centralized and workers of necessity were concentrated in factories and workplaces. Indeed, the factories of this era are now heavily automated, with robots performing many skilled tasks, often better, and certainly faster, than humans. Hence knowledge-based skills that facilitate mental agility in navigating changed conditions are more important than the narrowly focused skills for competently mastering repetitive tasks, as the economy moves more to a person-centered capability rather than masses of workers on production lines with limited skills. While teamwork and cooperative effort is certainly needed, this can often be accomplished through modern technology, with computer literate workers in full communication operating in diverse locations.

Primarily, this book is the history of how it all happened and why. It concerns the People, the Machines, and the Politics of the seminal events that created the Cyber Age. This book describes the dreams, the passion, and the commitment of the early pioneers of the computer and creators of the Information Age. This story is important as a stepping stone to the future. The world was prepared from the start for this kind of environment and has thrived in it. This book tells the story of how a few pioneers transformed every aspect of our daily lives, and impacted the future forever, offering lessons of broad applicability.

The economic, social, and political paradigms that served the industrial order well enough in the past are no longer sufficient in the global economy. The excitement and the risk will be that of inventing new technologies to meet the needs that are being created. America has done this before; it is now time to do it again. I hope my experiences, lessons, and relationships will help those who will take up the challenge. This book tells the story of how we got here to a Cyber Age through the tales of many of those who created the engines of progress and ends with a crystal ball look at the future.

Like writing a book, innovation and invention draws on many sources. The inventor of the computer is an ancillary question handled by many other books. This book is unique because it handles the creation of the Cyber Age- the people who made it a reality; the machines which were created, developed, and witnessed the test of time; and the politics which seriously impeded progress, present in the corporate, university, government, and even personal levels as some individuals sought to gain fame, fortune, or both. Thus, this book is about the creation of the Cyber Age and not just the computer.

Rocco Leonard Martino
Villanova, Pennsylvania

People, Machines, and Politics
of the Cyber Age Creation

INTRODUCTORY

THE HISTORICAL PERSPECTIVE OF THE COMPUTER

Nature abhors a vacuum. So does human progress, which comes as a result of harnessing the winds of fortune that sweep across timelines. The end of the Second World War was a unique time in history. The destruction of that mighty war followed on the heels of a devastating world depression through the decade before. The world in 1945 had almost two decades of growth to catch up on. In the Unites States, an energized and organized military force that had been geared to creating weapons to speed up victory was ready to re-enter the civilian ranks.

With them came a re-born "can-do" attitude that I believe is a key component of the American culture of innovation and invention that has its roots in the invention of America itself. It was almost an awakening to meet new challenges and opportunities. The computer was born at this time, and the economic and human forces of the day served as catalysts in setting the stage for the Information Age that followed.

"The old order changeth, yielding place to new." – Alfred Lord Tennyson[8]

Since the end of the Second World War, global economic growth and income realignment has eclipsed by a wide margin to that of any comparable period of history. Moreover, the pace of growth and dispersion of the benefits is accelerating. This growth has been paced in parallel by increased linkages for trade and cultural exchanges. The catalyst for this prosperity has been the computer and its "children" – communications and visualization techniques. Recently, Alan Greenspan observed that:

> A number of global forces have......altered the world as we know it. The most visible....has been the increasing transformation of everyday life by cell phones, personal computers, e-mail, Blackberries, and the Internet. The exploitation after World War II of the electronic characteristics of silicon led to the development of the microprocessor; and when fiber optics combined with lasers and satellites revolutionized communications capacities, people from Pekin, Illinois to Peking, China saw their lives change. A large percentage of the world's population gained access to technologies that I, in setting out on my long career in 1948, could not have imagined, except in the context of science fiction.

> These new technologies not only opened up a whole new vista of low-cost communication, but also facilitated major advances in finance that greatly enhanced our ability to direct scarce savings into productive capital investments, a critical enabler of rapidly expanding globalization and prosperity.[9]

At the beginning of this book, it is vital to define terms. There are many forms of computers- special purpose, general purpose, machine control, ignition control, GPS, and on and on. In this book, the word computer- unless otherwise stated- always refers to the general purpose electronic digital computer, always controlled by some program, where program is a set of instructions followed by the machine to perform any one of a set of tasks.

The computer is undoubtedly the greatest of the great inventions. Learning how to control fire made it possible for mankind to survive more comfortably and, in time, to construct modes of transport powered by fire. The invention of the wheel made it possible for humans to span distance. But the invention of the computer gives us the ability to span a universe of ideas, discovery, labor, arts, and literature. The computer's handmaidens – Internet, cellular communications, and techniques of graphic, scientific, and knowledge visualization – permit anyone to see and be seen, hear and be heard: anywhere, at any time.

Today's world is an on-demand place, as stated in Thomas Friedman's 2005 bestseller, The World is Flat[10]. Yet Friedman's analogy only partly captures the modern essence. The world today is really a small flat plate made of sand – the silicon making up computing, communication, and imaging devices. I call it the Glass Triangle. The modern world is made of silicon. When the history of the world is written centuries from now, it may well refer to this era as the Silicon Age.

Our times mark the transition from the Industrial Revolution, where the accumulation and increase of wealth was mostly generated from physical labor, and work moved from the farm to the factory, to the new era where wealth came mainly from products of the mind, and the work place was the world. With this transition came the major changes in how people live, work, play, and think. While information has always been with us, everyone's ability to have immediate access to any knowledge, anywhere, anytime, is certainly new. For some, it is an on-demand world; for others, a threat to the status quo; and for most of us, a time of continuing mystery and revelation. A large portion of us know more, have more, do more, and live longer with more variety. The so-called "Digital Divide" that creates new occupational challenges for those lacking computer literacy is acknowledged and must be addressed.

The pivotal changes occurred in a few short years starting essentially as a consequence of the Second World War. As part of the wartime military effort, most of the major belligerent countries allocated funds to find ways of improving their weapons to defeat their enemies. Efforts were made to decrypt the secret messages of the enemy, to direct artillery more accurately, to see the enemy at a distance even in the dark, and to maximize the destruction of the enemy with reduced risk to the attacker.

One of these efforts culminated with the unveiling of the first operational digital electronic computer on February 14, 1946. The machine was ENIAC – Electronic Numerical Integrator and Computer – a machine soon labeled a Giant Brain, as indeed it was a giant if not a brain. It was the brainchild in turn of giant human brains.[11] In the timeline of history's technological developments, ENIAC began operations that day in a ground floor laboratory of the Moore School of Electrical Engineering at the University of Pennsylvania in Philadelphia. Over the more than sixty years from that day, the world has entered a new era spawned by that computer. This father of the modern computer continued in operation at the Aberdeen Proving Ground facilities until 1955. Once moved to Aberdeen, ENIAC was enhanced to include the stored program and conditional logic capabilities envisioned and planned for, by its original creators, Pres Eckert and John Mauchly.[12]

That was the start of the Information Age. Giant Brains – human and electronic – have dominated worldwide development since.

History is a dynamic story. It is replete with patterns of events and it is nonlinear. Changes often repeat themselves and can by cyclical. But they do not suddenly materialize. Changes are foretold and there are always signs and signals that precede both large and small changes. Identifying these portents can provide an advantage that can lead to fame and fortune. This book details concrete examples of such changes and illustrates both those who gained and those who lost in the process. These lessons are important to individuals and as a nation, as we find ourselves under attack in a new form of warfare. This time the weapons of choice are intellectual and economic rather than the customary bullets, bombs, and other ordnance.

Evidence is all around that we are entering a new phase of closer intertwined international cooperative effort. The emergence of the European Union is such an example, as are national and regional trading partner agreements. Forces are being unleashed that will initially propel such cooperative efforts in industry, commerce, and finance; and rapidly bring about the formation of new and altered power structures, quite independent of the structures of individual nations. For the foreseeable future, such effort will be the ongoing historic movement propelling the labor, commercial relations, and political structure in most of the world. This is a movement that will not be denied until, like all other movements in history, it runs its course, perhaps over centuries or millennia. At this stage of globalization, some have embraced it, some are trying to cope with it, and some are ignoring it. Many of the political and military conflicts we have recently seen, from riots over cartoon depictions of religious figures to opposition in the U.S. to foreign ownership of domestic seaports are, in large measure, conflicts over such international cooperative effort. We must face up to this necessary force of our times, but what do we do with it? We cannot wish it away. It will be with us indefinitely, and it will dramatically affect the lives of everyone in the world.

We must examine the forces of the past to understand the genesis of the globalization movement and to establish some gauge for its future path and impact. The greatest empires and civilizations of the past have risen and fallen inexorably, giving way to the new wave.

So, how did this movement to cooperative international effort come about? Where is it going? How will it affect us?

George Santayana, that most perceptive Harvard historian, noted that to ignore history is to be condemned to relive it. History is ever moving forward, as it accumulates the yesterdays of today, but much of recorded history from our perspective seems relatively static. In certain periods, change is rather slow; in others, change speeds up, and is tremendously fast. In the 1930s, the U.S. was static because of the Great Depression. Then, with Pearl Harbor, the pace of things exploded with the Second World War. In recent years, despite the War on Terrorism and the conflicts in Afghanistan and Iraq, the U.S. has been in a relative pause, while much of the rest of the world has been moving apace.

While we are all creatures of history, today we have the opportunity to have a profound effect, in our lifetimes, in molding the world to a new historical era. Since the 1990s, we have been in the midst of a new cycle of historical development and growth loosely called Globalization. Even as we act, history can shift and take on its own momentum. It might be noted of historian Arnold J. Toynbee's 12-volume Study of History[13], the twelfth volume of which, Reconsiderations, written years after the first eleven, tended to debunk the earlier works. Others, too, have been critical of his work. The Time Magazine article, "Toynbee Revisited", in particular was critical, with comments that included, among others, "ignorance, dabbling in mythology at the expense of fact, distorting fact to bolster false theories"[14]. Whether such comments are justified or not, the fact is that civilizations do rise and fall, that the mightiest have not lasted, and that there appear to be cycles that permeate history. At the very least, we should accept the concept.

In his work, Toynbee summarized the historical cycles of the rise and fall of empires and civilizations. Toynbee described and analyzed the macro forces behind the cycles of history, paying minimal attention to specific events.

For him, it was the great forces that created and triggered events, while events affected but did not necessarily bring the forces into being. Historian Edmond Taylor furthered Toynbee's analysis of historical cycles in his insightful 1963 book, Fall of the Dynasties[15]. In it he traced the collapse of Europe's Old Order, as he called it, from 1905-1922. He then outlined the succession of the old European empires – Germany, Austria-Hungary, and Russia- by the tyranny of the dictatorships before September 1939, when the cataclysm of the Second World War erupted.

For all its misery, that war gave birth to two of the major events, indeed forces, leading to the closer intertwined international cooperative effort of today. One was the invention of the electronic digital computer, and the other was the coalescing of nations in common cause to defeat the Axis Powers. To achieve this objective, hundreds of millions of people worked together regardless of national origin. The effect of this can most clearly be seen in the area which many see as the war's fulcrum – Europe. The rigid nationalism of the early twentieth century there has been replaced by the European Union (EU).

This EU may have its good or bad points, but it is at least an economic and social federation with an evolving common culture. Its analog, of course, is the United States, with its disparate geographic regions, ethnicities, conflicts, and cultures, yet stitched together in a common federation. Although it often does not seem to be so, the United States is really one nation. And so it seems that Europe is now headed toward a true federation, a nation of Europe. But there is more to those twin stories. Along with continent-wide unities, forces are pushing Europe and America into a global comity. To see the proof of this, one need only reflect on how a citizen in New York City today might have as much affinity with a citizen of London, Paris, Lagos, or Buenos Aires, as with someone in Ohio.

The Cold War was both a variant and a continuation of the Second World War, as imperialistic Communism sought to expand its power, influence, and wealth. Yet the subjugation of people behind the Iron Curtain ended as the resources of the United States bankrupted the Soviet attempt to match it in the military and economic spheres. This triumph was aided in no small way by "the power of the electron," as Radio Free Europe, Vatican Radio, and other outlets sent views varying from the official party line into Eastern Europe. An electronic tsunami intensified and widely spread the West's counter message and efforts. All helped dispel the Soviet myths of the evil West and of Soviet invincibility and inevitability.

The fall of the Berlin Wall in 1989, significant though it was, only underscored the titanic force toward the Global Village that had been envisioned years before in 1962 by the Canadian communications theorist Marshall McLuhan, under whom I had the privilege of studying. McLuhan prophetically perceived the bridging of cultural gaps through the technological forces of jet travel and modern communications. He conceived of the idea in the 1940s and explained it with increasing clarity into the 1960s. During this period, McLuhan's thinking was paralleled with the most remarkable invention in history- the computer. While he went about his work, the computer was en route to siring instant worldwide communications. When mated with visual technologies such as television, it created a cultural juggernaut that coercion and bureaucratic tyranny could not and cannot ever stop.

He perceived this bridging of cultures as a major transformation in the evolutionary history of humanity. McLuhan's introduction to his 1964 book *Understanding Media* summarized this concept of the Global Village:

"Today, after more than a century of electric technology, we have extended our central nervous system in a global embrace, abolishing both space and time as far as our planet is concerned."[16]

It took McLuhan years to crystallize his thoughts this way. He started thinking, talking, and lecturing about it ten years before this book. I am still awed by his prescience.

The computer was and is the ultimate extension of electrical and electronic technology and its real revelation is not in its stunning speed or sublime design. The computer's structure and function mimic the human mind and expand exponentially the mind's potential. It is the first and only machine ever invented that enhances any and all functions of the brain-retention, storage, analysis, consideration of alternatives, use of logic, communication, and modeling.

To know where we are headed, we need to know how we got to this place at this time. This I hope to explain as I recount my career, which began in the early 1950s working with room-sized computers that laboriously completed their tasks, and today that involves handheld, Internet-linked devices which instantly obtain vast amounts of information. I have lived and worked through this historic cycle, and had some part in creating the tools of Globalization. Throughout my career, I have worked in the trenches and the office suites and was involved in many economic and technological transformations that cleared away the dead hand of old habit and bureaucratic resistance. Further, I personally knew many of the people who were pioneers in this new era of challenge, risk, and opportunity, people like Sir

Robert Watson-Watt, the inventor of radar; computer pioneer Admiral Grace Hopper; and Eckert and Mauchly, the synergistic *what if* and *why not* team that was the moving force behind the first general purpose electronic digital computer. Among other roles, I served as a business partner in Mauchly's often groundbreaking, often chaotic firm and as a consultant to Watson-Watt and to his colleague, the Swedish Electrolux tycoon Axel Wenner-Gren, who owned, among many other companies, the Logistics Research Corporation that made the ALWAC computer. This book is autobiographical but also biographical of the life of the computer so far. It is also a saga of the personal rivalries one might expect in any rapidly growing field. With the glory comes the gold, and with either comes the possibility of defeat or ruined health.

My credentials are important in the text of this book. When the computer was born in Philadelphia in 1946, I was an undergraduate at the University of Toronto. My career has spanned much of the history of modern electronic devices and other devices of the globalized world. In Toronto I benefited from an array of "philosophers of the humanities". In addition to McLuhan, there were Jacques Maritain and Etienne Gilson, respectively the philosopher and the historian who brought the work of Thomas Aquinas into modern times. There was my personal friend and mentor, Father John Kelly of the Order of St. Basil, and many other brilliant men of science I encountered as I pursued my technology-related studies. Leopold Infeld, the Polish physicist and close colleague to Albert Einstein[17], was one of my teachers, as was Gilbert de Beauregard Robinson, who headed Canada's Examination Unit of decoders in World War II, and H.S.M. (Harold Scott MacDonald) Coxeter, whose work in polyhedrons inspired the surreal art of Escher and the geodesic-domed architecture of Buckminster Fuller. For a young person seeking to expand intellectual horizons, these giants provided inspiration indeed.

One of the first computer developers, I wrote my first program in 1949, at the University of Toronto, on the FERUT machine.[18] I have been involved ever since in many critical aspects of computers, telecommunications, aerospace, and finance. In the 1950s, I worked with the co-inventors of the digital computer, the University of Pennsylvania's Mauchly and Eckert. I was also instrumental in developing the mathematical formula behind the construction of the heat shields for the Apollo moon missions of the 1960s. Later, in the mid-1970s, I was one of the chief inventors of electronic funds transfer. As part of this effort, our team created the first local area shared networks, a key step toward democratizing the computer and toward the networked world of the Internet. By permitting the immediate transfer of any currency to any spot on the globe, we created the first form of electronic universal currency. It has since become the glue for international commerce and finance.

As my career progressed, I worked with leading international organizations with a need for absolute continuity in their operations; and this necessitated and led to inventing and installing disaster-tolerant information systems. These systems were, are, and will be critical to the peace of mind and reliability of business and governmental functions. Needless to say, they are essential to the continued functioning of society in the event of manmade or natural catastrophe. In the 1980s and 1990s, I helped to computerize various departments of the Roman Catholic Church for the Vatican, which provided a further exposure to and education in the breadth of global forces and needs beyond commerce and finance. More recently, as Chief Executive Officer at the XRT and the CyberFone companies, I have been intimately involved in the explosion of the Internet and the cell phone – connected movements that have supplied the toolbox for the growth of international contact and global commerce.

My experiences have given me an awareness of a new cycle of history in which we are living that is driving us towards multinational cooperation far beyond the charter and founding dream of the United Nations. This common effort will ultimately break down the barriers of language, geography, and culture as we learn and appreciate more about each other, understand our common problems, and work together in self-interest while creating common benefits. Our ultimate success, despite many challenges, will be fueled by technology.

Historically, we have always had forms of globalization. Up until the birth of the computer, most globalization flowed from efforts to balance power between competing groups. Hence the great alliances of the early twentieth century which led to the cataclysms of two world wars. Under the umbrella of Mutually Assured Destruction (MAD) with nuclear arms, protective alliances were forged, most notably in Europe through the North Atlantic Treaty Organization (NATO). In turn, these led to trade agreements which proved mutually beneficial. Success breeds success, so more and wider agreements were considered. The computer's impact made it possible to handle ultra-complicated movements of goods, control delivery schedules, and assure payments. The computer-communication revolution further created electronic currency that supplanted the age-old systems of delivery and payment.

This intensified capability for trade in turn fueled the expansion into the new industries that were created in the post World War II period. Historically, it was and is a phenomenon without comparison in recorded history. Since our nation's founding, the genius of the Atlantic market-driven economy has been the spirit of adventure and innovation that has led to the creation of new products, new techniques, and whole new industries. My catchphrase for the most important of these ongoing changes is "The Cyber Triangle", the nexus of computers, electronic communications, and instant visualization techniques. This concept will be explored more fully as the story unfolds. The Glass Triangle, noted earlier, is a metaphor for the silicon-based connective tissue that bonds these phenomena together.

In the modern Western world, our leadership and economic independence are at risk from the emerging nations of India and China. Whether we reject or embrace it, we are moving rapidly into a world more akin to a village than was imagined when Marshall McLuhan first coined the term "Global Village"[19].

Today, Americans ask themselves, "Is the glass half-full or half-empty?" Does disaster or opportunity loom around the corner? With societal and economic challenges in abundance, the temptation is to see the glass as half-empty. The giants of my day saw the glass as half-full, seized the opportunity, shook the trees, and let the fruit fall. The results are that in absolute terms, more of us live longer, better, and therefore happier as a result.

We made history – often unheralded in what we did, but profound in its impact on life, commerce, and communication on earth and beyond. My work in many parts of the world solved in whole or in part some specific problem; created mutual understanding of problems and possible solutions between diverse people; and educated us about each other, about different sides of the problem, and about the needs beyond technology. My teachers were leading figures in government and business. I acquired a broad sense of finding ways to achieve the possible.

From the lessons of the past come the trend lines. For nations, organizations, and persons, there is a need for a clear-cut understanding and appreciation of the past and present in order to create the future and to thrive in it. While armed conflict is still a factor in global politics, by and large the power struggles of the future will undoubtedly be heavily economic in nature.

This book describes the creation, the current extent, and the potential for personal and national growth, or loss, in a world dominated by the Cyber Triangle. For pleasure, profit, and power, this combination has spawned a new era of technology-centered wealth creation. While Globalization is the term used to describe these phenomena, the reality is much greater than the accepted meaning of the term. What exist are the embryonic stages of the universally connected Global Village.

I write this history in the hope of providing instruction and to help construct a successful outcome scenario for a society that has grown dangerously too comfortable with the status quo. This is a challenge for a society struggling mightily to rise above the human inertia that presents a barrier to overcoming the status quo, when failure to do so spells economic subservience. Taking up the challenge to change means giving up the sense of entitlement that permeates much of the Western World.

Safety nets are necessary for a responsible society, but there must be a distinction made between a legitimate safety net for the demonstrably weakest and the safety net that insures comfort for an otherwise enviable standard of living. As Fareed Zakaria pointed out in a Newsweek Article in 2006:

> History has arrived in the form of Three Billion New Capitalists[20], as Clyde Prestowitz's recent book puts it, people from countries like China, India, and the former Soviet Union, which all once scorned the global market economy but are now enthusiastic and increasingly sophisticated participants in it. They are poorer, hungrier, and in some cases well trained, and will inevitably compete with Americans and America for a slice of the pie. A Goldman Sachs study concludes that by 2045, China will be the largest economy in the world, replacing the United States.[21]

As a nation that loves to watch sporting events, we have difficulty understanding and accepting in everyday life what the players on the field clearly understand - that is, that the outcome of any contest can never be assumed. Players are not entitled to win; they must prove their merit at all times, on every play. The game is often not decided until the clock runs out. In real life, the clock is unknown, and the winner is not always the team with the highest score at any given moment. Moreover, today, the playing field has no fixed shape and the rules have no easy definition.

Today, the on-demand and directed-information world is available for those who can and know how to use it. Delay times between an event occurring and knowledge of it can be fractions of a second. This deluge of facts and options can overwhelm and lead to knee-jerk reactions before another deluge of facts arrive, some contradictory and some representing totally new scenarios. There is often insufficient time to correlate and assimilate a situation before a new problem emerges. For centuries, science has been based on four phases: observation, correlation, deduction, and conclusion. There is no shortcut to this process, just the need to complete the process faster. The Theory of Relativity was not fashioned in a few moments because of some new fact, but the arrival at a conclusion could well have been speeded up through the use of a computer. This major change has impacted our modern world much more than we realize.

Is there a place for the individual in today's world? Of course! The past and present are full of stories of leadership, greatness, and accomplishment. The question is how and where one uncovers opportunities. In the mid 1890s, the superintendent of the patent office was alleged to have said that he was concerned for the engineers of the day since everything that could be invented had been invented; his was a glass half-empty. Then came air travel, medical marvels, antibiotics, television, computers, space flight, electronic communication capability, and on and on. Those developments, unanticipated by that administrator who lacked imagination and vision, spawned whole new industries, created opportunities for Ford, Sloan, Jobs, Gates, Hewlett, Packard, and the other greats of the twentieth century, and provided the livelihood for millions around the globe.

I will consider this book a success if it engages the reader to ask, formulate, and answer such questions as: Why should I be interested in the information technology revolution? I use my computer every day, and I just buy the latest that I need, why do I have to understand how it all happened? Are we bound to become an economic colony of China and India? As we produce less and less ourselves and buy more and more from overseas, will we be able to find new products and technologies to sell so our economy can endure? If we have always allowed our ingenuity and inventiveness to give us economic, commercial, and military dominance in the world, can we assume this will continue? Is our national security at risk as well as our standard of living? What can I do to ensure that my health, standard of living, and security is protected, as well as doing what I can to protect our nation's prosperity and security?

One of the difficulties inherent in this notion of protectionism is the concept of progress. Rather than view the life of an individual or a nation in terms of an undulating sine curve, since the depression of the '30s we in the United States have come to view everything that constitutes a standard of living, economic, health, and social standing, as a trajectory that "should" move inexorably upward and to the right on a scale that measures the level of that standard over a time horizon. This arbitrary notion ignores reality and is all the more reason to recall, once again, Santayana's admonition: "Those who ignore history are condemned to repeat it".[22]

With that in mind, we must ask ourselves, how does one train for success, recognize the openings, and seize the initiative? In this book, I have tried to describe what worked for me and how I benefited from my teachers – in the classroom, but more importantly, in work rooms and boardrooms – often under stress, sometimes at leisure. Throughout this journey, I never felt that I was entitled to anything other than what I could personally produce through individual effort. I hope the reader may find this useful as well.

Many economic, social, and political paradigms that served the old industrial order in the past are no longer sufficient to answer the questions that the global economy presents. For this reason, we need to create new models for problem-solving by trial and error, a process that requires risk-taking.

The excitement and the risk worldwide will be inventing new technologies to meet the needs that are being created. America has done this before; it is now time to do it again. I believe America's corporations, universities, and government labs must leverage their strengths in innovation to continue to thrive in and to lead the world. Pre-college institutions must do their part to help students exercise their native imaginations while developing the basic critical thinking skills they will need to succeed.

When Apple Inc. co-founder Steve Jobs addressed the graduates at Stanford University's commencement exercises, he related that dropping out of college was one of the best decisions he ever made because it forced him to be innovative - even when it came to finding enough money for dinner. Decades later, his bout with a rare form of pancreatic cancer reemphasized the need to live each day to the fullest. Jobs noted that, "Your time is limited, so don't let it be wasted living someone else's life."[23] Jobs had dropped out of college after only eight months because it was too expensive for his family. He said his real education started when he "dropped in" on whatever classes interested him - including calligraphy. Few of his friends could see the value of learning calligraphy at the time, but the same painstaking attention to detail involved in mastering different fonts was what set Apple's Macintosh computer apart from its competitors.

When he was diagnosed with cancer in 2004, Jobs said his doctor told him he only had three-to-six months to live. He later found out he had a rare, treatable form of the disease - but he still learned a tough lesson. "Remembering you are going to die is the best way to avoid the fear that you have something to lose," he said.[24] He recovered. He fathered the iPhone and the iTablet and redefined the Cyber Age, as defined in the Preface of this book.

When I read this speech, despite a generational difference, I felt a certain kinship with Steve Jobs. I offer this book as a battle-scarred, but hopeful, look at the past for the clues to securing a brighter future for Americans seduced and paralyzed by Chicken Little's cry, "The sky is falling."[25] It is not.

CHAPTER ONE

BRINGING COMPUTING TO FRUITION

The computer was a consequence of one man's quest for the ability to solve complex problems. History is replete with many others seeking the same kind of solutions. This chapter presents examples of the step-by-step efforts to find solutions to the numeric puzzles and riddles all around us, and of ways to generate and control the flow of numbers. It includes a description of the driving force of these quests, which were sparked by intuition, thought, inventiveness, and dedication – the innovative spark that has always lit the path for humanity.

These developments were possible because of the computer-communication-visualization triad that is the catalyst of the Flat World Creation.

But what is a computer and who invented it? There are many Challengers to Fame and Fortune for this. In this chapter we introduce the idea of the Men and Women who labored over centuries to invent the Computer Age; and finally the men and women who built the first truly general purpose electronic digital computer. They invented and created what we think of as a computer. This is challenged because of terminology. What cannot be challenged is that they invented the industry.

<u>The Wheel of the Modern World</u>

The (general purpose programmable digital) computer is the wheel of the modern world. How it came to be in a time of great national and international stress can be a beacon lighting the way to the future. The ENIAC was that first computer and it was and is an example of innovation at its best. This invention created the Cyber Age, and ushered in dramatic changes to how we work, live, communicate, and just about anything else you can think of.

A by-product of the invention led to the greatest growth of worldwide wealth that ever occurred in such a short period of time throughout recorded history. To ignore this case history would be both foolish and perilous.

This book has as its main theme the background of why the invention came to be when it did, the mentally restless men and women who made it happen and the fallout in their own lives and careers, and in the creation of the information-centered global economy of today.

These are useful lessons from history; we ignore them at our peril.

This book is not an autobiography. It is the story of people and how they created both the hardware and software industries that permeate our life today. I knew and worked with many of these people. I am one of the workers in that early vineyard. As such, my recollections and work are often interwoven with telling this story. Multiple objectives are defined in the early pages of the book. The main story of this book is how we truly made the world a village. The book recounts the invention of the Computer Age and is directed to the exposition and examination of events and many of those men and women who participated in them. Descriptions of certain events of this period are at odds with those put forward by others and it is my hope to finally set the record straight.

Why the Global Impact?

As the "wheel" of the modern age, the computer is the definitive invention of the immediate past that has and will transform all aspects of life in the present and the future. The story of how it was conceived and invented is compelling. It is the story of people, their dreams, their work, and their anguish.

As individuals, the inventors and the team they assembled were driven by various needs, but the results of their efforts changed the world forever. The inventors had innovative vision and drive and were deeply dedicated; they had "fire in the belly." Some were creative dreamers, others were creative doers. In a few cases, the two characteristics were present, creating something akin to a lovely symphony. This combination of diverse skills and objectives led to ultimate success, often unrecognized at the time and in fact, even afterward. We owe much to these remarkable men and women, though they were often treated without ceremony and reward.

Through the years, others have sought to gain undeserved fame and fortune from this invention, distorting the truth, plagiarizing, and even maligning the true creators. There were also colossal institutional and corporate blunders that changed the economic welfare of major international companies, regions in the United States, and nations around the world. Sadly, people of vision and accomplishment are often swept aside by the seekers of fame and fortune.

It has always been so. The acceptance of innovation and invention is often slow, contentious, and unrewarding. Just as the first wave in a military operation suffers the most casualties because the opposition's resistance is greatest, so do the "pioneers" of a field of endeavor suffer from being the first to break from the norm. History is replete with examples of society's early resistance to new ideas from Galileo[26] to Joseph Lister[27].

Traditional and existing paradigms often remain so until they no longer have sufficient utility. When that point is reached, resistance to new concepts diminishes and the pace of acceptance quickens. Acceptance and reward soon becomes an avalanche, sweeping all before it, and often rewarding the followers rather than the creators.

The milieu of the creative years of the computer was vastly different from the human, moral, economic, and international environment of today. By and large, the groundwork for the creation of the computer occurred in the decade surrounding the Second World War (1939-1945).[28]

The first general-purpose digital electronic computer to function productively was the ENIAC-Electronic Numerical Integrator And Computer. As noted earlier, the co-inventors of the ENIAC were John William Mauchly and John Presper "Pres" Eckert. The story of their work, vision, and dedication is compelling and can serve as a case history of innovation with all its joys and frustrations.

Initially, the prime mover in this effort was John Mauchly who began tinkering with circuits in the 1930s. John Mauchly was an unlikely inventor who thought outside the box but lived outside it as well. Pres Eckert thought outside the box as well, but lived his life within it. John's widow, Kathleen McNulty Mauchly Antonelli, wrote of his tinkering in his early years in a memoir entitled <u>John Mauchly's Early Years</u>[29], which was penned after his death in 1980. In the 1930s, the paradigmatic machine was the Bush Differential Analyzer[30]. It worked to the extent required. It was essentially an analog machine that generated answers just as an old-fashioned speedometer showed speed on a dial instead of digitally as most cars do today. Dreamers with revolutionary concepts, then as now, met with resistance. They were, and are, usually more or less ignored by peers. Such was the case in Philadelphia with John Mauchly. As will be told in detail in Chapter Two, Mauchly quietly worked away until he found a willing listener who became an enthusiastic co-worker and co-inventor, John Presper Eckert. Their partnership blended the skills of vision and engineering genius, to create a computer that was a first, from which the modern computer has evolved. It continued to function for ten years after it was first "turned on" and put into operation on February 14th of 1946.

These two individuals built a team of men - and women. As will be recounted in Chapter Three, the "girls" had a significant hand in the computer revolution. While the men built the machines, the women created the software. These two teams actually laid the foundations for both the hardware and software industries as we know them today.

The first half of the twentieth century wrought inventions that enabled the rise of transportation capability in all its forms, especially automotive and aeronautical. Industries were born and thrived based on these inventions and capabilities. Chief among these were the mass production capabilities associated with automobiles, airplanes, and ships. These in turn accelerated wealth creation, spawning a host of ancillary industries. On a parallel path, there was an immense demand for energy of all kinds, leading in time to a significant redistribution of international wealth. Since then, the exploding global demand for energy and the means of mechanized transportation created an almost exponential world-wide demand that accelerated dramatically towards the end of the twentieth century.

Globalization has leveled the industrial playing field as production has become global in nature and fact. There were twin catalysts to the forces of globalization. The obvious one is the reduced cost of transportation. Not so obvious initially, but quite apparent now, is the impact of the computer on the creation of the Cyber Age. With the application of the initial computers in the '60s, satellites were placed in orbit for communication. The limited use of the research oriented ARPANET [31] network of the '60s became common as the commercialized Internet grew. The introduction of low-cost computer power via the PC, the laptop, the handheld Personal Digital Assistant, and the cell phone provided all the instruments needed for a symphony of technological and material progress to emerge. The computer capabilities provided the means of control. Rapid, inexpensive, and universal communication capability provided the means of managing geographically spread sales, production, and finance, treating these functions as if they were immediately visible in one place. This ubiquitous communication capability has accelerated what was described in the '50s as "The Revolution of Rising Expectations".[32]

The nature of the creation of wealth also changed. As an adjunct of the mind, the computer allows full rein to the creative genius of human beings.

As a result, the products of the mind now have become vital factors in wealth creation[33]; intellectual property rights could become as valuable, or even more valuable, than assets "in the ground", such as deposits of ore and oil. This wealth creation by the computer was twofold - first as the dominant economic industry on the globe, and second, through the ancillary information industries associated with the computer and its offspring, especially software and computer packages.

From its humble beginnings before, during, and immediately after the Second World War, major changes have occurred as a result of the computer. Depending on one's definition of the word "computer" (see Introductory for the definition I offer), in some sixty years, the computer population has grown from a handful of ultra-large machines to hundreds of millions, and even billions- most of them mobile and hand-held devices. Currently, there are over three billion cell phones in the world, all of which have more computing power than the computers of the 1960s.

Moore's Law[34], which has been proven quite accurate, projects that the performance of chips doubles about every twenty-four months. With this exponential growth has come an equally dramatic reduction in the cost. In this day and age, communication is immediate. Text, voice, pictures, video, music, and information are immediately available on demand, or directed to specific persons singly or in groups.

Wealth is now generated significantly by products of the mind rather than from physical effort. The number of billionaires in the world has risen from a handful to close to a thousand – and growing steadily. Monopoly is now achieved by product advantage rather than by force or coercive agreements. The advantage is usually gained by precedence, capability, and user demand. This is the time for products of the mind rather than products of the factory or the soil, including energy and food, which are still important, but of lesser importance than are the products of the mind.

In today's environment, unprecedented demands for energy, entertainment, information, and wealth are releasing forces unknown in prior history. Affluence, and the dream of affluence, is driving individuals globally to expand the horizons of the Cyber Age with new products and new services.

Where is all this going? What is good? What is bad? How can we direct these forces to maximize the benefits of prolonged continuity of development and growth? Will the phenomenon that is the high tech era we live in today known as the Cyber Age[35] be viewed in the context of a zero-sum game in which there are only winners and losers, or will the Cyber Age be seen in the context of a rising tide that lifts all boats?

To a large extent, the answers lie in the history of the past, especially the immediate past that has witnessed the creation and rise of the computer as an accepted necessity in the world.

Humans struggled for eons to find better ways of understanding and controlling the world and their environment. From the dawn of history, the innovative spark of mankind – men and women – made possible by the uniquely human ability to think in the abstract, fueled by curiosity and need, led to major discoveries and inventions.

Why should we take to heart Santayana[36]'s warning about repeating the past mistakes? Throughout the ages, mankind has sought to find ways to explain the universe, and to predict the path of stars in the heavens. This desire led to the development of geometry, arithmetic, and methods of calculation. The quest expanded over time to the nineteenth century when efforts nearly resulted in the creation of a calculating engine. The leap into the twentieth century produced that first general purpose electronic digital computer, the ENIAC, in 1946.

The explosion since then has put computers, vastly reduced in size but greatly magnified in speed and power, into nearly every location and aspect of life on the globe. Practically everyone and everything is touched by the computer. In my estimation, the future seems to beckon brightly as the computer comes of age. Understanding the history of this remarkable machine and its role in our lives is vital to imagining how it could shape our collective future as the 21st century unfolds before us.

The facts of the story will provide valuable lessons for inventors, entrepreneurs, lawyers, teachers and public policy makers, and anyone else charged with preserving and protecting the creative genius that has been the cornerstone of the development of history's most powerful free market economy. In this book, valuable lessons can be gleaned from the description of the power politics and personality struggles of those who sought to enhance reputations and wealth.

Of all the various ideas that have been advanced on how to revive the US and world economies, one of the most dominant is that of ingenuity, innovation, and the creation of new products and industries.

<u>What is Innovation? What are the Factors that Lead to Success?</u>

We can't teach people to innovate – if we could, we could write an expert or artificial intelligence program that would innovate. But we can encourage it, provide funding, and promote adoption of new ideas.
We can and should establish the environment to encourage innovation and innovators and recognize and reward innovation.

Innovation means a new way of doing something. It may refer to incremental, radical, and revolutionary changes in thinking, products, processes, or organizations. Essentially there are three types of innovation: 1) radical—e.g., vaccination, fuel cell; 2) incremental—aluminum instead of chrome on a car, cell phone, the Internet, satellites; and 3) revolutionary—leading to disruptive technologies (the digital computer, nuclear power, asymmetric warfare, and innovative explosive devices).

One of the greatest innovations in history, the ENIAC—the Electronic Numerical Integrator and Computer—happened over sixty years ago in Philadelphia. The world's first general purpose electronic computer, it encompassed radical, incremental and revolutionary innovations. It is the grandfather of the computer and of the information transformation of our world. It was the first machine ever invented that amplified the mind rather than physical strength.

Newton saw an apple fall, Einstein knew there was a problem with speed of light experiments, and Mauchly wanted to predict the weather and the stock market. All had an idea. They nurtured it; they chewed on it, wondered about it, and went about solving the problem.

There are a number of factors involved in innovation. There is the environment of need (war, depression, epidemic, poverty); capability (industry, Babbage, Lister); and funding (government, private, corporate) support, both psychological and financial.

There is "passion": the guts and "fire in the belly". There is little chance of a breakthrough with a revolutionary/disruptive innovation without intestinal fortitude. Bill Gates slept in a kneehole of a desk. Steve Jobs worked in a garage with Steve Wozniak until the first showing of the Apple Computer. Bill Hewlett and David Packard built their devices in a garage until they built a factory and launched the Hewlett Packard Instrument Company. John Mauchly bought used gas tubes with his own money, soldered circuits, and built counters from 1936-41 until he convinced John Presper Eckert to join him in building a computer in 1941. There was no funding until they won a government contract in 1943.

There has to be an idea: disruptive (cell phones, iPod, video, IED), incremental (wing design, FM, laptop, Internet); or revolutionary (jets, antibiotics, atomic energy, the computer, personal medicine, nanotechnology).

Financing is needed. This often comes from the government (SBA, R&D, DOD, CIA, Energy) for basic science, and was the initial source for computer efforts. Government funding can be cautious, slow, and bureaucratic. There is also corporate support, which is success-oriented, profit-oriented, and also cautious, sometimes political, and product-oriented, often covering applied research. Academic research relies heavily on government support, along with individual (angel and venture capitalist) support, which is success-oriented, return-oriented, adventuresome, and has supported major breakthroughs of the last fifty years (Microsoft, Apple, Google, Yahoo).

Of course, an innovation must have impact—it must be worth doing. In particular, a truly revolutionary evolution will be highly disruptive, creating new products, industries, and redirection to political and economic ways of doing things. It must be focused—buckshot often misses, but a well-aimed rifle in the hands of a marksman usually hits the target. Much time, treasure, and energy is lost in the absence of focus.

There is a great deal of interest in how to revive the economy of the United States and of the world. This is a pressing problem of great concern to many. Various ideas are advanced. One of the most dominant is that of ingenuity, innovation, and the creation of new products and industries. If that indeed is a solution, what could this mean to the future of the United States and to the Delaware Valley?

There are four parts to this analysis.

As we will see throughout the story, innovation begins with a "fire in the belly," a powerful desire to understand something that cannot be understood through existing methods or protocols- the "box" within which conventional thinking occurs.

The essence of this book is the invention, creation, and use of the first general purpose, electronic digital computer – the ENIAC. The book traces the roots of this machine and links its development to historical efforts to create other calculating engines. The story advances to the later developments in the 1940s and '50s, up to the delivery of UNIVAC and the first production computer of the early fifties. The book skips forward to the 1973 trial between Sperry Rand and Honeywell, that produced highly questionable findings and decisions as to who "invented" the computer and who would profit from its invention.

The book ends with an evaluation of the Computer Age from the first UNIVAC to the present day when the number of "computers" is rapidly approaching the number of people in the world.

When the history of this age is written, it will start with the birth of the computer and all the technology it has spawned. Without the computer, there would be no space program, no Internet, and no high tech revolution. Many of the wonders of modern engineering and medicine would not be feasible, electronic movement of money and global commerce would be impossible, and there would be no global communication capability. By the same token, there would be no e-mail, no rapid design of products, no e- shopping, no video on-demand, no chat rooms, no blogs, or other means of global instantaneous idea exchange. In the Cyber Age, we are once again at life's starting line, but as Freidman indicates, there are ever more participants in the race.

Without the computer, a major part of our daily experience would be absent. The void is unimaginable. But this is only the start. The orchestra of computing instruments I mentioned earlier has only played its first symphony. In musical terms, I am reminded of the famous line "You ain't heard nuthin' yet," uttered by the great American entertainer, Al Jolson, in the first sound movie, The Jazz Singer[37].

While the computer's birth was worked on, planned, hoped for, and finally achieved, the quest and struggle took many decades over a number of centuries. It started with various philosophers going back to Pascal in the 17th Century[38]. Babbage brought the dream along in the mid 19th Century[39] and ENIAC was born and began operations in the middle of the 20th century.

The birth of ENIAC and the years that followed it were full of rejection, controversy, lawsuits, and slow acceptance. The natural conflicts associated with pioneering leadership - pride, monetary gain, and even chicanery - were intensified by the age-old adage first coined by Niccolo Machiavelli (1469-1527):

"There is nothing more difficult to take in hand, more perilous to conduct, or more uncertain in its success, than to take the lead in the introduction of a new order of things."[40]

This is often paraphrased as:

"There is nothing more uncertain and likely to fail than a new enterprise (or invention) since it will receive only lukewarm support from those who will benefit, and intense opposition from those it will affect."

And so it was with the computer. In addition, the normal natural conflicts between constituencies were intensified because of the sweeping potential, and later sweeping impact, of the computer and its offspring. Today we can call this the Information Age, if not the Cyber Age, as all aspects of technology associated in some form with information, computation, and visualization bear some relationship to the digital computer.

Think for a moment. It took thousands, or perhaps millions, of years to move from the cave to the tribe to the village to the city to the city-states and then to nations. The twentieth century's cataclysmic wars led to nation groups – political and economic – all in less than a hundred years.

In the same vein, it took centuries to create the agrarian societies that reached a peak about the 12th century. In the following five hundred years the Industrial Revolution flourished. Coincidently, it got under way with the start of the Renaissance; in the next two hundred years it moved to mass production concepts; and since 1946, it has evolved into the Information Age. Then, the Internet exploded from its nascent state into a global force still not totally adsorbed or reckoned with. That was the birth of what we may ultimately call the Cyber Age, a vibrant offspring of the Information Age.

The Information Age Overload Versus The Cyber Age Information Control

The Cyber Age refers to the control of our environment and things about us not through force, but through the extension of each individual mind to other minds to form consensus and understanding. While this may seem altruistic, in reality, the computer, as the first and only adjunct of our intellects, has created a whole new realm of control; that control is manifest through devices, communication, visualization, and consensus. It is all brought about by the computer with its connection to communications and the process of visualization over distance of people, things, and events as they happen. The term CyberSpace[41] referring to the Internet is only one part of the concept of relationship.

The element of choice is the real thrust of the Cyber Age. We choose because we can. We select because we have many choices available to us. We can communicate with others, seek their opinions, share opinions, and even try to change opinions, and in the political sphere, we form a consensus.

That is the context of the Age that is emerging, coming of course as an outgrowth of the birth of the computer, but marking an entire Age or epoch that separates it from others that preceded it.

For some, the Cyber Age heralds a new golden age of mankind, one in which familiarity of cultures and religions facilitates mankind's ability to live in understanding and harmony. This utopian vision is far removed from the truth. Knowledge does not necessarily bridge barriers and gaps, especially if there are firm opinions and religious beliefs that are poles apart. Indeed, the flood of information might even create a glut, an overload. Today, the availability of instant information often heightens the demand for the instant response. Instant response is not always possible, or desirable. Thinking time, digestion time, and quiet time are often needed and just as often not possible because demand is intense and availability is immediate.

In today's world, we are ever more aware, and on a shorter time frame than ever before, of changes, threats, opposition movements, and support mechanisms and people. But recall Machiavelli's caution – for any new cause or system, support is thin while opposition is strong.

The impacts are manifold. For example, classical Biology has led to the current approaches in Microbiology and Genetics. The power of the computer provided the basis for the human genome solution, which will in turn create waves of change in humanity. Now we hear of Nano[42] Robots that will be small enough to invade and traverse the human body, seeking to find and correct disease; but, in the wrong hands, there is danger that this can lead to creating human robots controlled in a new form of slavery. These and other developments have created discussion, controversy, fear, rejection, and tremendous conflict among people and nations. This fear in turn is magnified and spread via the Internet. Furthermore, cloning, stem cell research, genetic change, genetic disease forecasting, and invasion of medical records are all technically possible with significant support for action both pro and con.

Genetic change is only one of many new forces and fears. In the mid-twentieth century, the greatest problem in the schoolroom was chewing gum and talking. Now it is murder – children killing children – and children using the Internet to plan and collaborate on crime. Certainly there are forces at work either using technology or based on technology that must be addressed. Technology can both harm and benefit either side of the discussion.

We stand at a crossroads in history. One path leads to the Golden Age for humanity, the other leads to a decline and decay of our civilization similar to what occurred with the collapse of the Roman Empire. We can refer to this age in which we live as the Cyber Age – the dawn of the second renaissance of mankind, or we can refer to it as the Death of Culture, if not the Death of Nations, the very Death of History, and the negation of civility among persons, institutions, and nations.

In global socio-political history, modern economies have evolved from tribes, to city-states, to nations and groups of nations, such as exist today. Economically and socially, these modern economies have moved from agrarian society, to the Industrial Age, to the mass production age, and now to the Cyber Age. Modern economies have emerged in slightly more than a century from a time when each new discovery of science inspired awe to today's ho-hum attitude towards everything, accepting and rejecting the news as we see fit.

Technology has brought great benefits and potentially great perils. To achieve the full potential and the promise of what is possible, we must examine the perils, analyze the nature of the threat, and establish an effective strategy for continued growth to achieve the fruits our hard work has created for us.

But what kind of perils do we face? What is the promise of the future? How will history view this age? The answers lie in considering what kind of world we live in. What are the forces that move us now, and what are the forces that got us here? Technology is certainly one of these forces.

Are we moving to a technocracy where civility, individual personality, holistic personhood, culture, and life must be measured only in terms of progress? And if so, how do we measure progress – by wealth, by the quality of life, by personal gratification, by moral values, or by what? Is Cyber Space the new addictive drug? Are instant gratifications via sex, pornography, and drugs to become our norm? Or is there an alternative, where technology is taken in stride, controlled, and directed to be our tool rather than our master? No doubt we stand before this moment of history as a troubled people – full of promise and potential, yet threatened by a whole new set of perils that never existed before.

Of course, the old perils of thirst for power and domination, relentless personal and national pride, and greed are still with us. The threat of warfare – big and small – is still with us. But now we face the old forces with new potential. Spawned by the computer, instant communication and visualization of anything anywhere has added whole new dimensions and potential for mischief to the old problems, and increased the potential for harm. The analogy is almost akin to the damage wrought by a small bomb to that created with a nuclear explosion.

Before examining the major perils before us, and how to tame or eliminate them to achieve our potential promise, we must address where we are and the driving forces that brought us to this age we live in.

There is rising demand for government support – via welfare, workfare, medical insurance, safety nets, reparations, projects that serve special interests (pork barrel), and bailout grants even to major industries.[43] This Culture of Dependence on government is proceeding side by side with decreased trust and belief in government. Government support is demanded as a right without individual or corporate accountability – not as a privilege, not as "noblesse oblige". Once again, the demands are strident using all of the tools of the day – Internet, media, computerized letters, computerized phone calls, and video calls.

Even with all this support, and even with the affluence of our times, there is a breakdown of family and personal relationships. We have almost become a Disposable Society; casting off moral and cultural norms, people, parts, and relationships, as we move relentlessly forward in search of the next form of wealth, personal gratification, and power trip.

Bill Bennett wrote two seminal books – <u>The Book of Virtues</u>[44] and <u>The Death of Outrage</u>[45]. They were an attempt to revive Civility, Morality, Courage, and Virtue.

In the midst of the greatest surge in economic power in history, the rise of people power, increased personal wealth, and the dream of a second Renaissance, we are inundated with the perils to the promises that technology can provide. The sheer power and potential of the forces for technological good are under attack on many fronts. The human genome project is a significant major development in human knowledge. As noted above, the possibility of Nano Robots circulating in our bodies to track and overcome disease is a startling dream with personal potential beyond easy comprehension.

Instant communication with loved ones anywhere by sight and sound, the ability to transact personal business at a distance, the potential for a re-emergence of the electronic analog of the cottage industry, learning at home via distance learning, classrooms without walls, medical diagnosis and treatment of the highest caliber in the remotest hovel of the world - all these and more are the promise of technology. We must not let this promise fail as we become inundated and sidetracked with real perils that must be addressed. These perils can be ameliorated, if not overcome, by technology, even the very technology that spawned the threat.

In particular, we must address the growing divide and discontent between the haves and have-nots. We can, must, and will overcome the Digital Divide with technology itself – creating Digital Union rather than a Divide.

In <u>Julius Caesar</u>[46] Act IV Scene III, Shakespeare wrote:

"We, at the height, are ready to decline.
There is a tide in the affairs of men,
Which, taken at the flood, leads on to fortune;
Omitted, all the voyage of their life
Is bound in shallows and in miseries.
On such a full sea are we now afloat;
And we must take the current when it serves,
Or lose our ventures."

This is often shortened and paraphrased as:

"There is a time in the times of the tides of men when taken at the flood lead on to greatness and victory."

The time is now. We can achieve the Potential and the Promise.

The global community is at an historical crossroad. Let us examine where we are, how we got here, what stands in the way of a glorious future.

The hope is that this book may serve as the baseline for and the roadmap to the future that may enable us to create a Digital Union that avoids the dire consequences of a Digital Divide.

Let us be clear about this quest for power over the environment. It did not originate in modern times, for it can be seen as a basic attribute of the human species. It may or may not extend beyond the individual's need to understand the nature of the environment in which he or she must function. When this quest does extend beyond the need to understand, psychological, practical, acquisitive forces present themselves that drive what we call progress. But all of this "progress" must begin with dedication, desire that builds to become a burning need that translates to an idea that may evolve to an invention that typically has a practical purpose in mind. That purpose often is directed at control of time, energy, and effort. By common definition, an invention is considered to be unique. Nothing like it has been conceived before. As such, it represents an innovation in the way something is accomplished.

As will be discussed in later chapters, it is my contention that the United States and the Western World have grown and flourished through a spirit that seeks to innovate, to improve on what exists, typically in the interest of conserving time, energy, effort and other resources. In the global economy, this may be the Unites States' competitive advantage that must be nourished if the promise of technology is to be generally realized by this and other societies.

It should be recognized that as far back as can be determined, man has always been driven by an unquenchable need to know. This intellectual need to understand is often coupled with the needs of others to provide a measure of control over the forces of the universe that impact human life. Sometimes, these needs reside in the same person, more often, they do not. As you will see later, John Mauchly, a central figure in the history of the modern computer, was essentially driven by an intellectual curiosity – a desire to understand - manifest in a relentless need to know, that rendered him vulnerable to the less attractive needs of others.

But what of this need to know and how has it impacted the computer technology we take for granted today? Let us review some signal events that helped to advance understanding of certain fundamental principles on which much of our knowledge of calculation is based

For example, Anaximander[47], the Greek philosopher of Miletus, lived between 611-546 BC. He is said to have made a map, perhaps the first, of the world. His treatise in prose, "On Nature" is lost. But like the "star wheels" attributed to him, most of the evidence of his work is in the form of references from Aristotle and his pupil Theophrastus. Few of Anaximander's opinions about the stars have survived. Perhaps the best way to imagine the star wheels is as a conglomerate of several wheels, each of which has one or more holes, through which light shines, which we see as stars. It is likely that the sum-total of these star wheels resembles a sphere. The only movement of these star wheels is a rotation around the earth from east to west, always at the same speed, and always at the same place relative to one another in the heaven. This early speculation about the motion of the universe has evolved into the star wheel in use today and whose concept of identifying certain relationships had been utilized in commercial activities.

Archimedes[48], a Greek mathematician, Geometer, Inventor and Engineer, in addition to discovering the value of Pi and the Principle of Buoyancy, is believed to be the first to invent integral calculus, some 2000 years before Newton and Leibniz.

An abacus[49], a later device that appeared after 500AD, is a device used for addition and subtraction and the related operations of multiplication and division. It does not require the use of pen and paper, and it is useful for any base number system. There are two basic forms for the abacus: a specially marked flat surface used with counters (counting table), or a frame with beads strung on wires (bead frame).

The abacus seems to have appeared in the Middle East region and its use spread around Asia and to Europe. In Europe in the 1700s, it was supplanted by the introduction of the Hindu-Arabic notation of numbers. It is still in use in Asia.

In the early 1600s, Scottish mathematician John Napier[50] invented logarithms that were a great assist to arithmetic calculation. He created a tool called Napier's Bones that consisted of multiplication tables inscribed on strips of bone.

Succeeding Napier and employing his logarithms, William Oughtred[51], an English mathematician, invented the rectilinear and circular slide rules that remained in effective, everyday use for over 350 years.

In the 1670s, Leibniz[52] took mathematical calculation to a higher level than any before. He is reported to have said, "It is unworthy of excellent men to lose hours like slaves in the labor of calculation, which could be safely relegated to anyone else if machines were used". Building on Pascal's ideas, Leibniz introduced the Step Reckoner. This machine could add, subtract, multiply, divide and evaluate square roots by a series of stepped additions. Moreover, Leibniz advocated a binary number system that forms the basis of the modern digital computer.

In 1834, Charles Babbage[53] a British mathematician and inventor, originated the principle of the analytical engine and conceived a device that was intended to use Jacquard's punch cards[54] to control an automatic calculator that could make decisions based on the results of previous computations. However, the machine never worked. It was intended to run on steam power. It has been considered to be a forerunner of the modern electronic computer, since Babbage envisioned several features employed in modern computing including sequential control, branching, and looping.

Lord Byron's daughter, Augusta Ada Lovelace[55], was a brilliant mathematician who designed a program to run on Babbage's Analytical Engine to compute a mathematical sequence known as Bernoulli numbers[56]. With some, she is credited with being the first computer programmer and in 1979, a modern programming language was named ADA in her honor. Perhaps! No doubt she conceived of a methodology for calculation using a machine that was neither built nor operational. But there is more to programming than theory. The first true programmers were the young women who programmed ENIAC. One of these was Kathleen McNulty, future wife of John Mauchly, and afterwards of Severo Antonelli after John Mauchly's death in 1980.

An issue to be discussed later is the efforts during the Second World War of encrypting[57] on one hand, and decoding (decrypting) on the other. Here, there is the exciting story and controversy over the ENIGMA machine of the Germans, the Japanese machines, the Colossus of the British, and the visionary efforts of Alan Turing in the 1930s.

Elsewhere, television was born in the 1920s but only achieved some form of widespread use in the 1940s after the Second World War ended. The visualization concept of TV was based on images carried as modulations of regular short-wave radio waves. This was an analog[58] concept as opposed to the digital or binary bit concept.

In the early days that followed its invention, television was an independent development from the computer through the Second World War, but today it is a fully intertwined step-child. It is the triumvirate union of computers, communication, and visualization that has created the technological catalyst and foundation of the Global World, the Flat World, we live in today.

One further major point to remember. The concepts of standards of digital representation of data were established in the 1930s and 1940s, if not even earlier. The concepts and designs of circuits to handle timing pulses and the manipulation of data streams were also completed in the 1930s and 1940s. The genius of the inventors of ENIAC, John Mauchly and John Presper Eckert, was to assemble all these known elements into new forms to create the first stored-program computer.[59]

The analogy is to compare radio and television. Radio contains many of the components and circuits that exist in television. But add a few more circuits, a picture tube, and suddenly there is sight as well as sound- a remarkable difference. Hence, in the 60 years since its invention, speed, miniaturization, and components have widened the capability and usefulness of the computer. The basic concepts remain as the foundation of CyberNetics to this day. From these fundamentals the widespread use of digital representation techniques so prevalent today for music, pictures, conversation, and electronic images in digital form has grown.

The Bush Differential Analyzer was invented and patented in 1935 by Dr. Vannevar Bush and his team at MIT.[60] This analog calculating machine, call it an analog computer, was the standard being used at the University of Pennsylvania's Moore School and at other universities, like Harvard. Its purpose was to perform what were, at the time, the most rapid calculations possible by a machine.

Other machines, including the ABC developed by John Atanasoff, have also claimed to be the first computer. The British created the Colossus machines during WWII and used these for decrypting encoded messages of the Germans. But ABC, and the Colossus machines, were special purpose. Only the ENIAC was general purpose, and it worked on many problems of diverse nature productively for ten years after its unveiling at the University of Pennsylvania in Philadelphia on February 14, 1946.

The ENIAC was an electric machine as well as electronic. The end product was a calculation which resulted in numbers understandable to us- that is, values represented in decimal form. Other electric machines predated the ENIAC and also produced values in numeric form. The distinction lies in the manner in which these calculations were completed. Confusion lies in truly looking at what is being claimed to have been invented before we can truly assess whether the claims are valid or not.

There is an ancient proverb that goes: "Success has many fathers, but failure is an orphan." ENIAC was the first general purpose electronic digital computer that worked, and continued to work for ten years beyond its public unveiling. There is no doubt that John Mauchly and Pres Eckert were the masterminds and the driving forces behind the building of that machine. The issue is clouded as to whether or not that invention was patentable, whether or not prior art existed upon which the design of that machine rests, and whether or not others deserve the accolade as "inventor" of the computer. This particular topic is dependent upon different contributions of different people at different times. It also depends to a large extent on facts, opinions, and claims that emerged after the famous (or infamous) trial in 1972. This trial is considered in detail in Chapter Seven. At this point in the narrative, however, it becomes important to make a distinction between ENIAC and the differential analyzers which were prevalent for calculations in that period of time- the late 1930s and the early 1940s.

The primary distinction is that the differential analyzers were analog, and ENIAC was digital. That seems like a simple thing to say now. But in the thirties and forties it was not so obvious. Today, we have digital readout for time, car speedometers, body temperature, and on and on. But before these digital displays we had analog devices - devices that measured by analogy. A wheel turned a dial, and we read the number off the dial. Secondly, the ENIAC was electronic[61] rather than electro-mechanical, and thirdly, it was designed as a general purpose computer.

This distinction of general purpose versus special purpose is very important. It is a crux of the argument between the claims of priority by those supporting Dr. John Atanasoff as the inventor of the computer, and those who do not. He was concerned with a special purpose machine, whereas Eckert and Mauchly were concerned with a general purpose machine, a machine that could be used for anything. A special purpose machine can do only one thing. Both can be called a computer. As a matter of fact, a slide rule can also be called a computer. To some extent, a slide rule is almost a general purpose computer, but it cannot do every form of calculation. More important, a slide rule often called for the reentry of data by repositioning the slide stick. So, too, in most cases the same requirement exists for special purpose machines. This was true of the ABC machine built by Atanasoff.

Rotary desk calculators were also available, whether mechanical, electrical, and later digital. These too were general purpose to some extent in their ability to handle diverse problems. To some extent, desk calculators had the ability to retain intermediate answers which could be used. So the argument can be made that ENIAC was not the first general purpose computer. This is not totally true. The important considerations, and those that were extremely important to Eckert and Mauchly, were the ability for the machine itself to regulate the entire process according to a program loaded onto the machine. That is what we have come to know as the "computer", but in reality, we are talking about a general purpose electronic digital computer. ENIAC was definitely the first such machine. Hence, the computer, as we understand it today, was born in the ground floor lab at the University of Pennsylvania's Moore School of Electrical Engineering. It was military need that provided the resources to undertake and actually build John Mauchly's dream, and it was American business and industry that subsequently mastered it.

The ENIAC machine was the first truly stored program machine based on the representation of data in digital form. Initially it was not. Programming was done by cables and switches which were set up when a problem was loaded. The calculations were done in decimal (all except for square rooter, designed by Kite Sharpless). Eckert and Mauchly determined how to make it a stored program machine. This means that numbers and letters are represented each by a unique set of zeros and ones- also known to programmers as Binary Code.[62] This was subsequently done when ENIAC was moved to Aberdeen. Whether the program was stored or not (as pulses stored on tubes or with patch-cord and relays- internal or external program), ENIAC was programmable from the very beginning as a general purpose computer.

ENIAC stored data and programs in about 20,000 electron gas tubes. Each tube stored one bit of data, and each character needed six bits (or tubes). Hence, the full "memory" of this machine was less than 3K in total, but less than 2K was available to the programmer. Contrast this with the up to 16,000K (2 million times the "memory" of ENIAC) in a modern laptop. Note that the early machines all had names like ENIAC. Others were Whirlwind at MIT, MANIAC at Michigan, ENIAC's "son" UNIVAC, and ENIAC's "father", ORDVAC. ORDVAC (1942), or Ordinance Virtual Automatic Computer, used electronic circuits for calculations, but used a board with wires for its program. As such, while it was an electronic machine with computing capability, it was not until ENIAC that self-stored programs controlled the computer. More importantly, ENIAC was the first machine to be able to switch logically. There were many "firsts" enumerated by Eckert in an interview before his death in 1995. This is presented in detail in Chapter Seven.

Thus, John William Mauchly (1907-1980) and John Presper Eckert (1919-1995) were the co-inventors of the electronic digital computer ENIAC. Mauchly and Eckert later created a partnership to manufacture computers. John and Pres Eckert formed the Eckert Mauchly Corporation in 1948 with John as President. The two began work on the Universal Automatic Computer (UNIVAC) in 1948, and secured contracts to deliver the system to the US Census Bureau, the Army Map Service, and Metropolitan Life Insurance Company, among others.

By 1949 they were desperate for cash. With the death of their Financial Vice President in an airplane crash, it became essential to merge or sell all or part of the company. IBM rejected the opportunity, but James Rand of Remington Rand Corporation was encouraged by John Patterson- a deal maker of the day, an early version of an investment banker in the computer community- to buy the Eckert Mauchly Corporation in Philadelphia and Electronic Research Association in St. Paul. Discussions took place over months. Finally, the officers of Eckert Mauchly agreed to a final meeting, and all agreed not to leave the room until a decision was reached. The final offer gave Mauchly and Eckert each $34,000 plus a percentage of future royalties on the UNIVAC patents, which ultimately paid virtually nothing. So Mauchly earned $34,000 for inventing and patenting, together with Pres Eckert, the greatest invention in history up to now. Mauchly told me he was fighting for more but desperately had to go to the bathroom and could not until a decision - yes or no - was reached.

UNIVAC was completed and became the first commercially available general-purpose computer in 1951. For his efforts, John Presper Eckert received the National Medal of Science in 1969. As you will see later, John Mauchly was denied the accolades for the theoretical and experimental contributions he deserved.

I have presented this chapter as both a stage setting and an overview to the history to be related in more detail in the later chapters.

There are many lessons to be gleaned from this early modern phase of the computer's history. I think these lessons will be helpful in selecting the path to the future the United States must take, and I will endeavor to point them out as they appear.

But let me be clear at the outset. The generalized cultural of *material entitlement* that has emerged in the US since the invention of the modern computer is simply antithetical to the realities of a globalized world. In my judgment, if this view is maintained, it will present a serious obstacle to our continued economic success.

What is to be done to provide the guidance needed at history's crossroads? We must demand leadership from those who purport to lead, for it is this collective group that creates policy and shapes opinion.

Moreover, the policies needed at the crossroads must fit an overarching strategic plan aimed at maintaining, if not exceeding, our current living standards. In my estimation, any lesser pursuits than these will fall short and today's living standards will most likely continue to erode.

CHAPTER TWO

CREATING THE FIRST COMPUTER-
THE INVENTION THAT CHANGED THE
WORLD

The invention of the computer is a case history of the trials and tribulations of inventing and innovation. The story of ENIAC's creation is one of driving ambitions, towering achievements, petty jealousies, mistaken assumptions, and two men's grand vision.

True Inventors

The true inventor of general purpose digital computers was cheated of his place in history. It was John Mauchly who with his vision convinced J. Presper Eckert to join him in building the first electronic digital general purpose computer. The partnership of Eckert and Mauchly created the "perfect team" of visionary and engineer. This compelling story is based on the author's personal knowledge of Mauchly's work and family. The chapter portrays the scientist as an archetype of the kind of creative, team-oriented entrepreneur required for success in a globalized, technical world. The impact of greed, plagiarism and incompetence is outlined as it affected history's official view of what happened. That view is flawed.

Without computers Globalization would be difficult if not impossible. The Global Village[63] would be a rustic slow moving caricature of medieval times with air transport replacing the horse-drawn cart. With the computer, of course, there is instant communication independent of distance and time, on or off the globe, with complete visualization. Needless to say, the control capabilities of the computer permit instant response to orders, deliveries, payments, receipts, and plans. The invention of the computer has made the Global Village possible.

This chapter details the story of the digital computer's real inventors – John Mauchly and Pres Eckert. This story has much relevance to our story of how we truly made the world a village, and made the Globalization a reality. We owe much to the technologies which will, and which have, propelled us. We owe much to the inventors of this mind expander.

Unfortunately, greed, caprice, pride and plagiarism prevented the person who was the prime moving force from being recognized for his brilliant contributions. This is the story.

The computer, as mentioned in the previous chapter, is the "wheel of information" on which our globalized, digitized planet turns. Our economies, our countries, our mores will increasingly be built upon it and the computer's handmaidens like the cell phone and the Internet.

The tale of the computer's real inventors touches on many of the themes of Globalization. It is the tale of how true innovation operates – by following one's dream, by thinking and acting outside the box -- against the confirmed opinion of established thought and entrenched bureaucracies. It is the tale of a birth of a new industry that revolutionized parts of the nation that embraced it, while leaving behind other regions that failed to grasp, or seize, its potential. It is the genesis of a machine that would make countless clerical and factory jobs obsolete, while opening up higher-level employment for even greater numbers of employees, especially those with the kind of education that would enable them to prosper in the new field.

The story captures the continuing tension amongst an entrepreneurial industry focused on profits, universities geared to basic and applied research, and a federal government attuned to social goals. It displays the revolutionary effects that a smart emphasis on scientific research can produce. In our tale, the chief inventors were driven by their vision, while their chief rivals, although certainly having their own interests in self-promotion, also looked to an academic ideal of shared research as opposed to one based around patent rights and entrepreneurship. While many of the researchers in the project work were true capitalists, working for personal satisfaction, wealth, or glory, the federal government picked up much of the tab for the work that was done.

The breakthrough technology invented soon leaked out to Great Britain and to the rest of the world, underscoring the fast-moving, international nature of the modern scientific enterprise. Like the contemporaneous Bletchley Park [64] code breaking project in England, which used an early form of computers to help crack the Nazi ciphers, the story describes an initiative that was in many ways the prototypical software company. Also like Bletchley Park, it demonstrates the strong role the military played in creating much of our modern know-how, from computers to the Internet to nuclear energy. This role was often put into effect, as in our story, by close collaboration between the military branches of the government and our research universities.

The project that devised the first digital, general purpose computer had an utterly modern feel to it. It had a free-wheeling management style, and it was characterized by crazed work schedules in a frenetic rush to "get to market." It was a socially progressive workplace, one in which all the programmers were women! And like today's research parks that are centers of youthful technical innovation, the hard work was broken up by inventive pranks, the more mechanically astute the better.

Still, the invention of the computer did take place in a very different time, and a very different culture; a time and a place that can teach us many lessons for dealing with Globalization. Compared to many in today's information technology industry, the men and women of the project, though many were surely profit-driven, worked much more for the war effort, out of intellectual curiosity, and personal fulfillment than for money. This was partly so because the tenor of the times put on a pedestal of honor the nation's scientific, industrial, and medical heroes – the Jonas Salks [65], the Charles Lindberghs [66], and the David Sarnoffs [67]. This is in stark contrast to today's society, which unduly worships the ephemeral and the sensational: pampered sports stars, starlets, rap stars, and celebrity for celebrity's sake. In each instance, cherished ideals are replaced with false idols.

This is also a personal story of two brilliant men's ceaseless struggle to bring to life a unique vision – while being unfairly undercut and discredited by jealous colleagues. Before the ENIAC project was picked up by the military, the great majority of John Mauchly's university brethren dismissed his ideas as absurdly impractical. Rather like those who thought that Bill Gates' and his start-up firm Microsoft were foolish to take on giant IBM. Or that Craig Venter's[68] start-up firm could sequence the human genome ahead of a vastly larger federal effort. Or that Cal Tech trained aeronautical engineer Burt Rutan could out-design the NASA behemoth in shooting his privately funded, reusable, Spaceship One some 62 miles above the earth.

But it was Mauchly and Eckert who, like Bill Gates or Marshal McLuhan[69], perceived the convergence of innovations and societal changes that were enabling the emergence of a revolutionary new technology.

Our story - as an archetype of modern technical creation, the creation of the greatest human invention, the computer - is a model of how to succeed in the current cycle of history. It is a new parable of the talents. It indicates how America can wield one of its greatest strengths, pushing the new frontiers of technical innovation - a strength I am convinced is a key to its prospering in a globalized culture. Through this advantage, the United States can exploit its many inherent talents to win again on the world stage. If used wisely, the tools of Globalization can accelerate growth for the United States, allowing it to reclaim its dominance over resurgent nations like China.

I personally knew, and was a close colleague of, John Mauchly. Since his death in 1980, I had continued my long friendship with his widow, Kathleen "Kay" Mauchly Antonelli. Indeed, interviews with Kay Mauchly Antonelli, who was John Mauchly's devoted spouse during his landmark innovations in digital electronics, make up some of the research material on which the following narrative is based.

The narrative takes many twists and turns and in view of what I know, I would like to begin the story with an exchange between two young school boys on a research report assignment.

Young Sebastian Mauchly was thrilled when he went to his middle school in Berwyn, Pennsylvania, one sunny morning in the spring of 2001. Sebastian Mauchly is the grandson of John William Mauchly. Andrew, Sebastian's close friend in their seventh-grade class, had recently been asked to do some research on a scientist and acquaintance of Grandpa Mauchly, one John V. Atanasoff.[70]

Sebastian's dad and grandmother had told him all about John Mauchly, who had dubbed his computer ENIAC, for Electronic Numerical Integrator and Computer. So Sebastian was startled when Andrew told him a teacher said John Mauchly had stolen his ideas from Atanasoff. It was Atanasoff, the instructor told the boys, who was the real creator of the computer.

But the teacher was wrong. Atanasoff, like Mauchly, had novel ideas about computers. Unlike Mauchly, however, he never built a full-fledged machine, but rather a prototype[71]. John Mauchly and John Presper Eckert *did build* the ENIAC, the very first fully functioning, general-purpose, electronic computer. And ENIAC not only worked as designed but, after its creation in 1944-45, it worked on cutting-edge subjects for ten years.

ENIAC's sixtieth anniversary took place on February 14th of 2006. The room-sized machine had spawned our Cyber Age with its hundreds of millions of world-wide computers

- connecting, informing, employing, educating, and entertaining over a billion people every nanosecond. ENIAC started it all.

Yet its true creators have been blocked of their rightful place in history. It is as if Newton[72] was denied title to the theory of gravity, and Einstein to relativity. It is high time to set the record straight.

John William Mauchly: The Brain Behind The Giant Brain

John William Mauchly was born on August 30, 1907 in Cincinnati, Ohio. Even as a young boy, he strove to understand how things worked[73]. A natural tinkerer, he took apart locks and studied the components of telephones. Climbing into a telephone company ditch outside his home in Chevy Chase, Maryland, he would hook up wires from the trunk line to his room, and even fashioned an intercom system for his pals. To read past his bedtime, he furtively placed a sensor under the steps leading to his room, alerting him of his parents' approach. His curiosity for electricity was in his blood, as his dad, Sebastian J. Mauchly, worked with the Terrestrial Electricity and Magnetism section at Washington, D.C.'s Carnegie Institute, devising gear to measure electrical fields over land and water. As a high-school student, recalled John Mauchly's future wife, Kathleen "Kay" McNulty, he worked nights and weekends helping his father with scientific calculations.

At Baltimore's John Hopkins University, Mauchly entered on an engineering scholarship but found it to be "cookbook stuff" and not interesting to his inquisitive mind. Thus, wishing to see "the big picture," he moved over to Physics and graduated with a doctorate at age 25. Although the Great Depression was in full swing, he was offered an Associate Professorship of Physics at small Ursinus College, 25 miles from Philadelphia, for $3,800 a year.[74]

Mauchly's initial studies on weather prediction drew him to computing. In 1936, he was doing painstaking protracted research on how sunspots might affect the weather. With funds from President Franklin D. Roosevelt's National Youth Administration, he employed students to pore through the Carnegie Institution's mammoth collection of atmospheric observations. But sorting through the data by hand, or even with punch cards, would have taken decades. This drove Mauchly to find ways of simplifying and speeding up his calculations.

He knew the limiting factor for timely weather prediction was calculations — the mathematical tabulation of temperature, wind, and precipitation data required to make accurate predictions fast enough to be useful. But John, in his typical "reaching out" fashion, was interested in much more than weather predictions based on charts of pressure and temperature, the usual approach to weather forecasting in his day. It is worthless, after all, to predict today's weather tomorrow.

In particular, he was deeply interested in the impact of sunspots upon the weather, phenomenon which was known through observation but unknown with regard to cause and effect. John wanted and needed a machine fast enough to handle the complex calculations which he envisaged to tackle this and other problems associated with weather forecasting. Today, with the giant high speed machines available, extremely complex relationships are used to forecast more than just the temperature and potential rainfall the next day. John pioneered this concept and pointed the way with his work on ENIAC. He was interested in much more than calculations alone. The need he foresaw was for some form of intelligence in a process that would branch according to intermediate findings. He not only influenced

Pres Eckert in the development effort, but he also spear-headed the approach to the solution problems using the machine that he and Pres Eckert were building. In later years, in the mid '50s, he headed the UNIVAC Applications Research group for Sperry Rand, where he was instrumental in initiating the genesis for the Critical Path Method and Object Programming by encouraging and counseling his staff in developments of that nature.

Archives at the University of Pennsylvania reveal that Mauchly began dreaming of a machine to do the work of a mechanical calculator but automatically, with electronic switches for retrieval and storage, and electronic tubes to do math at speed-of-light pace. His concept was a fully electronic machine, with no moving parts, that would take a problem from beginning to end. It would do so without intermediate recording, and then re-entering of any number, as must be done with any machine that has no memory capability. In the mid-1930s he set along the path of creating such a machine by building counting devices by hand, using parts he acquired with his own money from second-hand stores.

Mauchly knew that scientists had recently devised electronic instruments for counting cosmic rays. The challenge was recording hundreds of "cosmic events" per second, a rate that overwhelmed electromechanical recorders. In response, physicists came up with so-called scaling circuits using high-speed vacuum tubes to bring the pulses down to a manageable number. As Augarten put it: "When, say, eight events struck the sensors, the first set of circuits dispatched four electrical pulses to the second set, which sent two pulses to the third ring, which in turn issued a single pulse to the recorder."[75] Mauchly was to apply such circuits to his electronic calculator.

Invention is often a solitary, even artistic, task. For example, Mozart once stated he would go for a long walk, and new music would begin circulating in his mind. Then he would write the music out as his mind dictated it. Einstein also spoke of invention as a form of art, and referred to other great scientists as artists[76]. He spoke of conceiving his notions of relativity by imagining that he was traveling along a light beam through space. In similar fashion, Mauchly conjured most of the logic behind the first digital, general-purpose computer as he imagined the ideal way to perform tedious calculations.

To a creative thinker like Mauchly, the construction of devices and systems took place through a process akin to composing a poem. Poetry is an economical, harmonious assembly of words directed to a desired purpose or theme. The poet needs to know how to fit together many complex pieces to create a compelling whole. In a similar way, Mauchly envisioned the solution to an intricate puzzle, and set about making the right pieces to fit within the solution.

In the provincial world of Ursinus College, Dr. John William Mauchly rapidly became the most popular teacher on campus. He always found ways to make his lectures exciting and understandable to his students. To explain the concept of a flip-flop he would use a balloon that he would squeeze at either end to show the flipping of the bulge from side to side. I can still see the grin on his face as he recounted the story saying, "See — flip–flop." One day he wore roller skates to demonstrate Newton's third law. Standing on the desk in the front of the classroom, he threw a ball forward and went backward, almost falling off the table. I can just imagine the grin of satisfaction on his face as he probably said, "See — action and reaction."

Outside his teaching hours, Mauchly labored mightily to absorb the creative ideas of other scientists. In that pre-Internet time, scientific developments were disseminated only by technical journals or word of mouth.

Mauchly was a student during the '30s. In autumn 1936, he enrolled in an evening graduate course in Electronics at the Moore School of Electrical Engineering, part of the University of Pennsylvania in Philadelphia. The School, endowed in 1923 by a maker of wire for hoop skirts, was located in a squat, two-story building on the sprawling campus. The electronics class proved too theoretical, however, for a practical tinkerer like Mauchly. Nonetheless, he had plenty of free time to talk with Eckert, the lab instructor.

Therefore, toiling alone during free hours, he devoured the few sources of electronics knowledge then current, among them the *RCA Radiotron Tube Manual*. He also pored over the *Review of Scientific Instruments* and the *Journal of the Franklin Institute*, as well as Electronics magazine.

From 1936 to 1938, Mauchly studied the scientific computations performed on plugged-together IBM machines by Dr. Wallace J. Eckert (no relation to John Presper Eckert), and steeped himself in the electromechanical advances of the large, analog, networked computers that Bell Telephone Laboratories and Westinghouse were designing.

Using electrical pulses to count ones and zeroes, Mauchly fashioned binary "flip-flops" of the kind used in computers ever since. To go beyond binary counting, and count up to 10, he put together a group of flip-flops for a "decade counter." Still dissatisfied, Mauchly wanted to direct these pulses for the complex tasks of storing numerical data for future use, as well as for division and multiplication. Mauchly "was obsessed with finding ways to make these calculations less painful," one of his physics students, John DeWire, later recalled.

The young professor had no grant money, so with the little cash of his own he bought up components, mostly used ones from electrical stores. There is a famous episode of the original "Star Trek" series in which the crew time-travels into Depression-era America. Like Mr. Spock in that episode, Mauchly, years ahead of his time, turned the day's primitive vacuum tubes into functioning electronic devices.

The 1800s English mathematician Charles Babbage also wrestled with the problem of conceiving ideas that outpaced the technology needed to build the concepts. Mr. Babbage had conceived and was able to build models of a calculating machine, called the Analytical Engine, employing some of the concepts later used in digital computing. Yet apart from a working mechanical calculator, his computing insights remained unrealized since the materials and know-how of the day were not refined enough.

Mauchly bought neon bulbs from General Electric that cost eight dollars per hundred. From these, late in 1936, he fashioned digitized circuit controls. According to his wife Kathleen's article, "John Mauchly's Early Years", Mauchly "wired up two neon bulbs with three resistors and one capacitor (condenser) and created, by interrupting the current through the circuit, the off-on action of a switch."[77] Mauchly built an encryption device with the neon devices, and the following year showed it to the legendary William Friedman, of the Army Signals Intelligence Service in Arlington, Virginia, the unit that broke Japan's diplomatic code during World War II. Some of these counters still exist in the Special Collections section of the University of Pennsylvania's Van Pelt Library.

Toward the end of the 1930s, Irven Travis, a Moore School instructor, directed Mauchly through a continual dialogue to the school's giant differential analyzer; an analog computer constructed in 1927 by Vannevar Bush, the future head of the U.S. wartime science effort. In retrospect, Mauchly was truly a giant standing on giant's shoulders. By 1941, he had become an instructor at the Moore School, which he and Eckert and their ENIAC creation would transform for a time into one of the world's leading centers on computing, if not the leader, since MIT and Harvard were pursuing improvements in the differential analyzer.

Globally, work was going on in other countries, especially in the United Kingdom and Germany. The UK efforts were mainly directed toward special purpose devices directed to breaking (decryption) the codes of the Germans. Alan Turing was an English mathematician who, on May 28, 1936, submitted a paper on the concept of a computing machine. His work was essentially associated with algorithms for computing and decryption of codes. For some, he is the father of computer science, but in reality he was not concerned with building a machine so much as specifying how such a machine would be used. The British coordinated their efforts and built 10 machines called "Colossus" to break the German codes. These top-secret machines were at Bletchley Park in the UK — the headquarters for the code breaking and a place where Alan Turing worked during the war. The Colossus machines, which were top secret until years after WWII, were special purpose devices geared to code breaking and not general-purpose machines as conceived by Mauchly and engineered by Eckert.

Meanwhile, having mastered a means of counting — by tallying pulses of electricity — Mauchly grouped together individual counting devices to form circuits for a "carry operation" where sums exceeded 10. He labored long hours soldering the circuits himself. Then he conceived of, and later on he and his colleagues were to solve, the vital problem of electronic storage. This landmark step permitted the storage of intermediate results without having to enter and re-enter the results for additional calculations. Piece by piece, over ten years- 1935-1945- he kept at it until he had put together his electronic symphony, and most of the major parts of the modern computers.

As the 1940s began, Mauchly's correspondence made his ambitions clear. On Dec. 4, 1940, he wrote Mr. DeWire: "I expect to have, in a year or so, when I can get the stuff and put it together, an electronic computing machine."

His colleagues were skeptical of his endeavors. Most professors and administrators at the Moore School believed large-scale digital electronics were far too unreliable, and not worth the large effort and expense. The notion that thousands of failure-prone vacuum tubes could be strung together and made to work almost error-free seemed foolhardy indeed.

At about this time, at the Ames, Iowa campus of Iowa State University, Dr. John Atanasoff also wrestled with the notion of automatic calculating machines. Like Mauchly, Dr. Atanasoff was a brilliant professor of physics. Unlike Mauchly, who was developing a general-purpose computer that could work in various fields of study, Dr. Atanasoff tried to build a special-purpose calculator, aimed at solving simultaneous linear equations.[78]

The two met in December of 1940, at a conference in Philadelphia of the American Association for the Advancement of Science. There, Mauchly delivered a paper on his calculating machine. After the speech, Dr. Atanasoff approached him. They spent some 20 minutes together, with Mauchly drawing diagrams of his counters, made of resistors, gas diodes and a condenser. Dr. Atanasoff left Mauchly with the mistaken impression that he, Dr. Atanasoff, was working with a completely electronic computer.

Starved for funds, Mauchly was forever fretting about cost. Thus, he was fascinated by Dr. Atanasoff's claim of having devised a cheap way of storing data, for two dollars per bit. For 1940, this was a remarkably low expense. Atanasoff failed to tell Mauchly that his cost reduction came not from electronics, but from a mechanical contrivance of a rotating wheel or drum. The following June, an excited Mauchly took off on a long drive. In a letter he noted, "I am going to Ames, Iowa to visit with Dr. Atanasoff … and to discuss with him the pros and cons of his electronic computer versus mine."

During a five-day stay at Dr. Atanasoff's home and at his office, Mauchly was disappointed by Dr. Atanasoff's machine — the Atanasoff Berry Computer, or ABC. It had yet to achieve its goal — solving simultaneous linear algebraic equations. Moreover, although the ABC had a digital add-subtract unit, built from vacuum tubes, its coefficients were stored on a slow, mechanical, rotating drum. The computer's calculations were no faster than those made by hand.

Mauchly discovered that the work of Atanasoff to a large extent was associated with a special purpose computer, which was little more than an advanced calculator, and that storage was not electronic but electro-mechanical. Mauchly was not impressed. Being the consummate gentleman, he did write back to Atanasoff in September 1941 as follows:

> "A number of different ideas have come to me recently about computing circuits--some of which are more or less hybrids--combining your methods with other things, and some of which are nothing like your machine. The question in my mind is this: Is there any objection, from your point of view to my building some sort of computer which incorporates some of the features of your machine?"

According to the Scott McCartney book, *ENIAC The Triumphs and Tragedies of the World's First Computer*, [79] Dr. Atanasoff's response was cordial, but reflected a concern over intellectual property rights that would lead, some thirty years later, to a contentious trial over patent claims. "Our attorney has emphasized the need of being careful about the dissemination of information about our device until a patent application is filed," Dr. Atanasoff wrote. "This should not require too long, and of course, I have no qualms about having informed you about our device."[80]

Mauchly's letter has been taken totally out of context. Those who champion the cause of John Atanasoff as the inventor of the computer use Mauchly's letter to buttress their claim that Mauchly's idea for a computer came from Atanasoff.

This is patently unlikely. Mauchly was lecturing in Philadelphia on computers in 1940 when he was approached by Atanasoff. Mauchly was deeply interested in low costs, but high speed, storage. The $2 per bit piqued his interest. When it turned out that such storage was not electronic, he was disappointed. Mauchly's goal was weather forecasting. That goal could not be achieved with a special purpose machine, nor could it be achieved with a machine heavily dependent on stop and go input of data, and on electro-mechanical storage. Since Atanasoff did not have the answers, Mauchly had to conceive and invent other ways to meet his objectives.

By his very nature, Atanasoff was very secretive. Whether this was protective of intellectual property or defensive because of inadequacy is subject to conjecture. McCartney's book goes to great lengths in pointing out the deficiencies in Atanasoff's designs, follow through, and perseverance. Atanasoff apparently abandoned the ABC machine completion, the patenting, and the claims. As detailed in many places in the McCartney book, Atanasoff never made any claim of priority of concept for years, but erupted with claims and innuendos after the Larson opinion. He claimed that he knew nothing about ENIAC but this was not true. He insinuated foul play in the suicide of his associate, but this was absolutely bizarre. On the whole, the claims made after the Larson opinion are extreme to say the least. This is especially tragic since, as shown in this book's section on the trial (Chapter Seven), the opinions are questionable as matters of law.

In his letter to Mauchly, he even requested complete secrecy because of the patent rules. John Mauchly, on the other hand, was very open at all times with regard to his ideas and aims.

In my opinion, it is unlikely that Atanasoff revealed all his ideas to John Mauchly; but I am firmly of the opinion that John Mauchly revealed all of his ideas to John Atanasoff. There is no proof of this assertion. It is based entirely on my knowledge of the individual character of these two brilliant men. Both deserve a great deal of credit for their forward thinking. Great attempts have been made by many people to diminish the contributions of John Mauchly in the creation of the Cyber Age. This is wrong! History is not a football game where we cheer for one side or the other.

Meanwhile, Mauchly doggedly pursued his own lines of research. He even attended courses, including a Moore School class on electrical design. But he needed a partner. He was aware of his strength, innovative thinking, but also knew his weaknesses, particularly in design engineering. He found it laborious to fabricate circuits. A collaborator, however, might make up for his deficiencies while sharing his zest for innovation. In 1941, he found such a partner in John Presper Eckert, with whom he teamed to produce not only the first ever electronic computer, ENIAC, but also the first production machine, UNIVAC. While Mauchly was the conceptual genius who "traveled the light beams of space," Eckert was the gifted genius who could make music from wires and tubes. The physicist and the engineer made history. Together they dreamed, worked, designed, built teams, built computers, and changed the world forever.

John Presper Eckert, Jr.: The Engineering Legend Who Created The Computer

John Presper Eckert, Jr. had had his own unique childhood. Born April 4, 1919, "Pres" Eckert grew up an only child in the Mt. Airy section of Philadelphia. His successful, affluent family later moved into a larger home in Germantown.

As with the Mauchly clan, learning and ingenuity ran in the Eckert family. Eckert's grandfather ran a small print business in Philadelphia, while his father, John, whom he greatly admired, operated a successful construction company. In place of a children's encyclopedia, his parents bought Eckert an Encyclopedia Britannica. He would frequently walk through the woods with his granddad, discussing all that he had learned from it. At his dad's construction sites, Eckert eagerly watched how his father, with great attentiveness and through a constant stream of questions, managed and coached the workers. The elder Eckert made sure each job was done correctly without cutting any corners. Eckert would employ these lessons throughout his life.

He also gained a love for math through those who raised him. On rainy days, Eckert and his dad would sit down, with the father calling out numbers and the son adding, multiplying, or dividing them as quickly as he could. Further, when his mom sent him to the grocery store, Eckert would constantly repeat each item on the shopping list over and over in his mind, instead of writing them down. In that way, one would "turn your short-term memory into long-term memory," Eckert later recalled, a concept he had employed in designing the first stored computer memory.

Because of Eckert's thriving construction consulting business, the family traveled around the world frequently for four months a year. Exposed to different cultures, Eckert's horizons literally broadened and may have helped foster his strongly independent streak of thinking.

"I'm not easily snowed by what other people tell me [what] the facts are in a situation where there's any uncertainty," Eckert explained. "I have to come to my own conclusions."

Like John Mauchly, Eckert was an inveterate tinkerer, constructing things like his own phonograph amplifiers by age thirteen. In such projects, his dad would stress the importance of finishing the task. His father's work philosophy, remembered his son, was, "If you started putting a building up, you had to make it work." Eckert further recalled, "My father used to say that all complicated things you come up against can be broken down into … consecutive steps. He said, 'What you want to be good at is … learning how to break things down … and thinking it through, because the individual steps are probably easy to do. Just because there are a lot of them, you shouldn't get too bowed down by it.' That is, of course, exactly what a computer does. He anticipated the computer in his philosophy."

MIT was always the top college choice for this natural-born engineer. Eckert's parents, however, could not bear having their only child attend class in faraway Boston. They preferred a prestigious local school, such as the University of Pennsylvania's Wharton School of Business in Philadelphia. But after a few days of class there, Eckert recalled, "It was putting me to sleep. They were grinding over the same ideas about ten different ways in each setting. I thought, 'God, I can't go through four years of this.'" He tried transferring over to the Physics Department, but it was full. So Eckert found the next-best solution: Penn's Moore School of Electrical Engineering. His class work was at first mediocre, then improved markedly — a C average turning into an A by senior year. Mauchly later said, "He didn't make top grades, but some people don't because their heads are so full of interesting things to think about and interesting things to do."

One of the interesting things Eckert did in his student days was to work at the World of Tomorrow for the 1939 New York World's Fair, where he was hired to set up a sound system for the E. G. Budd Company. At that time, the Budd Company was the pioneer maker of stainless-steel railroad cars, automobile frames and, when war broke out, the Bazooka anti-tank gun. At the futuristic Fair, Eckert deeply appreciated the economic importance of technological progress. He said, "If somebody makes an improvement, then somebody who remains the same is going to go down." In other words, constant innovation and technological improvement is crucial to staying ahead.

Despite his budding technical wizardry, Eckert was a bit of what a later generation called a "space cadet." A friend of his family, Tom Miller, remembered Eckert was notorious for driving over to the University of Pennsylvania and forgetting where he parked the car. His mom's chauffeur, Sam, would drive around the campus grounds until he found the vehicle.

Nearing graduation in 1941, Eckert received several job offers from top companies like RCA Labs and Philco; one firm offered him three times the normal starting salary. Realizing a higher education would prove more beneficial in the long run, he stayed at the Moore School to pursue a Masters in engineering. There, fate brought Eckert and Mauchly together in a partnership that would literally change the world forever.

So how did they go about it? In an interview in 1989, the interviewer, Alexander Randall V, asked Eckert, "So what did they give you? Did they say, 'Here's a room? Here are some tools. Here are some guys — go make it?'" Eckert replied, "Uh huh. Pretty much."

In the same interview, Mr. Randall went on to ask who invented the computer. Eckert replied, "Someday I'll write a book on who really invented the computer. It wasn't [Drs. John] Atanasoff or [John] von Neumann ... we did it."

Mauchly and Eckert Create the ENIAC

At the Moore School, Professor Mauchly was taking a summer engineering course, a class for math and physics majors to learn electrical engineering, as a more useful skill given the upcoming probability of war, and Eckert ran the class lab. The graduate student, under less pressure to be "practical" than some of his peers, leapt at the professor's proposals for collaboration. The young men complemented each other perfectly—Mauchly providing the concepts and logic, Eckert the skills and practicality to bring a dream to fruition. Besides, their different personalities further enhanced their complementarities. His forgetfulness aside, Eckert could be hot-tempered and argumentative, and was a painstaking perfectionist. Mauchly – calmer, friendly, talkative -- made a good foil.

The pair quickly realized they "both had a passion to build some kind of computing device," recalled Mauchly. Often, one could find them in Linton's all-night restaurant on campus, jotting their ideas on napkins. While many of his co-workers laughed at his ideas, remembered Mauchly, Eckert's extraordinary confidence kept his dreams going. "If it weren't for Eckert, I probably wouldn't have been encouraged to proceed."

By 1941, with America on the verge of war, Professor Mauchly attempted to apply his newfangled machine to a critical war-time effort -- improving the calculator tables for aiming field artillery. In August 1942, he wrote out a seven-page memo, "The Use of High-Speed Vacuum Tube Devices for Calculating". Mauchly proposed building an "electronic computer" that could perform 1,000 multiplications a second, and calculate the trajectory of an artillery shell in 100 seconds. Mauchly and Eckert certainly discussed everything that was known and being done in this new field of electronic computers. Mauchly wanted a self-directed machine with sufficient memory to handle any kind of problem more rapidly than otherwise possible. In particular, he rigidly insisted that intermediate or new numbers could not be manually entered into the process as it unfolded. This was certainly different from the direction taken by Atanasoff in the creation of his ABC computer. The ENIAC bore no relation in its foundation for its development to the work of Atanasoff. To claim otherwise, based upon the facts, would be akin to claiming James Watt invented jet engines since he was concerned with an expanding gas- steam. In particular, whereas Atanasoff used an electro-mechanical means for storing data, Eckert used electronic tools. Both store data, but what a difference! Eckert recalled, "We finally came to the conclusion, that if you're going to do this, you ought to do it whole hog and make everything in sight digital."[81]

The path-breaking use of subroutines was also to be built into the device. A subroutine is a set of program steps, separated from the main program, which can be invoked at will. "This idea was first proposed to me by Mauchly," said Eckert decades later in a speech, "and it became immediately clear that it was absolutely essential to the design and construction of the ENIAC." In this, Eckert returned to his essential notion of always breaking down a large task into smaller subtasks, in this case a master program into component subroutines. Today, just about every useful computer function, from currency converters to spell checkers to mortgage calculators are in fact subroutines. "Without this," noted Eckert, "the modern computer would be a bust."[82]

In the fall of 1942, Lieutenant Herman Goldstine was assigned as Army liaison officer to the Moore School, and there, headed up an Army ballistics office for "computing", that is, calculations. A 1936 math doctoral graduate from the University of Chicago, Goldstine was intrigued by Mauchly's work. In a lecture years later, he recalled Mauchly's emphasis on the "great gain in the speed of the calculation...if the devices which are used employ electronic means...very much higher than that of any mechanical device." Goldstine lobbied for the School to submit a proposal to the Army for a digital calculator. Mauchly and Eckert worked on the document, aided by the School's head of government contracts, John Brainerd.[83]

On Eckert's 24th birthday -- April 9, 1943 – Eckert, Mauchly, Brainerd, and Goldstine filled up the tank of a Studebaker, courtesy of some gasoline ration cards, and drove over to the Army's Ballistic Research Laboratory at Maryland's Aberdeen Proving Ground. Mauchly and Eckert revised their proposal on the way. There it was presented by Brainerd and Goldstine as a *Report on an Electronic Differential Analyzer and Computer*. The key person at the lab was Major Oswald Veblen, a noted mathematician from Princeton's Institute for Advanced Study. Veblen was ready to be impressed.[84]

Requests for ballistic firing tables had reached 40 a week, and with up to 500 variables a table, the Army was only turning out 15 tables a week. It took a squad of human calculators a month of cranking out numbers on such factors as wind speed and gun velocity to generate a single table. For the Americans then fighting in Africa and Europe, recalled Eckert in a 1988 interview with the Smithsonian, "the shells did not land where you wanted them to. The people there using these guns had to make guesswork corrections on the tables to hit anything."[85]

Driven by war-time pressures and impressed by the potential of Mauchly's design, Veblen heartily endorsed the proposal, and in June 1943 the Army formally awarded the University an initial six-month, $150,000 contract for the ENIAC[86]. A pilot computer was to be built at the Moore School, and a second, identical device for the Army's Ordnance Department at Aberdeen. Eckert was made chief engineer of the effort, code-named Project PX. Goldstine was appointed the Ballistics Research Lab's technical liaison, and Brainerd the project advisor, according to Augarten's book. Mauchly was dubbed principal consultant while he continued to teach a full load of classes.[87] With government monies flowing, the ENIAC team grew to 14 employees, 12 of them engineers.

While the government was strictly interested in an electronic machine to help with ballistic firing tables, Mauchly and Eckert were adamant about building a "very broad and universally applicable" machine capable of a wide range of tasks. Reflecting on his childhood learning experiences, Eckert said, "Everything in the past that I'd ever heard of that really ended up being worth anything was something that had a very general applicability."

Nuts and Bolts of a Historic Project

Throughout the project, requirements changed as engineers added more powerful features. "We originally expected to build the machine with 5,000 [vacuum] tubes," recalled its designer. "As it turned out, we built it with over 18,000 [A state-of-the-art B-29 bomber had less than 800 tubes]...The government changed from wanting one function table to three. They changed from wanting ten accumulators to twenty...The original plan was just to use an accumulator by repetitive addition. We decided to build a separate multiplier to greatly speed up multiplication by fifty times or something." The 100,000-pulse-per-second computer possessed twenty ten-digit memory slots.

By the time of its completion, after nine contract supplements, the project cost $486,804, and took two-and-a-half years, ending in fall 1945. Despite many changes to individual features, however, the team stuck to Mauchly and Eckert's overall vision of a fully digital, general-purpose device, a strategy critical to the eventual success.[88]

Caught up in the war effort, trying their utmost to support relatives fighting on the front lines, team members kept a frenetic pace, working seven days a week. In bouts of frustration, they renamed ENIAC the MANIAC. According to the article, "The Story That Doesn't Compute", by journalist Dale Keiger[89], they "relieved tension with pranks. Eckert fell asleep one night on a cot beside the growing machine. Two technicians picked up the cot, carried him to the second floor in an elevator, and placed him in an identical but empty room. When he awoke, he thought ENIAC had been stolen."[90]

Ensuring reliability among the huge number of vacuum tubes was a major hurdle. In a lecture years later, Goldstine reflected on the daring challenge: "The machine was a synchronous one, receiving its heart-beat from a clock which issued a signal every 10 microseconds. Thus, once every 10 microseconds an error would occur if a single one of the 17,000 [vacuum] tubes operated incorrectly; in a single second there were 1.7 billion (1.7 x 1,000,000,000) chances of a failure occurring and in a day (about 100,000 seconds) about 1.7 x 1,000,000,000,000,000 chances."[91] But Mauchly and Eckert and their team beat the odds.

From researchers at RCA, Eckert learned that lowering the current of the tubes not only greatly extended their lives but reduced the possibility of error. He had the voltage for the ENIAC's tubes reduced 5 to 10 percent. To build in further reliability, the circuits were designed to operate independently of component tolerances. "Man had never made an instrument," summed up Goldstine, "capable of operating with this degree of fidelity or reliability, and this is why the undertaking was so risky a one and the accomplishment so great."[92]

In January 1944, Mauchly and Eckert, the latter drawing on previous experience with pulse circuits used in radar, figured out the landmark process of how to store the computer's instructions in memory, in addition to the numbers. In its work, the ENIAC team outstripped the era's other computing efforts, such as the IBM Mark I at Harvard University. In comparison, even the Colossus I computer, built in 1943 at Bletchley Park, England with the help of math genius Alan Turing,[93] had limitations. Designed to help decipher Nazi codes, the Colossus[94] could not work on subject matter unrelated to cryptanalysis.

Some of ENIAC's woes were prosaic. The Moore School room hosting ENIAC was plagued with mice, which ate through some of the wires of the machines. Eckert, taking after his father's meticulousness, made sure that before a type of wire could be approved for use, it was put in a cage with a mouse that had been deliberately placed on a meager diet. The wire was approved only if the mouse could not chew through it.

Today's computers are exceedingly reliable, while ENIAC was frequently forced off line. However, the downtime was not totally ENIAC's fault. Aberdeen's military regulations enforced a "turn-off rule" when the computer was not working out a problem, according to Barkley Fritz' work, ENIAC-A Problem Solver[95]. The goal of the rule was to conserve scarce war-time electricity, and to bank the salary of the guard required to baby-sit, per Army regulations, any "unattended hot electrical device."[96]

When completed, the 10-foot-tall ENIAC weighed 60,000 pounds, sucked up 150 kilowatts of energy, and filled up 1,000 square-feet of Moore School floor. Its makeup, according to an ENIAC press release, included 6,000 switches, 17,486 vacuum tubes, 70,000 resistors, 10,000 capacitors -- and 500,000 soldered joints. A card punch was used for output, and to input data, programmers used an IBM card reader. Mauchly's grand vision of an all-digital, general-purpose computer was fulfilled.[97]

During this period, the Moore School also made engineering and cultural history by hiring the first computer programmers --all of them women. For these information tech pioneers, project advisor Brainerd pushed through a training course, one of the first classes dealing with computers. The leader of this group was Goldstine's wife, Adele, who made quite the contrast with the other ladies, typically from farms or small towns. Heavyset and cigarette smoking, Adele Goldstine would stride into a room, swing a leg over a desk, and start lecturing in a thick Brooklyn accent. Unusual for a woman of the time, she had a degree in Mathematics from New York's Hunter College. Swiftly taking charge, Mrs. Goldstine had three retired professors on the project removed, and had eager young computer instructors hired in their place.[98]

In summer 1945 six women, having completed their training, began work as ENIAC programmer-operators. As math majors, these women were chosen from the rankers of the "computers" at Penn, doing hand calculation of ballistic tables for the Army. Among them were Kay McNulty, a graduate of Chestnut Hill College in Philadelphia, who would become the future Kay Mauchly (later remarried, after her husband's death, as Kay Mauchly Antonelli) -- and grandmother to Sebastian Mauchly. Another of the programmers, Betty Holberton, noted, "Most of the men were away fighting. So we were left in charge." In 1946, Adele Goldstein wrote the Manual for the ENIAC,[99] laying claim to being the world's first technical writer for the computer

On February 14, 1946, with fanfare, ENIAC was introduced to the public. Before a gaggle of reporters, engineer Arthur Burks prepared a live demonstration. As related in Patrick Sweeney's book, Pioneer in Early Computer Development, Burks dramatically announced to the assembled scribes, "I'm going to add 5,000 numbers." He pushed a button. In three-one-hundred-sixtieths of a second, ENIAC multiplied 2,500 pairs of 10-digit numbers. The journalists looked up from their notepads to watch the calculation, and realized with surprise the calculation was already over. The women programmers bustled about in their dresses, throwing switches and plugging cables. Burks executed another command, and ENIAC calculated the trajectory of an artillery blast in 20 seconds, less time than a real shell took to travel. "That's when the speed really hit them," recalled a programmer.[100]

In addition to its work with the Army, the ENIAC team was rushed into service on the Manhattan Project. However, ENIAC's 20 10-digit memory slots were not adequate for the huge amount of information needed to crunch numbers for The Bomb. So Mauchly's team devised various workarounds, and one of the computer's first programs performed a computer simulation for Los Alamos.

In the end, a second ENIAC was not built for Aberdeen. Instead, in1946 the original one, modified with a stored program capability along the lines conceived by Mauchly and Eckert, was moved there from the Moore School, through a big hole in its wall, relates author McCartney.[101] Into the mid-1950s, it worked on hydrogen bomb design, missile tables, wind tunnel construction, and how weather conditions might affect nuclear fallout in Russia. The machine was employed far longer than are its modern successors.

Stealing Mauchly and Eckert's Thunder

Meanwhile, others outside the original ENIAC team took a hand in the project, eventually leading to great dispute. In the summer of 1944, Herman Goldstine had had a chance meeting at the north-bound platform of Aberdeen's railroad station. He bumped into John von Neumann[102], one of the many Jewish scientists who had fled Hitler's Europe, and now were working on weapons to defeat him. The Hungarian-born mathematician was world-famous for his papers on quantum physics and on the brand-new field of Game Theory. When Goldstine told him about ENIAC, von Neumann listened with rapt attention. His curiosity was spurred by his work with colleagues at the Manhattan Project. Von Neumann figured that calculating machines might solve that program's daunting challenge of modeling gigantic, nuclear explosions.

The following year, in June 1945, the Moore School team was planning a successor to ENIAC, called EDVAC. Von Neumann, now a consultant sitting in on many of the team's meetings, wrote up the thinking behind the revolutionary devices in a 101-page, mimeographed text, called *First Draft of a Report on the EDVAC*.[103] The document was published under von Neumann's name only. Eckert and Mauchly at first paid little heed to it as it was seen to be an internal summary of their team's classified project labors. "It appeared to be purely a characteristic of Goldstine and no one else that in producing this mimeographed version, Goldstine put no one's name on it except von Neumann's," Mauchly later recalled.[104]

According to the acting supervisor of the EDVAC project, S. Reid Warren, Goldstine asked him if the report material could be mimeographed at the Moore School - for use solely by von Neumann and project staff. "I asked Dr. Goldstine," recalled Warren, "whether or not the material should be classified, and he stated that since it was for use only within the group working on the EDVAC and since it was considered to be a formal report, no classification was necessary."[105]

However, shortly after, according to McCartney's book, Goldstine sent two dozen copies to colleagues of von Neumann in Britain and the U.S.[106] The report's language, in von Neumann's appealing style, was changed slightly to sidestep military censorship. As other copies, soon up to several hundred, were sent out, the false notion took root that von Neumann had generated most of the manuscript's ideas. This seemed a logical assumption, given that the Hungarian polymath was well-known to the press and was already a legend for his other achievements. To this day, most computers are said to be built around "von Neumann architecture". They should be more properly referred to as the "Eckert-Mauchly architecture".

Goldstine later asserted of the report, "Not everything in there is his [von Neumann's], but the crucial parts are."[107] However, Von Neumann himself never claimed such sweeping credit for the first stored program computer. Three months later, Mauchly and Eckert crafted their own *Progress Report on EDVAC*, which got little notice, partly because it was classified, by Goldstine, as a text documenting a top-secret project.[108]

Patents Pending

As the war drew to a close, patent disputes over ENIAC and EDVAC heated up. Mauchly and Eckert's first confrontation over this matter was with the University of Pennsylvania.

In 1943 the University's President, George McClelland, had made an agreement with Mauchly and Eckert, whereby individual inventors could hold title to patents. At the same time, the University could license ENIAC technology to the Government or other non-profit institutions. At war's end, however, the University's contracting officer, Irven Travis, overturned that pact, ordering Mauchly and Eckert to relinquish all patent rights, including commercial rights.[109]

Travis was likely influenced by growing collaboration between research universities and the government agencies offering them funding. According to the Howard Rheingold book Tools for Thought[110], Travis modeled the University's revamped patent policy after programs like the MIT's Department of Industrial Cooperation, and another at Johns Hopkins' Applied Physics Laboratory. The new policy required faculty members to hand over all patent rights. Asserting that a prior, good-faith agreement had been unilaterally breached, Mauchly and Eckert protested, to no avail. Dismayed, in 1946 they left the University to build computers in the private sector. (Eckert was to turn down an offer from von Neumann to be chief engineer on the latter's computer project at Princeton.)[111]

As it happened, Eckert and Mauchly actually filed just one patent application in 1947 for the overall ENIAC system[112]. Ironically, around the time they left the University, the Army Ordinance office granted the University of Pennsylvania funding for EDVAC, but a successful EDVAC was never constructed. "They got the funding, and then they couldn't build it," recalled a close former colleague of Mauchly. "The geniuses were gone." According to David Richie's book, The Computer Pioneers-The Making of the Modern Computer[113], this "was a foolish and short-sighted decision on the University's part, for with the departure of ENIAC's makers, the Moore School lost its preeminent status in the field of computing."[114] Indeed, some believe southeastern Pennsylvania thereby fumbled its chance to be a mid-Atlantic version of Silicon Valley or Boston's Route 128. On the other hand, this action, states author Fritz, "helped to move computer development from universities and dependence on U.S. government contracts to the eventual emergence of the major new industry of the second half of the twentieth century."[115] Moreover, according to Fritz, Mauchly and Eckert "came up with new ideas and more advanced technology, which, although not often immediately applied, led not only to future changes and enhancements to ENIAC, but also to a number of computers (e.g., EDVAC, BINAC and UNIVAC),[116] designed and developed later by many of the same team and others."[117] The EDVAC design proved very influential in its use of magnetic tape storage. The famous UNIVAC was the world's first commercial computer. It was designed by the Eckert-Mauchly Computer Corporation. By 1951, it was already in "production" (and failing to meet its goals due to a loss of financing when they sought Remington Rand as a buyer.

Mauchly and Eckert's second fight over patent rights was with Goldstine and von Neumann. In April 1947, with Army attorneys hovering in the background, the four men sat down to try to thrash out the patent dispute. At the meeting, the four men could not agree on assignment of credit for ENIAC's technology. The assemblage broke up with ill feelings, and Mauchly and Eckert did no further work with von Neumann or Goldstine.

According to Goldstine's book, The Computer from Pascal to von Neumann[118]:

The upshot...was that von Neumann's *First Draft* was treated by the ordnance lawyers as a publication...the distribution given to that report had placed its contents in the public domain, and hence anything disclosed therein became unpatentable…The Ordnance lawyers thereupon withdrew from the task of preparing patents on the EDVAC work in behalf of Eckert and Mauchly.[119]

In other words, Goldstine's failure to classify von Neumann's *First Draft,* two years previously, contributed to voiding Mauchly and Eckert's patent, and any of their related patents thereafter.[120] Soon after the intellectual property brawl, tragedy devastated Mauchly when his first wife, of seventeen years, drowned while swimming off the coast of New Jersey in 1946, leaving Mauchly with two young children, ages 7 and 11. [121]

Personality disputes and rivalries played a part in the schism. Eckert was miffed at a von Neumann lecture series where, Eckert asserted, the mathematician "rarely" accorded credit to those "who actually produced the ideas" for ENIAC. According to Goldstine, both Eckert and Mauchly were disappointed with Brainerd, for his perceived failure to publicly acknowledge their technical breakthroughs.[122]

High-Tech Controversy

Based on historical records and interviews with survivors, the credit unduly accorded von Neumann and denied Mauchly and Eckert for the invention of the digital computer is founded on a series of apparently deliberate acts by von Neumann and Goldstine. It is past time to set the record straight.

According to Goldstine, von Neumann deserves a lion's share of credit for inventing the technology behind the ENIAC.[123] Yet this is patently untrue, as Goldstine himself writes. "Eckert and Mauchly unquestionably led on the technological side," his book states[124]. Von Neumann was not an original member of the ENIAC team, but he was surely aware that Mauchly and Eckert were the chief architects behind the effort. He was also aware of the landmark lecture series on the computer at the University of Pennsylvania, a series built on the ideas of the Moore School duo.

Von Neumann 'inadvertently' failed, according to Goldstine, to give due credit to the work of Mauchly and Eckert. Goldstine writes that the reason for this was that the [EDVAC Report] :

…was intended by von Neumann as a working paper for use in clarifying and coordinating the thinking of the group and was not intended as a publication…Its importance was so clear, however, that later as its fame grew many outsiders requested copies from the Moore School or me. Through no fault of von Neumann's, the draft was never revised into what he would have considered a report for publication. Indeed, it was asserted several years later that he did not know that it had been widely distributed.[125]

This account stretches credulity. With his famously gregarious nature and his hundreds of contacts in various countries throughout the scientific realm, it is hard to imagine that the world-famous von Neumann did not quickly receive feedback on the report.

In any event, von Neumann had countless opportunities to "correct the record," but never did so. He could have written an explanation to his many friends and colleagues in different nations, granting Mauchly and Eckert due credit. He could have attached a cover letter to this effect in the original report. He could have laid out the true facts in a lecture, or in a book. However, he did none of these things. As time went on, he was well aware that his reputation as "the computer's inventor" was growing. He benefited from this false renown, and did nothing to dispel it. With all due recognition to his undoubted accomplishments in various scientific fields, one can only conclude that, in the matter of the computer's invention, von Neumann, and Goldstine, were apparently disingenuous.

Goldstine also contended that he and von Neumann's real interest lay in keeping the ideas and innovations behind the ENIAC in the public domain for the benefit of the academic and scientific communities and the free pursuit of knowledge. Goldstine's view implicitly paints the patent seekers, Mauchly and Eckert, as materialistic, even greedy men, while portraying himself and von Neumann as big-minded men upholding the public interest. In his book, Goldstine argues he and von Neumann wanted to keep computer technology free and open, thus blocking Mauchly and Eckert from gaining financially from a scientific feat belonging to all. But Goldstine and von Neumann's own actions flatly contradict this view. They also applied for patents -- for the EDVAC, in 1946.[126]

This was hardly the action of men motivated by idealism. It also should be noted that other actions of theirs undermined their very own patent application. Their dissemination, and *de facto* publication, of the EDVAC report might very well have constituted "prior art," a legal status that precludes granting of ownership rights to previously published material.

The most damning thing about the behavior of von Neumann and Goldstine may have been their approach to security. Mauchly was to be unfairly brushed, during the EDVAC project, and the McCarthy Era, with false allegations of Communist sympathies.[127] Yet Goldstine committed real and potentially damaging breaches of national security by failing to classify the EDVAC report. Not only did Goldstine neglect to classify this paper, which contained an overview of the most cutting-edge, militarily-related technology of the time, but Goldstine sent it to dozens of colleagues, including those outside the United States. And these men sent it out to dozens and dozens more, until hundreds were in the know about what should have been kept secret.

It is known that the nascent computer sectors of friendly countries, including the United Kingdom and Canada, benefited greatly from the information in the EDVAC "blueprint". As Maurice Wilkes, the head of a leading computer initiative in England, put it, "For some reason, the draft EDVAC report was not given a security classification and a number of copies, including the one…showed me, were given away." Given that the technology behind ENIAC/EDVAC was practically made public by its widespread dissemination, nations such as the Soviet Union, soon to be a Cold War adversary, could easily have benefited as well. Yet no investigation was ever made of, nor reprimand given, to von Neumann and Goldstine.

For years after, relations between the two sides remained frosty, as the publication of Goldstine's book in 1972 showed. The publisher, Princeton Press, sent Mauchly an advance copy to elicit his comments. "So John read it," recalled Kay Mauchly Antonelli, "and he was pretty incensed about the things that Goldstine was saying about him." Mauchly noted 10 substantive factual errors, and sent them to the publisher. Princeton Press wrote back, said Antonelli, "that the author refuses to accept these corrections and the book will be published as Goldstine said."[128]

Disputes over intellectual property continued to dog Mauchly. Remington Rand, and its successor Sperry Rand Corporation, had acquired the ENIAC patent rights upon buying the Eckert-Mauchly Computer Company. Sperry Rand engaged in a long patent dispute with Honeywell Inc., which culminated in a noted 1971 trial in Minneapolis. The trial verdict unjustly denied Mauchly's patent rights stemming from his work on ENIAC, and has had a lasting negative effect on Mauchly's place in computer history.[129]

An Impact Undeniable

Still, the impact of the ENIAC, and its two inventors, on our world is immense and undeniable. The notion of its fully digital, general-purpose computer registers "is the origin of our modern Random Access Memory or RAM," Eckert once stated[130]. The ENIAC's creation of subroutines is the structural basis of modern programs. The project's rigorous testing of components was a procedure that "really did not adequately exist to any great extent in consumer electronics before ENIAC," noted Eckert. Yet another of ENIAC's revolutionary notions was the idea of electronically stored instructions, with their elimination of time-consuming, labor-intensive setup.[131]

Another important aspect is the ENIAC 's impact on the business world. In the spring of 1946 Tom Watson, the son of IBM's president Tom Watson, Sr., visited the ENIAC. He quickly appreciated the potential of sophisticated electronics and advocated the development of computers at IBM—originally for government use and later commercial. Within 15 years IBM became "the dominant supplier of digital mainframe computers," as stated in James W. Cortada's The ENIAC's Influence on Business Computing, 1940s— 1950s.[132] During this period, businessmen began to investigate what the computer could do for the nonscientific and nonmilitary world. Companies sent teams to attend seminars and visit the ENIAC and other similar computing devices in hopes of gaining as much knowledge of this new industry called "computers" as possible. Shortly thereafter, many corporations were doing their own in-house research.

In 2000, Kathleen (McNulty) Mauchly Antonelli, one of the first programmers in history and widow of John Mauchly, summarized the lives of Eckert and her husband as follows:

"Eckert and Mauchly remained fast friends throughout their lives. They complemented each other. Mauchly was always the teacher — highly intelligent, witty and compassionate. Described by many as the 'visionary of the computer age,' he was interested in developing people as well as ideas."

Mauchly died in Jan. 1980 from complications of an inherited disease of the blood vessels. Speaking at John Mauchly's funeral, Eckert said, "He inspired me and he inspired many others. He was not tied down by inhibitions or tradition. He was certainly one of the most brilliant people I ever knew."

Eckert stayed with the company he had co-founded and retired as vice president of Unisys. This brilliant, original, no-nonsense engineer and spellbinding speaker died from leukemia on June 3, 1995, just a few months before the 50th anniversary of ENIAC celebration sponsored by the University of Pennsylvania on Feb. 14, 1996. The contract to build ENIAC had been signed in May 1943, shortly after his 24th birthday.

In his later years, Eckert had become a spokesman for the computer industry. He claimed in his speeches that he and Mauchly were the Wright Brothers of computing. Eckert was undoubtedly the Engineer of the Century, even if not designated officially. Kay Mauchly Antonelli made significant efforts in the latter part of her life to have Eckert so designated.

Mauchly and Eckert changed the world forever with their work. We must all be grateful for the inventive genius of these two men.

Had ENIAC not been developed, another machine certainly would have. However, the ENIAC project was totally unique for its time. While AT&T was developing computers in the 1950s and Britain had designed their infamous Colossus, neither was brought to the attention of the public at that time; the latter was entirely unknown until the late 1970s. The ENIAC was widely known, and as a result, a demand for such computing capabilities in the private economy developed. This sharing of information and collaboration simply for the sake of intellectual curiosity has impacted billions of humans across the globe and truly jumpstarted the greatest technological era in world history.

CHAPTER THREE

THE WOMEN OF ENIAC

It is necessary to recognize the work and tireless efforts of the first programmers that made possible the computer as we know it today. This chapter highlights the dedication, brilliance, and credit due to these tremendous women. I cannot stress this enough.

Admiral Grace Murray Hopper : Striving for Natural Computer Language

Computers have a language of their own. It is normally incomprehensible, cumbersome, and difficult to use. In fact, it is almost impossible to use correctly. Hence in the early days of computers, programming took almost forever. You had to fabricate instructions using code symbols that the computer would understand, and indicate the exact position in memory of the data or numbers you wanted to manipulate. Estimates were that each instruction that was ultimately correctly produced cost from ten to sixty dollars depending on the complexity of the task; and those dollars were 1950s dollars.

Almost immediately with the advent of the computer, efforts were made to harness the power of the computer itself to writing code. Today, we can virtually talk to our computers and get what we want accomplished - whether it be an item of data, a song, a movie, a telephone call, or even building a new system to do any of these - and more.

Two giants of the computer age were heavily involved in starting this era of automatic programming. One was Dr. John Mauchly, co-inventor of the ENIAC, and the other was Dr. Grace Murray Hopper, later to be the oldest serving active duty officer in the United States Navy when she retired in 1986 with the rank of Rear Admiral[133]. In 1996, four years after her death on January 1st of 1992, the US Navy christened a destroyer (DDG-70) the "USS Hopper". The ship has been nicknamed, just as she was, "Amazing Grace". This is one of the very few naval vessels named after a woman.

I first met Grace in the late summer of 1956. I walked into her group's office at Remington Rand UNIVAC where she was director of the automatic programming group, headquartered at 19th and Allegheny in Philadelphia. This was the site of the UNIVAC I production facility. At this location, LARC- Livermore Advanced Research Computer- was created and assembled. LARC was the most advanced machine of its day, going into full operation in the 1958-1959 time frame. What is significant is that it was the first client server system utilizing two CPU's (Computer Processing Unit) with one handling the input and output of data, and the other doing the background calculations. Much of the work associated with the operating system for this machine was done by Grace's group.

   She was sitting on a high stool, at a drafting table laid flat for her use as a desk. She was tapping the desk with a thick ruler, giving directions to a host of people who wandered in and out of our meeting. Finally she dismissed everyone and we got down to work designing automatic programming systems. It was the beginning of a life-long friendship and collaboration that lasted until her death on New Year's Day of 1992. Grace Hopper has established herself in the history of computers and information technology as one of the foremost exponents of computer language that can be readily used. The stories and legends about her are vast. Grace had a brilliant analytical mind and a no- nonsense feisty personality that added color and dimension to her work and accomplishments. She also had a way with words, perhaps enhanced by her marriage, from 1930 to1945, to Dr. Vincent Hopper, Chairman of the NYU English department.

   Grace Brewster Murray was born in New York City on December 9, 1906. She graduated from Vassar College in mathematics and physics in 1928; and went on for graduate work at Yale University, receiving her master's degree in 1930 and her Ph.D. in 1934 in mathematics. She taught mathematics at Vassar until December 1943 when she volunteered to serve in the WAVES, "Women Accepted for Volunteer Emergency Service", a division of the US Navy organized in August of 1942. She was posted to the Naval Reserve Midshipman School at Smith College. After graduating first in her class in 1944, she was assigned to the Bureau of Ships Computation Project at Harvard University, as the third person to join the staff of the Director, Dr. Howard Aiken. Lieutenant Hopper, with her usual energy, immediately became expert at programming the huge Mark I machine.[134]

   Unlike the ENIAC, the Mark I was not fully electronic but rather an electro-mechanical machine of vast proportions - 51 feet long, 8 feet high, and 2 feet wide. It was used to solve large and complex mathematical problems. It could perform three additions per second, very slow compared to the ENIAC. The basic calculating units had to be synchronized mechanically. This was done using a 50 foot shaft driven by a five horsepower motor.

   The Mark I was not a general purpose electronic digital computer.

   With her brilliance Grace quickly became an important part of the group and co-authored three papers with Howard Aiken. She even put together a 500-page Manual of Operations for the machine. After her request for transfer to the Regular Navy at the end of the war was denied, she stayed at the Harvard Lab with Dr. Aiken until 1949.

   The Mark I was soon replaced by the Mark II in 1947. Like the Mark I, and the Mark III and Mark IV afterwards, these machines were built by IBM directed by the design of Dr. Aiken. It was while Grace was working on the Mark II that her coworkers noticed that a moth stuck in a relay had interfered with the computer's operation. In her log book, Hopper wrote that they were "debugging" the machine, and the term gained wide currency.[135] The log books, and the moth's remains, are now at the Smithsonian. The term "debug" has become synonymous with solving programming errors, or 'bugs', in a computer program. Thanks Grace!

In 1949 she joined the Eckert-Mauchly Computer Corporation as a senior programmer. It was during this time she began working on language structures to make computers more readily programmable. Under the direction of John Mauchly, she devoted her energies to cracking the problem of making computers easier to use. There were and are three ways to handle such a problem. They all involve the use of an artificial language, or pseudo-code, to replace the use of the real computer codes. The three approaches are called assemblers, interpreters, and compilers. In all cases the computer reads the pseudo-code. The obvious preferred pseudo code is our everyday vernacular language - English, Spanish, French, or whatever. For scientific calculations, the obvious approach would be to use formulas. That was the goal. How did we go about it?

In an interpreter, the pseudo program stays in the memory of the machine, and triggers various code segments to act as the computer interprets the pseudo instructions to function. In the assembler system, the computer replaces the pseudo code with actual machine instructions and locations. In compilers, the computer converts the pseudo code into real computer code which it then performs.

BASIC is the best known of the interpreters and compilers; and COBOL (Common Business Oriented Language) is the best known compiler. The assemblers were the cornerstone of building interpreters and compilers, and soon were used only by the professionals, and even then their use diminished rapidly.

I was fortunate to work on both interpreters and compilers in the early fifties; and to collaborate extensively with both Grace Hopper and John Mauchly in their work with automatic programming.

If the reader will forgive me, it becomes necessary to interject a few brief technical remarks to make it possible to truly evaluate Grace's contributions to humanity. Grace's group was developing what is called Automatic Programming and it is in this area that she did some of her famous work in developing compilers. Automatic Programming consists of various attempts to simplify the development of the code that runs the computer. Every computer has its own unique real code or operation code. These are abstruse characters or a combination of characters - letters, numbers, and symbols. Computers also have to function with data that is stored in specific locations. Early programmers had to know, among other things, the addresses and sizes of the data, so writing real code for a machine becomes very complex. The alternative is to use automatic programming approaches. For example, a programmer could write statements in English, and from them, the compiler would create actual programming code.

This all started in 1949, and some results were beginning to be achieved by 1952. By 1956 we had a number of systems completed, in use, and ready for the next stage of development. Consider the world of 1949-1952. There were no satellites; computers were gigantic machines that filled hundred and thousands of square feet; only a limited number of people were adept at computers, or even knew what they were; and programming was cumbersome to say the least. Now imagine the difficulty of actually critiquing a program that would create programs! That's what Grace and a few other intrepid people set out to do. From these rudimentary steps taken then, we have progressed to today where we can talk to our machine in many languages, have the machine do our bidding, and even carry on a dialogue with it. As the Virginia Slims cigarette ads used to say, "You've come a long way baby!"

Computer compilers are an attempt to deal with this problem.

As previously mentioned, there are three kinds of compilers: interpreters, assemblers, and the true compilers. The programming language is built around "pseudo code". Pseudo code has a great resemblance to natural, English-like language, and thus is relatively easy to write, and to use.

With interpreters, the program interprets, or processes, each instruction of the pseudo code in turn. This is slow, since there is a constant back-and-forth between a pseudo code and the block of real code that runs the particular instruction. The speed reductions can be as great as 10:1. However, when the time required to create a program is cut from days or even weeks to hours, then reduction in machine efficiency may be very worthwhile.

In this vein, the work of Grace Hopper and her Philadelphia-based, automatic programming research group of Remington Rand UNIVAC involved computer compilers. It was divided in the so-called A-track or series, the A standing for arithmetic, or scientifically oriented, automatic programming, and the B series, standing for business automatic programming. Grace had begun her operations in this field for Remington Rand around 1952, about the same time as the University of Toronto was doing its own related work with Transcode, probably the first successful interpreter.

The A series was initially very successful, ultimately being released as the commercial product Math-Matic. The B series led to the release in the late 50s of Flow-Matic, which became the forerunner of COBOL - for Common Business Oriented language - the most successful of the early compilers.

IBM, with its superior marketing strategy and performance, outdid Remington Rand, initially releasing its FORTRAN, for Formula Translator. It soon became the standard in scientific enterprises. Grace's Math-Matic never really got off the ground, even though, in some respects it was a superior product.

During this same period of time, in the early 50s, Transcode was being developed at the University of Toronto by Drs. Pat Hume and Bea Worseley[136]. It was very fast, even though it was an interpreter. I used it extensively from 1953 to 1956, developing sophisticated systems for space vehicles, aerodynamic test instrumentation, and aerial navigation systems. In my opinion, it was far superior to all other systems then available.

Pat and Bea never received much credit or acclaim, which they really deserved for their very advanced, and very fast, application. In 1964, BASIC for Beginner's All-purpose Symbolic Instruction Code was designed by John George Kemeny and Thomas Eugene Kurtz at Dartmouth in New Hampshire. BASIC soon took the lead as the favorite interpreter. Later in the 70s it became a compiler as well. Bill Gates was an early developer of Basic Compilers when Microsoft was in its infancy.[137]

Assemblers are more direct and faster than interpreters. The real code is replaced with a mnemonic code; that is, one relatively easy to remember and manipulate. An assembler uses symbolic addresses with a tag pointing to the real address, which the assembler then assigns. This saves a lot of work updating addresses. Assemblers are much faster to operate, but their programmatic assembly code is harder to write. IBM was concentrating on its Autocoder assembler for business applications in the period from 1953 until 1956 when the Autocoder was supplanted by FORTRAN and later by COBOL in the late '50s.

The true compiler takes a pseudo code instruction and converts it into the real code of the machine. The real code is then used to process the application. More advanced versions optimize the generated code to make the code "tight" and run as fast as possible.

The B series became a forerunner of COBOL, for decades the major programming language of business. I was well aware of Grace's work on the B series. I offered to field test the system. At the time, 1958, I was in charge of UNIVAC Systems in Canada, and also utilized UNIVAC Systems throughout the United States. I selected a major client, the Ontario Hydro Electric Power Commission, as a test bed. Over time, we trained about a hundred people on creating pseudo code for the compiler's use. This was the first effective large-scale test of the concept of English-language programming for business systems. It set the stage for the founding of the Codasyl Committee of the Department of Defense which in turn led to the creation of COBOL. The rest is history

I believe the work we did at the Ontario Hydro was the forerunner of natural language systems, the languages the great majority of programmers use today, which was a very important thing. Those experiences set the stage for the United States Department of Defense to establish the Codasyl Committee. Codasyl was the acronym for Conference on Data Systems Languages. This committee oversaw the creation of COBOL. By the mid-60s, COBOL, besides being paramount as a business application, was the most widely used programming language in the world. Grace was a member of the Codasyl Committee. It is fair to say that COBOL was based very much on her philosophy. I sometimes wonder how much of our findings at the Ontario Hydro helped in her spearheading of the COBOL creation.

Grace and I remained friends over the years, sharing experiences and ideas. When she went back to active duty in the Navy in 1967 I was developing manpower systems for the Navy and I would often wander up to her fifth floor office in the Pentagon to discuss the realities of the task – system-wise and politics-wise. Grace was equally adept at both.

Grace was a brilliant woman, but you might say she was rather direct in getting what she wanted, and perhaps somewhat of a showboat. Like John Mauchly she liked to pepper her public speeches and appearances with memorable gimmicks. Her favorite was the Nano-stick, a piece of wire or stick that measured slightly less than a foot. It was the distance a beam of light would travel in a nanosecond, a billionth of a second. By comparison, the length of wire a light beam travels in a microsecond is almost 1000 feet long. This proved her point about miniaturization, and the impact on the speed of computing.

At one time, her office at Remington Rand was outfitted with a blue sofa, which she hated with a passion. At the same time the office of a fellow named Hermann Lukoff, an engineer who was Pres Eckert's deputy, had a green sofa. Grace preferred green to blue. Overnight, without notifying Lukoff, the green sofa appeared in Grace's office, and the blue one in Lukoff's.

I recorded almost twenty hours of video with John Mauchly's widow, Kay Mauchly Anontelli. During these reminiscences, we compared notes on people we both know, including Grace in particular. She told me that Grace was a real "party girl", full of vim. She had a wry sense of humor that helped in awkward situations. She also had a will of iron and always knew what she wanted. Kay told me that Grace never had enough file cabinets. She liked to have a lot of them. One time, she walked into John Mauchly's office, while he was President, and eyed his file cabinets. According to Kay, Grace emptied John's filing cabinets on the spot. She took them and put them in her office. Trained in math, Grace Hopper lived one of Euclid's precepts: the shortest path between points is straight line! [138] She was laid to rest with full military honors in Arlington National Cemetery; Section 59, grave 973. Rest in peace, Grace. We miss you.

Kathleen McNulty Mauchly Antonelli

Kay was brilliant. She was a caring mother, a steadfast and supportive wife, and one of the first digital computer programmers in history. It was my privilege to know and love her for almost fifty years until she died in 2006. She had an impact on all those she met, either with her quizzical smile, her always upbeat nature, or her keen and sharp intellect. Kay could discuss abstruse mathematics, modern art, Chestnut Hill College, or bringing up children at the drop of a hat.

It all started because Kay needed a job after graduating from Chestnut Hill College as a Mathematics Major in 1942. Of the 92 graduates, three had earned their degrees in mathematics. They all needed jobs.

Consider the world in 1942. The attack on Pearl Harbor had occurred on December 7th of 1941, in the middle of her senior year. Women mathematicians were a rarity, with the usual jobs open in teaching at the secondary school or college level. Actuarial science called for at least a Master's Degree, plus special examinations conducted by the Society of Actuaries. Research jobs were reserved for men. The professional world, especially in mathematics, was virtually a total male environment. The war changed all that as men went off to war or to industries backing up the war effort. As a result, jobs opened up for women as assistants to men in the male-dominated environment, whether in the services or in industry. Grace Hopper joined the Waves. Kay McNulty and her Chestnut Hill College classmate Fran Bilas went to work at the Moore School of Electrical Engineering of the University of Pennsylvania as 'computers' – people who performed calculations. John Mauchly (her husband-to-be), Kay and I often discussed the use of that word for persons as differentiated from its use with machines. We facetiously proposed that people be called 'computors', with the 'o' replacing the 'e;' to distinguish between persons with an 'o' and computers with an 'e'. Idle chatter in a way, but full of meaning for someone tagged with that title as a profession in 1942. It just shows that inventive minds can do more than just invent machines, computers, and languages or create algorithms for computation.

It is often said that behind every great man is a great woman. Here it was a case of the first six women behind a great invention. In the history I will present, it is fair to say that behind one of the 20th century's greatest inventions stood a group of extraordinary women. These were the human "computers" that so impacted the development of the ENIAC General Purpose Electronic digital computer that they were inducted into the Women in Technology International Hall of Fame in 1997. Kay was also inducted into the Chestnut Hill Hall of Fame during its 80th anniversary as a college in 2007. She was one of 80 selected from all the graduates since the College was created in 1927.

I am proud to say that my wife, Barbara, was also one of those selected. She graduated in 1960. I mention that because Kay was instrumental in our marriage. In 1960 she flat out told me one day I should get married. When I said I was too busy to date, she very firmly said, "I'll fix that!"

She did. She had known Barbara all through her time at Chestnut Hill College since she was a classmate of Kay's step-daughter, John's daughter, Sidney. Barb had often spent time at the Mauchly household. Kay invited Barb to dinner, and the following year we were married. I often refer to us as the first computer couple, picked not by the computer, but by the inventors of the computer. That is a neat way of saying thank you to both Kay and John Mauchly, who had a hand in engineering our introduction and subsequent marriage.

The women of ENIAC were always called 'the girls.' In February of 1946, after almost four years of effort in programming – first the differential analyzer and then the ENIAC – the 'girls' produced the dazzling and successful programs for the demonstration of ENIAC. These six young women programmed the world's first all-electronic computer, the ENIAC. Their ballistics program used hundreds of wires and 3000 switches. They created the first sort routine, software application and instruction set, and classes in programming. Their work dramatically altered computing in the 1940s and 1950s. They paved the path to the modern software industry. They programmed ENIAC to perform a ballistics trajectory, a differential calculus equation important to the WWII effort, and they succeeded brilliantly. When the ENIAC was unveiled to the public on February 14, 1946, their program captured the imagination of the press and made headlines across the country. Afterwards, the ENIAC became a legendary machine and its engineers (all men) became famous. Never introduced or credited at the ENIAC events of the 1940s, the story of 'the girls' - the actual Programmers - disappeared from history. They became invisible.

Forty years after the unveiling of the ENIAC, whose press coverage included the picture of women standing beside the behemoth of a machine, Kathy Kleiman, a documentary filmmaker who details these women's contributions, was told that the women in pictures with ENIAC (1946) were "Refrigerator Ladies," models posed in front of the machine.

As Kay McNulty Mauchly Antonelli said in a documentary filmed in 2001, "None of us girls were ever introduced...we were just programmers."[139]

Kay McNulty Mauchly Antonelli not only stood behind the ENIAC machine, but she stood alongside John Mauchly, her husband and co-inventor of the ENIAC through both the good times and the difficult times. After John Mauchly died in 1980, Kay set herself to right the terrible wrongs visited upon her husband by both individuals and circumstance.

I first met Kay in 1958 when I visited John in their home. She was a friend of mine for over 45 years until she died on April 20th in 2006. I saw her for the last time four days before her death. She was as chipper as ever even though we both knew it was only a matter of days. We had taped a number of joint lectures and then some twenty hours of video during the spring and summer of 2005, discussing the early days of the computer, the birth of ENIAC, and the after years of John Mauchly and Pres Eckert. The tapes are memorable as history; and for me, they are a memento of a class act. I refer to them as "Conversations with Kay." Some day perhaps they will be aired.

Kay's immigrant story is a classic American saga of accomplishment that supports the image Americans have of this country and to which those elsewhere likewise subscribe. This story begins with her birth, in the Irish speaking area of County Donegal. That very night, February 12th, 1921, her father was jailed for his participation as an officer who trained members of the Irish Republican Army during the Irish War of Independence.

When Kay was two years old, her activist father was released from prison in Londonderry and like so many others, sought a better life in America. As Kay would describe it, James McNulty came to America, settled his family in the Chestnut Hill neighborhood of Philadelphia, and became a successful entrepreneur in the stone masonry business.

As a child, Kay enrolled in the neighborhood parochial elementary school and graduated from Hallahan Catholic Girls High School in Philadelphia.

Chestnut Hill College for Women beckoned and Kay pursued its rigorous curriculum as one of the three seniors of a class of '92 to major in mathematics. Chestnut Hill College then, as now, is noted for achievement and high scholastic standards.

Kay was not interested in teaching, the traditional female occupation for math majors; and she sensed that other job opportunities for women math majors were not as easy to come by as they are today. Actuarial positions, typically filled by males, required a Master's degree.

As a college junior, the world of business seemed to hold opportunities and Kay prepared herself by taking as many business courses as possible.

Just six months before her graduation, Pearl Harbor was attacked and America entered the war. Shortly after graduation, as Kay was looking at employment notices in the Philadelphia Inquirer, she spotted a Civil Service Position under the headline "Wanted: Women with Degrees in Mathematics" at the University of Pennsylvania's Moore School of Electrical Engineering. Penn was working on a contract with the Army's Aberdeen Proving Grounds to compute ballistics trajectories that would be used for creating artillery firing tables. In those days, such computations were made using rotary desk calculators. It took 40 hours to perform one trajectory calculation. ENIAC reduced that to a minute.

Kay and fellow math major classmate, Frances Bilas were promptly hired. Josephine Benson, the third math major from Chestnut Hill, was not immediately available. To what post was Kay assigned? The official designation of her position was that of "computer."

For Kay and Fran Bilas, who started their jobs together, the math courses had not prepared them for the numerical integration methods required to integrate numbers to compute trajectories. The available textbook provided little help. They slogged on with the tedious work and mastered the required methodology; Kay achieving early prominence in the position. They created specific algorithms that would speed up the calculation process for trajectories in that effort, and later with ENIAC.

Shortly after beginning, Kay and Fran Bilas were set to work on the Bush Differential Analyzer, an analogue machine invented some ten years before by Vannevar Bush at MIT. An analog machine is not digital. For example, a needle that moves on a dial to represent the speed of an automobile is an analogue machine. The Bush Differential Analyzer[140] was a huge machine with wheels, pulleys, and arms that drew curves and graphs as the end product of a set of calculations. This analog machine at Penn was one of only a handful in the world at the time. It was the largest and most sophisticated analog mechanical calculator in existence at the time. It was soon superseded by the ENIAC and all the digital computers that followed.

The Bush Differential Analyzer was improved upon by the staff at the Moore School, to a point where the computation of a single trajectory could be accomplished in about 50 minutes as opposed to the forty hours needed to perform the same operation on the mechanical desk calculators.

Many years later, when we were creating and taping "Conversations with Kay" at Chestnut Hill College, Kay said that she was once asked the question, "What do you remember most about working on the differential analyzer?" That question was asked by the woman making a documentary film about the women "computers". Kay said no one had ever previously asked that question. She thought about it and said:

The most interesting part about that whole problem was the people I met. They had gone around the country recruiting 'computers' and there weren't that many math majors. There just weren't. Women weren't majoring in mathematics. Math majors were men. They would hire the men as mathematicians and then put them doing the computation work of different kinds. But there was a war on, so they recruited these women, the Catholic girls from Chestnut Hill, and these bright Jewish gals from Hunter College in New York - even someone from the wilds of Nebraska. They told me stories about what their lives were like and things like that. I had never met Jewish people before. I had never run into them. Their lives were different from mine. Having been an Irish Catholic, you know, and plunged into this environment which was so different, so culturally international, but I'd say it was national because it was from all over the United States, that was the thing I remembered the most about it. Not the boring stuff of the differential analyzer.[141]

In 1945, when the secret classified ENIAC project authorized by the Army at Aberdeen Proving Grounds in 1943 was at a stage where programming was required, Kay was one of the very first women to be selected to program the ENIAC. In 1945, Kay and several other "computers", about whom more will be written later in this chapter, were sent to Aberdeen between June and August to be trained in the use of IBM punch card equipment that would provide the input and output method for the ENIAC.

At first these women were not permitted to see the machine taking shape but they were given blueprints to work out the programming in another room. Once the extremely precise programming was done on paper, and once they received their security clearances, the women were allowed in the room to physically program the ENIAC. Betty Jean Jennings, Kay's colleague and close friend then and for 60 years, would recall that "as the first programmers, they had no programming manuals or courses, only the logical diagrams to help them figure out how to make the ENIAC work." As an interesting sidelight, John Mauchly walked Jean down the aisle when she married. In fact, it was at that reception that John Mauchly first approached Kay about dating.

The 'girls' had none of the programming tools of today. Instead, the programmers had to physically program the ballistics program by using the 3000 switches and dozens of cables and digit trays to physically route the data and program pulses through the machine. Therefore, the description for the first programming job might have read: "requires physical effort, mental creativity, innovative spirit, and a high degree of patience."

The programming involved setting up and running test programs to assure system integrity. Pres Eckert, the perfectionist and ENIAC's co-inventor, required that every vacuum tube and every electrical connection must be verified before a real problem could be run on the machine. He and Kay worked long hours. Kay would often take the last train at night to Chestnut Hill. Just as often, Pres Eckert was on the same train.

The trajectory problems to be programmed required a heretofore unknown level of complexity and precision with a machine that was still a work in progress. This was demanding, heady stuff, driven by everyone's awareness of its critical wartime need.

In February 1946, the war had ended without the immediate services of the ENIAC to provide firing tables for the field artillery. However, as a public relations decision by the military, it was unveiled to the public on two successive demonstrations beginning on Valentine's Day - February 14th to demonstrate its general-purpose problem-solving capability and speed. What a Valentine present to the world, made possible by people of passion, brilliance, and commitment.

Within seven weeks of its public introduction, the two genius creators of the remarkable machine had "left the building". This was unfortunate. An arbitrary decision forced Eckert and Mauchly to pursue their dreams elsewhere.

Kay McNulty stayed on at Penn as an employee of the Army and transferred to Aberdeen's Ballistics Research Laboratory, along with her classmate, Fran Bilas and joined colleague "computers" Betty Jean Jennings and Ruth Lichterman, when the ENIAC was moved there in the summer of 1947.

Meanwhile, Mauchly and Eckert had founded a small computer company in Philadelphia and had hired Betty Jean Jennings Bartik and other "computers" to join their new enterprise. Despite the bump in the road that saw Eckert and Mauchly strike out on their own with a commercial venture, their connection with these "best and the brightest computers" remained intact.

For Mauchly's part, his trips to Washington as the company's chief salesman enabled him to periodically stop at Aberdeen. There he could check on the ENIAC and its progress.

As one of the stars of this band of intellectually high-powered women "computers", Kay McNulty certainly had John Mauchly's attention as he and Eckert were assembling a technical intellectual powerhouse in Philadelphia in the guise of EMCC (Eckert Mauchly Computer Corporation), the first commercial computer corporation in the United States. The company had John Mauchly as President, and Pres Eckert as Chief Engineer. The initial funding came from a loan of $ 25,000 from Pres Eckert's father.

John Mauchly had been widowed in 1946, when his wife accidentally drowned and he was left with two children to raise; now he was responsible for a start-up business with limited resources. He found in Kay the wife, mother, and star mathematician he needed. So he proposed that they should marry. Once again, opportunity came knocking and Kay opened the door and walked through it to probably the most challenging life she could have imagined. Thus began a cycle of ups and downs - from the height of exhilaration to the depth of heartache. Raising seven children, five of whom she bore, sharing an intellectual life with one of the brightest lights of the century, and working on software design for the ground-breaking BINAC and UNIVAC 1 computer systems.

As mentioned, following the death of her husband in 1980, Kay Mauchly set out on a path to right the wrongs that had been brought upon John Mauchly in the aftermath of what I have referred to as the Intellectual Property Trial of the Century. Her smoldering anger at the treatment he received in a Minneapolis courtroom in 1972 and 1973 became a source for the passionate rational arguments she would construct to restore his good name.

When Kay was going through Mauchly's voluminous papers, notes, and experimental prototypes that were being donated to the Special Collections section of the Van Pelt Library at Penn, she came across a letter file from Mauchly's years at Ursinus before he went to Penn to teach and learn. These letters had been stored away for over forty years. For Kay, they provided clear evidence that Mauchly had been working on advanced concepts for designing what would later become the ENIAC, before he ever met the physicist at Iowa State University. That was John Atanasoff, the man who Earl Larson, the Minneapolis Federal district Court judge, declared had provided Mauchly with the seminal ideas from which the ENIAC was conceived. In such a declaration, the ENIAC patent was invalidated and John Mauchly's reputation suffered a mighty blow, from which he never fully recovered.

These discoveries were drawn upon as source material for an article Kay wrote entitled "John Mauchly's Early Years" by Kathleen R. Mauchly; and published in the Annals of the History of Computing, Vol. 6, No. 2, 1984. The Annals are published by the American Federation of Information Processing Societies, Inc.

Kay wrote that at the trial, those files were not used as evidence by the Sperry Rand attorneys in support of defending John Mauchly in the face of an incorrect and damaging judgment by the court. To Kay and others, it seemed that the company could live with the tarnishing of the reputation of this pioneer. They couldn't live with being held in restraint of trade, the other allegation made against them. Since the latter charge was not upheld by the court, Sperry Rand could still see the glass as half-full and walk away from the matter.

For the remainder of Kay's spirited life, she spoke at conferences, wrote articles, and even confronted her nemesis, Herman Goldstine. Goldstine was the Army officer who oversaw the ENIAC project at the Moore School. She accused him of helping to appropriate the rightful attribution for creating the "stored program" concept from Eckert and Mauchly. That concept is one of the key direct links between the conception of the ENIAC and today's computers and even smart phones.

My "Conversations with Kay" provided many details that filled in the blanks of historical stories John Mauchly would convey to me in his characteristic verbal shorthand during our time together at UNIVAC and later in Mauchly Associates. These conversations Kay and I had were much more than a trip down memory lane. They were like pouring gasoline on a fire that has been burning in me for years about the utterly disgraceful treatment to which John Mauchly has been subjected.

The world owes an unbelievable debt of gratitude to this pair of giants. John was the unlikely inventor who lived and thought outside the box. His vision has left its mark on the entire physical and cultural world we inhabit; giving substance to ideas like McLuhan's Global Village and Freidman's Flat World. Kay was a giant in her own right, developing procedures to harness the power of the machine to the practical needs of solving problems. She was also a strong wife and mother - the glue that held the family together.

Both John and Kay are gone now, and oh, how I miss them both.

"The Girls" of the Giant Brain

Kay McNulty Mauchly Antonelli was one of the first of the six women "computers" selected to program the ENIAC computer in 1945. Like many of them, she had started in 1942, fresh out of Chestnut Hill College as a mathematics major, into a man's world. Jobs open for women, especially professionally trained women, were limited. There was no equality of the sexes or equality of opportunity. With men at war, there was a shortage of skilled persons to produce the firing tables required for directing gun settings for artillery shells. A number of women were hired to use the tools available in that day to perform this tedious task. Kay and the others had used the differential analyzer at Penn, or rotary (desk) calculators. It took about 40 hours to complete one set of calculations. In 1945, even as the war was winding down, the ENIAC was finally nearing completion. While the machine wasn't quite ready for use, it was ready for the 'girls' to begin hands-on programming to perform these calculations 1000 times faster. Six were selected. The five other women were Frances Bilas (Spence) - Kay's classmate from Chestnut Hill, Betty Jean Jennings (Bartik), Frances Elizabeth Snyder (Betty Holberton), Ruth Lichterman (Teitelbaum) and Marlyn Wescoff (Meltzer).

Their job was to develop the methodology for harnessing the computing power of the machine to the task at hand. The machine performed its work through the setting of switches, running cables between bays, and entering hard wired constants. They not only had to enter the program into the machine, but they had to figure out how to break up the process into the steps the machine would follow. In large measure, they created the software industry just as the men - Mauchly, Eckert, and their team of engineers - created the computer hardware industry.

Like Kay, several, but not all, of the other women selected were mathematics majors in College. All six women were selected because they could either handle a rotary calculator, had an aptitude for mathematics, and most important of all, could think logically. On the job, training was essential for all of them because the college level math courses taken by some were not adequate preparation for helping to create a break-through capability. Recall that the ENIAC was to be at its unveiling in February 1946, 1,000 times faster than any machine then in existence.

When trying to come to grips with the contribution these extraordinary women made, and to provide the reader with a perspective that has relevance today, I looked to their writings, their recollections, and their opinions for guidance. They, more than anyone else, did the work then, and in some cases, continued to educate and inspire others to follow in their unique professional footsteps. I was privileged to know Kay, but through her, to meet her great friend over many years - Betty Jean Jennings Bartik. We three videotaped many hours of reminiscences of the early days of the computer. Jean also has written extensively of her experiences, and been interviewed widely. A few years ago, she was asked, in hindsight, to identify the reasons why these women should have been included in the Women In Technology International Hall of Fame in 1997, fifty-one years after the unveiling of the ENIAC.

Based on the criteria required for induction into the Women In Technology International (WITI) Hall of Fame and by her responses, I am able to present to you their contributions in the context of four distinct phases that consist of direct professional accomplishments and cultural accomplishments. These women were true pioneers and several have spent years in the public eye serving to educate all and inspire other women to pursue opportunity in the field of software programming that they invented. Not long ago, there was a debate about whether software or hardware was the more important component of the modern computer. While it is true that both are indispensable, it must be kept in mind that these women created what has become the software. Since there were no manuals for programming the ENIAC or debugging both the software and the ENIAC hardware, they had to develop those procedures and techniques. While they had some training, they had to teach themselves. They had no text books - they created them; there were no subroutines for repetitive functions, they created them; and there were no convenient computer stores with packaged software to help them, they created the industry.

It is very difficult to imagine what the world of those six women was like in 1945. Whether math majors or not, these women were young, brilliant, and eager to learn something new, exciting and enormously challenging. Most grew up in cultural environments that sheltered them from the wider world, but each of them had struck out to meet that wider world with a confidence that they could meet the challenges thrown at them. This was a can-do group and their respect for each other's talents had a synergistic effect that was probably not anticipated but which served them and the overall enterprise well. To see so many opportunities made available to men and so few opportunities, outside of teaching, fall to women of their drive, might have been taken in stride as "that's just the way it was." However, the war changed all that, and all of a sudden, these women of talent were in high demand, albeit with a low, sub-professional government pay grade. You'll recall Kay McNulty Mauchly Antonelli's comment that they were just "the girls".

As I noted previously, Kay McNulty mastered the Bush Differential Analyzer rather quickly in late 1942 and until selected as an ENIAC programmer when it was time to do so in 1945, found great stimulation from the company of these talented women who brought what seemed to her as exotic life experiences to the mix.

Kay McNulty was joined at the Moore School in the summer of 1942 by her Chestnut Hill College classmate and fellow math major Frances Bilas. Together, they toiled on the Bush Differential Analyzer and like the others there at the time, alternated every two weeks between the day shift and the swing shift. Six days on, one day off. While each of these women landed at Penn through different circumstances, each shared the sense that they were doing something very important as part of the war effort. Since the work was classified, they were not permitted to be in the room in which the ENIAC was being carefully constructed. The first programmers started out as "Computers" - the name given by the Army to a group of over 80 women working at the University of Pennsylvania during World War II calculating ballistics trajectories - complex differential equations - by hand.

It needs to be mentioned that the trainers of these six women and all the others that worked on the Differential Analyzer while the ENIAC was under development, were women as well. They consisted of Adele Goldstine, wife of Lt. Herman Goldstine who served as the liaison officer for the Aberdeen –Moore School contracts to build firing tables; Mary Mauchly, the wife of John Mauchly, until her accidental death; and Mildred Kramer.

When the need for these women "computers" outstripped the supply of them in the Philadelphia and Baltimore areas, Adele Goldstine became the recruiter who scoured the Northeast for as many qualified women as she could find. But the supply was insufficient so the pressure to create a much faster machine to calculate firing tables for every combination of gun, shell and fuse was the impetus and financial support needed to initiate the ENIAC project, code named PX.

The work of computing ballistics trajectories was incredibly demanding and it is worth briefly describing what these women were asked to do.

The gunner possesses one principal element of information, the location of a target, including its distance from the gun, and an angle from north. The gun can be rotated in both horizontal and vertical planes through predetermined angles. The gunner must convert the range into an angle in the vertical plane through the gun. The firing tables make this conversion possible and enable the gunner to properly elevate the gun to establish the correct arc of the projectile in order for it to hit the specified target. The horizontal angle is determined geometrically.[142]

The tables also enable the gunner to factor in to the calculation, information on wind speed and direction, air density and temperature, the weight of the projectile, and the propellant charges and their temperature. When these and possibly a few more elements of information are taken into account, the gunner's firing tables provide a final angle of elevation and deflection.

A typical trajectory or path required 750 multiplications. The Differential Analyzer could do this computation in 10-20 minutes. The individual using a desk calculator would take two hours on that multiplication and about twelve hours on the calculation of a trajectory and Aberdeen needed about 3,000 trajectories for a firing table.

The differential Analyzer required about 30 days to perform the trajectory calculations for a firing table. Thus the needs of the military were not close to being met with existing technology. The pressure on these women "computers" and the entire project was enormous considering the stakes involved. ENIAC performed the same calculations in a few hours.

Training for ENIAC

In the summer of 1945, this group of six women entered a training program in Aberdeen to learn about programming the ENIAC. The objective was to develop techniques of using the giant computer being built in Philadelphia - the ENIAC - to develop tables for the firing of artillery shells. The machine was to replace the tedious calculations performed by these six women, and by 74 others, using rotary desk calculators and the Differential Analyzer at the University of Pennsylvania. They not only had to develop the methodology of application of the machine to these procedures, but then they had to translate these steps into the switch settings and cable patching that would act as the program. There were no textbooks, no prior experience, and no road maps. These women had to learn all about the machine, and then do it. The objective was to perform these calculations 1,000 times faster than anything they had worked with before at the Moore School.

The ENIAC was the first all-electronic digital computer, a machine comprised of forty black 8-foot panels containing approximately 18,000 vacuum tubes, 70,000 junk resistors, 3000 switches, and dozens of cables.[143] Because the ENIAC project was classified, the programmers were denied access to the machine they were supposed to program to solve the ballistics problems until they received their security clearances. As the first programmers, they had no programming manuals or courses; they were only allowed to see the logical diagrams of the machine to help them figure out how to make the ENIAC work.

The women had none of the programming tools available today. Instead, the programmers had to physically program the ballistics program by using the 3000 switches and dozens of cables and digit trays to physically route the data and program pulses through the machine.

Who were these women?

Elizabeth "Betty" Snyder (Holberton) was a Philadelphian and a graduate of the University of Pennsylvania. At Penn, her math professor discouraged her from pursuing a degree in mathematics and suggested that she should stay home and raise children instead. Betty opted to study journalism because its curriculum let her travel to a wider world and because it was one of the few programs of study open to women at the University.

Before the war, she had been conducting statistical surveys of farmer buying preferences for the FARM Journal magazine. Like many other women, when the war broke out, Betty wanted to do her part, so she quit her $15/week job and was hired to become a "computer". This carried a GS-3 designation with a $1400/year salary.

Betty credited her liberal astronomer father who taught at Benjamin Franklin High School with instilling an interest in science. The school had an observatory and he was interested in atomic explosions on the sun, otherwise known as sun spots. He was her hero who treated her brothers and sisters the same.

Colleagues remember Betty as being adept at figuring out the best path for guiding the complex calculations through the ENIAC's electronic labyrinth. Jean Bartik recalled that, "Betty had an amazing logical mind, and she solved more problems in her sleep than other people did awake."

Betty Jean Jennings (Bartik) was born in Missouri in 1924 on a farm. The Jennings family saw education as a path to a better life and teaching as a safe, secure and somewhat respectable position. Her father was a teacher. Her six brothers and sisters were all good at math so she didn't stand out among them. Betty attended a one room School House. From an early age, Betty loved math. In 5th grade, she was told that if she passed the sixth grade test she would be promoted to seventh grade. Ultimately, Betty graduated from Northwest Missouri State Teachers College with a BS in Mathematics as the only math major in her class.

While teaching positions were available Betty wanted to live in a wider world than she had known. She applied for and was hired to work for Aberdeen as a "computer". Over the objections of her favorite teacher, Professor Hake, and her father, she paid the $35 train fare from Missouri and promptly appeared in Philadelphia in the summer of 1945 to report for training as an ENIAC programmer.

Betty's job designation was SP-6 that paid $2,000/year. Working on Saturdays paid an additional $400/year and with this compensation, she was able to repay her aunt who had provided her with funds for her first two years in College.

Frances Bilas (Spence) was born in Philadelphia in 1922. She attended Temple University and was awarded a scholarship at Chestnut Hill College. Like Kay McNulty, she too was a math major. Frances also minored in physics. Both she and Kay graduated from Chestnut Hill College in 1942. The two of them were hired by the Moore School to compute ballistics trajectories. Both she and Kay followed the same employment trajectory at the Moore School, beginning on and quickly mastering the rotary calculators and moving on to the Bush differential Analyzer where they would continue to perform the tedious calculations until 1945 when she and Kay were selected to train to program the ENIAC. As a team, Frances and Kay led the teams of women who used the Differential Analyzer to calculate ballistics equations. In 1947, after having programmed equations on the ENIAC for some of the world's foremost mathematicians, Frances married Homer Spence, an electrical engineer from Aberdeen who had been assigned to the ENIAC project at the Moore School. Shortly thereafter, she resigned her position to raise a family.

Ruth Lichterman (Teitelbaum) was born in 1924 and graduated from Hunter College with a BS in Mathematics. She was recruited by fellow alum Adele Goldstine to work for the Moore School computing ballistics trajectories, like the other women "computers" who preceded her.

Marlyn Wescoff (Meltzer) graduated from Temple University in 1942 and later in the year, was hired by the Moore School to compute weather calculations. Marlyn knew how to operate adding machines. In the following year, Marlyn was hired to perform calculations for ballistics trajectories. In 1945, Marlyn was selected to be one of the six women programmers for the ENIAC. Jean Bartik noted that Marlyn was highly valued because it was said that she never made a mistake.

The ENIAC programming group was divided into three teams of two. Jean Bartik recently noted that the situation was ideal because a team of two had the advantage of bouncing ideas off each other and checking each others' work in their particular areas of responsibility. The level of trust within a pair and throughout the entire group was high. These women knew what the stakes were and they were the ones who ultimately had to make the ENIAC solve the problems it was given. They succeeded.

Beyond Training

With training completed, the six women were divided into three teams of two each to address the programming issues.

Marlyn Wescoff (Meltzer) and Ruth Lichterman (Teitelbaum) were a special team that taught themselves and others certain functions of the ENIAC and helped prepare the ballistics program

Kay McNulty and Frances Bilas led the teams of women who used the differential analyzer to calculate ballistics trajectories and then used the ENIAC to perform the same calculations. This would serve as a test of the accuracy of the ENIAC machine and the program developed by the team

Jean Bartik and Betty Holberton formed the team that met the challenge of learning the master Programmer that directed the performance of all sequences of the ENIAC. They were the team that led the entire group in calculating the ballistics trajectory of the February 14, 1946 public demonstration

The merging of the work of all six created the success heralded by the press then and since

Following the successful demonstration on February 14th of 1946, even though the war was ended, work continued with the ENIAC as the computing work horse for the Army. Many complex calculation procedures were entrusted to the group and to the machine. ENIAC would become the center of the Army's Ordinance and other computing needs at Aberdeen. In addition, the long dreamed of engineering advancement to a fully internally stored program was also initiated. In 1947, the ENIAC was moved to Aberdeen and Ruth Lichterman moved with it, remaining in Aberdeen for two more years to train the next generation of ENIAC programmers. Marlyn Wescoff decided to get married and before that relocation took place, she resigned from her position

Both Kay McNulty (Mauchly Antonelli) and Fran Bilas remained on the job and relocated to Aberdeen with the ENIAC machine. At Aberdeen, they programmed equations for preeminent mathematicians who wanted use the power and speed of the ENIAC

Jena Jennings (Bartik) and Betty Snyder (Holberton) initially took separate paths but both led them to what Jean Bartik has referred to as Technical Camelot. Initially, Jean continued to program the ENIAC along with Adele Goldstine after it was moved to Aberdeen and was instrumental in the enhancement of the ENIAC to accommodate stored programs that enabled the computer to handle larger and more sophisticated programs. That was the "Holy Grail" of the invention that Eckert and Mauchly had envisioned back in Philadelphia but were unable to implement under the Army's wartime deadlines. Later, Jean married and moved to the Eckert Mauchly Corporation. Jean has described the firm as the Technical Camelot, because it provided the ideal environment for sharing ideas, working for peak output, pushing the envelope and enjoying the camaraderie of working with kindred spirits - brilliant men and women who shared the same goals. At this Technical Camelot, invention was the norm. There, Jean programmed the BINAC, designed logic and an electrostatic memory backup system for UNIVAC 1. After a 16 year hiatus to raise her family, Jean returned to the field to make computers easier to use. She continued her efforts into the era of the microcomputer (PC) by developing reports useful to business seeking to understand this new computer as a business tool.

Betty Snyder (Holberton) went to work for the newly formed Eckert Mauchly Corporation in Philadelphia. While there and later at Remington Rand, the company's acquirer, Betty developed the C-10 instruction code[144], the accomplishment she said she was most proud of, and the first sorting route for the UNIVAC. Betty also designed a control panel with a numeric keypad and suggested a color change to beige for the cabinet that became the industry standard. In 1953, Betty joined the Navy's Applied Math lab at the David Taylor Model Basin in Maryland where she was the supervisor of advanced programming. In 1959, Betty served on the COBOL Committee to design the first computer language to operate across computer platforms. Betty served on both national and international computer standards committees, wrote standards for the FORTRAN Computer language and helped develop the COBOL computing language

In a 1983 interview conducted for the Charles Babbage Institute, a computing history center at the University of Minnesota, Betty conceded some of the criticisms of the COBOL language she helped develop. It was criticized as a hasty, inelegantly designed programming language. But she added, "Cobol, I felt, was very important because of its ability to describe data.'

Betty joined the National Bureau of Standards in 1966 and worked there for two decades. Once at the National Bureau of Standards, Admiral Grace Hopper ran into a problem with a program she was using and requested that Betty be loaned to her department for a week to try to identify and fix the problem. Betty resolved the problem in three days and Admiral Hopper declared that Betty was the best programmer she had ever seen or worked with. Kathy Kleiman noted that Betty "took that hard won knowledge on the ENIAC and applied it over the next forty-years, in nearly everything she did in the field."[145] Betty was dedicated to making computers easier to program.

Kay, as previously mentioned, married John Mauchly in 1948, raised seven children, and continued to work on program designs and techniques for many years. Although never employed outside the home (except as a substitute teacher), she continued to have an influence on program design by serving as a sounding board for John Mauchly, who always liked to talk with her about everything he was working on.

The women who remained in the field or who took time out to raise families and return to the field, devoted years serving as evangelists for insuring that women deserved a rightful place in the field of Information Technology. They have served as mentors and role models for many young women who entered in and succeeded in the field.

It is regrettable that it would take years of tireless efforts by an attorney, Kathryn Kleiman, to bring these accomplishments into full public view. Finally, in 1997, these extraordinary women were recognized for their accomplishments by their induction into the Women In Technology International Hall of Fame.

They and the many other women who answered the call to help the war effort in the early forties are owed our eternal gratitude. They were successful pioneers. They paved the way for women to work side by side with men - as equals and often as superiors - in any field; they teamed to make ENIAC a success; and most important of all, they laid the groundwork for what has become the software industry as we know it today. Hats off to "the girls."

CHAPTER FOUR

BUILDING ON THE ENIAC INNOVATION

The chapter covers both the technical Legacy and the global impact of that legacy.

Technically, the need to instruct or program the machines was vital but initially secondary to the task of creating and building them. There was never any doubt that the programs ultimately had to be stored within the machine. ENIAC was designed to have this capability, but the priority of delivery delayed this feature until after the demonstration of the invention. Release of the information about the EDVAC machine that would have to wait encouraged copiers, imitators, and plagiarists. Controversy over potential royalties created a debacle which actually sped up the process of development, but economically diverted future rewards.

The Legacy of ENIAC

ENIAC was the start. It was a brilliant innovative concept that set the foundation for all the computers that have come since. What is the legacy of the ENIAC? Was it a one-of, something that worked but was completely superseded by developments that followed? Or was it the guiding light for all future developments of computers even to the present day?

It was the latter. It not only paved the way for the development of computer technology and information systems to what exist today, but it provided a global impetus to that initiative.

The following are excerpts from Eckert's speech delivered at the 10th anniversary of the Eckert Research International Corporation (ERIC) April 15, 1991 in Tokyo, Japan.[146] Pres Eckert addressed this question and elaborated what, in his opinion, the special characteristics of ENIAC were. These remarks of his have been amplified with my comments linking his analysis to the current day environment. Eckert's thoughts are what he believed were the most important firsts that came about through the development of the ENIAC:

1. The most important in the ENIAC was control of the sub-routines in programming. This idea was first proposed to me by Mauchly and it became immediately clear that it was absolutely essential to the design and construction of the ENIAC.

    Author's Comment: *Without subroutines, the concept of a program would be cumbersome and tedious, to say the least. This is a distinguishing feature of the general purpose digital computer compared to a special purpose digital or analog device. Even if subroutines were used in special purpose devices, it is unlikely that they would have the ability for nesting, reentry, branching, parallel operation, and the myriad of other nuances that distinguish the general purpose computer from the special purpose device. ENIAC showed the way. What is obvious today was NOT obvious in the thirties and early forties.*

    This capability was linked to the concept of using function table arrays to generate signals for varying the electronic path within the machine. As Eckert mentioned later, this, in his opinion, was John Mauchly's most significant contribution to the ENIAC design, and to the creation and invention of the computer.

2. The second important idea in the ENIAC was the idea of a general purpose register which could be used for many purposes and which could be read into and out of, at electronic speed. ENIAC ideas are the origin of our modern Random Access Memory or RAM.

    Author's Comment: *Once again, what is obvious today was a brilliant stroke of innovation at the time of conception and implementation. This register concept laid the groundwork for caching, buffering, reentrant code, multi-programming, multi-tasking, and system software for creating self-correcting operating systems and disaster tolerant systems.*

3. The concept of rerouting the sequencing process by examining the value or sign of a particular number and then choosing an appropriate subroutine as a result allowed the ENIAC to make decisions based on numbers it had calculated and this feature gave it both great programming power and flexibility.

    Author's Comment: *Without this feature, there would be no capability for logical choice, inference, or decision support systems, to name only three important byproducts. This ability is the cornerstone of much of the real-time control systems in operation today.*

    Just for a moment, think of the importance of being able to handle "What if...", and then remember this was considered, designed, and invented in the early 1940s.

4. The concept of nesting and interloping subroutines to produce complex results with comparatively little program switch equipment was intrinsic in the design of the ENIAC program system.

    Author's Comment: *See #1 above*

5. ENIAC had the ability to stop the process after each pulse time, after each addition or data transfer period, or at special points introduced in the subroutine process and in accord with some set of conditions or rules. The purpose of this was to facilitate troubleshooting of both the hardware and the software and to allow for human intervention in the problem-solving or decision-resolving processes being investigated;

    Author's Comment: *See #1 above. In addition, consider the vital aspect in modern hardware and software design for self-checking and redundancy in circuits and software. This capability set the stage for this.*

6. ENIAC had the ability to provide automatic input, on demand from the process, from a stack of punched cards placed in a suitable machine.

    Author's Comment: *Later, of course, this ability to have input on demand would extend to voice, telecommunication signals, disc, and other systems. This, in turn, created the automatic control type of systems that handle a multitude of incoming signals on demand from a switching capability within a program, using general purpose registers as conceived by Eckert and Mauchly.*

7. ENIAC also had similar output ability and could punch cards from data in the machine. These output cards could be sent to the tabulator for printing and for certain types of data checking, which otherwise would have tied up the ENIAC itself.

    Author's Comment: *The comments in #6 apply   equally to output.*

8. Each register of the machine had its own program control system built into it. This allowed each unit to be tested without too much dependence on other units. But it also allowed operation of several sections of the machine at one time. The ENIAC allowed for parallel operation of several processes at the same time.

    Author's Comment: *A classic understatement. This capability was the forerunner of multi-tasking so prevalent in today's environment, to self-checking of circuits and results, and on and on. The key features are the ability to have hardware check the hardware, and to control any manner of combinations of hardware components – then panels, later boards, and now chips – permitting complex processes without slowing down performance of the overall system of hardware and software. The objective was twofold – to create and produce completely accurate results and to use all components of the machine at maximum throughput at all times. Remember – this was prior to 1946!*

9. There were also banks of buffer relays between the punch card machines and the rest of the ENIAC which allowed data to be put in and data to be taken out, and data processing to occur; all three at the same time in order to save time.

   Author's Comment: *The universal concept of buffers is common today, but not only innovative with ENIAC, but not really implemented in the first large-scale IBM machines of the 1950s - the 700 series.*

10. The ENIAC's forty main panels and seven power supply panels for servicing and manufacturing reasons. These were plug-in units with special handles for forcing the units into or out of the back panels. No screwdriver to disconnect wiring from wiring terminals was ever required. Today's printed circuit cards that plug into motherboards are direct descendants of this idea, an idea not really exploited in electronic equipment before ENIAC.

    Author's Comment: *We thought plug compatibility was a major improvement in manufacturing of computers in the 1960s when IBM used this concept for building its 360 series of machines in different parts of the world. This groundbreaking capability of ENIAC was the forerunner of this capability.*

    Obviously, this also makes it possible to complete repairs by changing boards or panels, putting the machines back in operation immediately, and repairing or discarding the panels off-line.

    Finally, this isolation of individual panels made it possible for self-checking circuits and/or software to identify the problem in real time.

    Author's Comment: *A major factor in all operation and manufacturing of computers today. The genius and innovative skills of Mauchly and Eckert provided this in the ENIAC.*

11. The idea of testing parts and then designing to tolerate the variations in economically produced parts is still a part of the computer business today and this approach really did not adequately exist to any great extent in consumer electronics before ENIAC.

    Author's Comment: *An understatement*

12. ENIAC accomplished all of the above goals at speeds much in excess of all past human experience for devices which carried out complex sequential processes.

    Author's Comment: *For years, there was great speculation of the four-minute mile for sprinters. Then Roger Bannister, in 1954, accomplished this for the first time. Since then it is a common goal that is achieved. The same with breaking the sound barrier – Mach One. Now it is a common occurrence. This is by way of saying it is easy to copy but difficult to innovate. The ENIAC stands as a tribute to the innovation genius of two individuals – a partnership "made in heaven".*

Most, if not all, of these 12 items are still found in "astronomically improved" form in today's computers. The legacy of ENIAC is that of father of the computer industry.

Pres Eckert went on, in his presentation, to summarize the significant single contribution of both John Mauchly and himself:

"Mauchly's big idea, in my mind, was the sub-routine control concept."

For himself, he added:

"My big idea was the idea of the stored-instruction sequence or program, using a single fast memory for both data and instruction, with no distinction between registers used for many purposes."

Author's Comment: *ENIAC showed the way. It is always difficult to be first, but exhilarating in other ways. By pioneering, there can be an impact into the future. Some historic examples leap out: putting the car engine in the front of the car instead of in the back; putting an aircraft engine as a puller rather than a pusher until the jet came along (and even then engines were put in the front long before they were put in the rear); telephones which separated the voice box from the ear piece, even with the integrated units of today, until the speaker phones achieved prominence; and, of course, dieting via starvation instead of restructuring the diet and restricting quantities of only certain foods, as, for example, the low carb diet.*

We owe much to Mauchly and Eckert for their invention of the ENIAC – the father of all computers since.

The Global Impact of the ENIAC Legacy

As we have seen earlier, the primary source of financial resources that enabled the development of the ENIAC was the military's urgent need to rapidly create firing tables. In the UK, even earlier efforts were likewise directed and funded to meet wartime need. In the UK's case, that need was focused on breaking the German code.

In both instances, wartime need and financial support enabled some of the most brilliant physicists, mathematicians, and engineers to apply their remarkable talents to a particular problem.

Until the *First Draft EDVAC Report* of a classified US military project made its way to England, all previous efforts in the UK to build computing capability in that period were viewed as attempts to serve a special purpose. Dr. Douglass Hartree was invited to give one of the legendary Moore School Lectures[147]. Hartree was very forward looking and was excited by the mathematical potential of the stored program computer. Maurice Wilkes pointed out in his article in The Annals of the History of Computing that Dr. Hartree's colleague, L. J. Comrie, made a visit to the Unites States at that time and when he returned to England, he showed the *First Draft EDVAC Report* to Maurice Wilkes, who, in one evening's reading, saw where the development would inevitably go. Wilkes Annals Light bulbs were illuminated in the UK and a number of the scientists, mathematicians, and engineers who had labored in secret at Bletchley Park so long and so hard were able to rather quickly reassemble in university settings to re-channel their energy and talents to the post-wartime challenge to build the future as they could discern it, based on the *First Draft of the EDVAC Report*- the new Development Manual or "blueprint".

The importance of the Moore School Lectures in the summer of 1946 cannot be overestimated. The course itself was groundbreaking and was entitled "Theory and Techniques for the Design of Electronic Digital Computers". Organized in response to the Moore School's announcements and demonstration of the ENIAC in February 1946, the course brought together the leading theoreticians and practitioners working on the development of computers in the US and the UK. At that time, only three publications that addressed the design of the stored program computer were known to the leaders in the field. These were:

- *The First Draft of a Report on the EDVAC*, authored by John von Neumann (1945)
- *Proposed Electronic Calculator* by Alan Turing (1945)
- *Preliminary report on the proposal for an IAS machine* by A.W. Burks, H.H. Goldstine and John von Neumann. (June 1946)

Of equal importance, and perhaps even more so, in these early publications was the work authored by Eckert and Mauchly to counter the claim that von Neumann had originated the concepts outlined in his *"Draft Report"*. This Eckert-Mauchly report (September 1945) was classified as Top Secret by Goldstine. It seems strange that the von Neumann report, covering the same project, was not classified, and indeed, openly distributed by Goldstine.

This series of lectures drew everyone's attention to the problem of how to design and build a stored program computer. The "students" were often the teachers and vice-versa in this high-powered intellectual environment.

As we have seen earlier, the departure of John Mauchly and Pres Eckert from the Moore School in the spring of 1946 to form the first commercial computer manufacturing company in the US spawned the industry we know today. Had these two geniuses remained at the University of Pennsylvania, we can easily assume that the EDVAC would have been built there before the EDSAC, produced in the UK from the EDVAC blueprint. Indeed, since Eckert and Mauchly had contemplated and planned for the stored program in the ENIAC, whose further development was frozen by the exigencies of the war, the EDVAC as the first operational stored program computer probably would have been built at the University of Pennsylvania's Moore School. As it was, when the ENIAC was moved to the Aberdeen facilities the US Army Ordnance Department, this feature was promptly added to the ENIAC, as noted by Hans Neukom in his article The Second Life of the ENIAC. However, the world was not made aware of this advanced capability.

Had Eckert and Mauchly remained at the Moore School to complete the EDVAC, it is less clear that the US computer industry would have developed as quickly as it did. However, with a license granted from the University of Pennsylvania, IBM could have directed its resources to create the industry much sooner than IBM otherwise was able to do.

The actual building of the EDVAC computer at the University of Pennsylvania, under contract with the military, was not a successful effort because the principal architects had "left the building". In a similar fashion, the attempts to build this machine at Princeton met with limited success.

The English Competition

A major competitor was a British group that drew on the ideas of Mauchly, as well as the computer's godfather, Alan Turing, and that built on the legendary work of the wartime Enigma code-cracking team.

On to the Stored Program Computer

John Mauchly and Pres Eckert might have hoped for a respite. During the pressure cooker environment of World War Two, they had worked around the clock for two years to devise the first digital computer. But their labors were to prove just as hectic and demanding in the post-war period.

Having digitized automatic calculation, Mauchly went on to the next, epochal step – a stored-program computer, one that could keep data "in memory", instead of forcing human operators to continually load and reload information by throwing banks of switches and by pulling and inserting plugs. In attempting this newly daunting task, Mauchly was to face vehement competition and opposition from the rival development teams of two nations, from investigators in the Federal Government, from his former University employer, and even from a world-famous colleague. He would be accused, in this incipient McCarthy era, of Communist associations, and would begin a bitter 20-year struggle for the patent rights to his rightful inventions.

Disputes Over Patents

From the time he began winding up work on ENIAC, as the Second World War drew to a close, Mauchly was mired in patent disputes concerning who was the true creator of the ideas behind ENIAC and its successor machines.

Mauchly and Eckert were increasingly focused on a stored-program successor to the ENIAC, which would become known as the EDVAC, or Electronic Discrete Variable Automatic Calculator. There were some elements of a stored program concept within ENIAC from the very beginning, but the full-blown stored program capability was not built into the ENIAC until it was moved to the Aberdeen Proving Grounds in Maryland in 1948.

From his experimental circuits in the 1930s, Mauchly had always wanted to inhibit reentry of information once it was first entered in the machine. For example, when we have two groups of numbers, we perform operations on each and then combine the two sets of answers, by "re-entering" the results of the first set and combining with the result of the second set. For him, the ideal was never to re-enter the intermediate answer from the first set. For Pres Eckert, the necessity was to be accurate in the manner in which pulses circulated around the machine, with the timing interval of the pulses indicating what these pulses represented. Hence, his emphasis was on the purity of the signals generated and the absolute accuracy of the timing of the pulse transmits. The two men were in absolute synch as to how to build a machine to do calculations.

The ENIAC, because of the exigencies of budget and wartime pressures, was built as a compromise rather than the perfect result of their objective – to build a general purpose electronic digital computer to solve problems. Hence, while from the beginning they well understood the needs of keeping all information within the machine when once entered, and to keep the process functional without outside intervention, they compromised as they went to meet the deadlines of the project. Therefore, ENIAC initially was only partly a stored program machine. They conceived of how to make it a fully stored program machine and prepared a proposal to do so. In the alternative, they proposed building a newer machine that would have the benefits of the lessons learned with ENIAC. This led to the EDVAC proposal.

In April 1946, the Army Ordnance Department at the Aberdeen Proving Ground was to grant the Moore School at the University of Pennsylvania a $100,000 contract to build the EDVAC. This was later increased to $467,000, for a preliminary model of the machine. Meanwhile, simmering tensions between Mauchly and Eckert on the one hand, and Army liaison officer Herman Goldstine and famous mathematician John Von Neumann on the other, broke out into acrimony. At the crux of the dispute were the men's differing views over intellectual property rights to the ENIAC and EDVAC. And at the heart of the fight was a report, *First Draft of a Report on the EDVAC,* that Von Neumann had written in June 1945. If the reader will recall, it was Goldstine's efforts which spearheaded the original Army Ordnance contract which financed the building of the ENIAC. Indeed, without his efforts there might never have been an ENIAC; but he was not a factor in the design or production aspects of this machine. In a very important fashion he handled the contractual requirements and also acted as security officer for this classified military project. Eckert and Mauchly were the spear-head creators and inventors, and led the team that did the work. When the news releases were prepared, Goldstine inserted his name as one of the creators of ENIAC. John Mauchly reacted strongly, going to the Dean to have Goldstine's name removed. Hence, the credit for the developments in the news releases mentioned Mauchly and Eckert, relegating Goldstine to his proper position of military manager. This only intensified the bitterness between Goldstine and the Eckert-Mauchly team. In retrospect, Goldstine's role as the driving force for the funding of the contract certainly deserved greater importance and mention. It was a team effort all round.

Mauchly and Eckert, who had personally done most of the theoretical and technical work for ENIAC, which laid the groundwork for EDVAC, sought to take out patents for their labors. As detailed in Chapter Two, the University had originally granted them permission to apply for such rights, and then, at the end of the war, had backed off from its agreement, shifting its patent policy more toward the ownership rights of sponsoring government agencies and away from university scientists like Mauchly who actually came up with the inventions. Much of this controversy was caused by the newness of the linkage of patent rights with University research and positions. This relationship is more clearly defined in today's environment where multiple part relationships between scientists, universities, and corporations acknowledge patent rights and royalty splits. This was too new for that period in history. Hence the disagreements and false starts.

When the University of Pennsylvania had ordered Mauchly and Eckert to give up the patent rights to ENIAC, rights that the University had granted them during the early stages of the project, Eckert and Mauchly decided to tender their letters of resignation. They went on to apply for ENIAC patents, finally filing an application in June 1947.

Bidding adieu to the Moore School and to the Army Ordnance Department, Eckert and Mauchly founded a company to develop computers spun-off from their Moore School developments.

This latter action, states the book <u>ENIAC-A Problem Solver</u>[148], "helped to move computer development from universities and dependence on US government contracts to the eventual emergence of the major new industry of the second half of the twentieth century." Moreover, Mauchly and Eckert "came up with new ideas and more advanced technology, which, although not often immediately applied, led not only to future changes and enhancements to ENIAC, but also to a number of computers (e.g., EDVAC, BINAC and UNIVAC), designed and developed later by many of the same team and others."[149]

Racing for the Computer's Holy Grail

While Mauchly and Eckert's company tried to establish itself in the shadow of intellectual property disputes, rival efforts to claim the Holy Grail of the budding computer industry, the stored program, were proceeding apace.

Before considering this in greater detail than has already been done, a major discrepancy over the launch date of ENIAC should be clarified. Was it February 14th, 15th, or 16th of 1946? All, three dates have been used in different publications.

It is the common practice for any theatrical production to have a dress rehearsal. While individual actors practice their roles alone or with other actors, there is a need to have actors, stagehands, producers, directors, lighting, and music all work together to make sure that the entire ensemble interacts properly and on cue. Integrated timing is a vital part of any production. So it is with the computer, and especially a prototype computer.

In the case of ENIAC, tests went on for weeks until the full-function test, or "dress rehearsal" per se, was set for February 14th of 1946. In actuality, a stop and go dress rehearsal was conducted on the 13th for a select group with a lot of final tinkering to fine tune the machine. On the 14th, the staff of the Moore School and selected friends were invited to the integrated full-function test. It was a complete success. ENIAC worked as conceived, planned, and executed.

News releases were prepared by the Department of Ordnance and distributed to the press with a notation not to be released until February 16th. The world, then, became aware of ENIAC on February 16th, but for the professionals, February 14th was the true birth date. When the fiftieth anniversary was celebrated in 1996 at the celebrations held at the University of Pennsylvania, February 14th was picked and announced as the birth of the Computer Age.

To put ENIAC into perspective, it was the first general purpose digital electronic computer that functioned. Other digital machines were designed, many of them never built, and none of them worked as general purpose machines. For years, analog machines had been functioning, most notably the differential analyzer designed and first built by Vannevar Bush. Special purpose digital machines were also built, most notably the Colossus in England for decrypting Nazi messages. The ABC computer at Iowa was digital in nature but, designed by John Atanasoff for the solution of simultaneous equations, it never achieved productive efforts. ENIAC, on the other hand, continued to function for another ten years, first at the University of Pennsylvania, and later, after being moved and reassembled, at the Aberdeen Proving Grounds.

Two problems plagued the machine. Both were readily solved. The first was that it "blew" tubes – the high voltage of use caused them to stop functioning. In the words of the co-inventor, John Mauchly, ENIAC was "the biggest tube testing rack in the world". After studying the problem, the other co-inventor, Pres Eckert, established that the higher operating voltages were not necessary to establish the high and low, yes and no, zero and one, requirements for the machine to function. Hence, he reduced the operating voltages to half. Thereafter, blown tubes still happened, but on a more infrequent basis as part of routine maintenance as opposed to an operating nightmare.

The second problem showed up after the machine was moved to Aberdeen. While at Penn, the "uptime" or full operating capability of the machine was in the 90% range, remarkable for tubes and in that era. At Aberdeen, the operating percentages dropped precipitously, often to 50%. This went on for months until one day John Mauchly was told and solved the problem. Knowing John, he would react with a quizzical smile, scratch his head, look into space, maybe tell a story or two, and then, out of the blue, suddenly ask an unexpected question, as he did in this case: "Do they shut the machine down at night?" The affirmative answer confirmed his suspicion. The starting voltages in the morning knocked out scores of tubes. The machine had never been shut down at Penn unless it was for necessary maintenance. Even then, individual banks (there were eleven) could be isolated without shutting down the whole system. At Aberdeen the whole system was shut down. The penny wise pound foolish bureaucratic rulings were cancelled; the machine was kept running continuously and the myriad blown tubes were a thing of the past.

The popular reaction was one of incredulity. The term "giant brain" was bandied about, and many fanciful stories appeared of how machines would perform wonders – write poetry, think, overcome humans, and on and on, even when they weighed eleven tons and operated in eleven huge bays with tons of cooling for its 18,000 tubes. This wonder of the ages had less power and capability than is found in the modern hearing aid or wristwatch.

The detractors, especially those who had espoused other approaches, were very critical. (Harvard, MIT, etc.)

Remaining "What If?"s

McCartney voices a commonly heard view. In his opinion, if Penn had kept Eckert and Mauchly at the university, the university would have been the leading computing center in the U.S. But even if Eckert and Mauchly had remained at Penn, it is not clear that Penn would have been the dominant force in computing. One must remember that MIT had an exceptional staff and knowledge of electronics as a result of its wartime Radiation Laboratory; it had unparalleled ties to federal scientific leadership and industry, and it had a long and strong computing tradition that was deeply embedded in the mission of the university.

Disputes over intellectual property rights drive much of McCartney's narrative. The Army had given the University of Pennsylvania the right to file patents arising from the ENIAC project, so long as the government held a nonexclusive, no-cost right to the patents. Eckert and Mauchly arranged with the university in 1943 that the patents could be held by the individual members of the Moore School team who were responsible for the inventions. Eckert and Mauchly filed the only patent application, however---for the overall computing system (and only in 1947).

By 1946, when it came time to negotiate for the rights to the EDVAC patent, the university saw that the world had changed and that it must harden its patent policy. Universities had new opportunities to become strong through research sponsored by industry and the federal government, and Penn believed that it had to take steps to protect these opportunities. McCartney argues that this change in policy was not only unfair to Eckert and Mauchly, but was also exceptional among American universities. However, the new director of research at the Moore School, Irven Travis, had been a contracting officer for the Navy during the war. He modeled the Moore School's new patent policy after the practices he was familiar with from the Applied Physics Laboratory at Johns Hopkins and the Department of Industrial Cooperation at MIT. The new policy established by Travis required that faculty members sign over all patent rights to the university.

Rather than sign over their EDVAC-related patents, Eckert and Mauchly resigned from the university and started up a commercial venture to build computers based on their Moore School experience. Goldstine and von Neumann were not sympathetic with Eckert and Mauchly's hopes to trade on EDVAC patents, and argued instead that the technology should be placed in the public domain. In a 1946 meeting, Army officials determined that von Neumann's Draft Report on EDVAC constituted a publication, and since it had been circulated publicly for more than a year, all patent claims were rendered invalid. This ruling further strained the relationship of von Neumann and Goldstine with Eckert and Mauchly.

I am reminded of my first touchdown playing football in high school. I caught the ball behind the goal line and ran for a touchdown. As I came off the field, at fifteen, thinking I was quite a "hot shot", the coach vented a blistering attack on every part of my running style and field navigation. Finally, I quietly asked, "Hey coach, how was it for distance?"

In the same vein, later in life, as head of the UNIVAC Data Centers, I conducted a series of computerized management games. I was finally coerced into heading one of the teams in a competitive effort. I sensed I was fair game. Somehow our team won, and won handily. All six teams gave reports, the lowest scoring team first. Every report showed sound decisions, organization, rapid responses, and every normal attribute of sound management. As I listened, I wondered how we had come to win. Then I realized why – we had more imagination, and our decisions about the competition were more "gutsy". When it came my turn to report, I was very brief. I still remember what I said, some fifty years ago. "We analyzed the situation and made decisions aimed at winning. We did. We won."

So it was with ENIAC. John Mauchly conceived of how machines could be built to digitally solve problems of any nature – general purpose. First, he proved it could be built by developing counting circuits which he wired himself in the '30s, using parts he scrounged or bought second-hand because he had no spare cash. In the thirties, nobody did. He used these rudimentary circuits and devices to prove to Pres Eckert that his dream was practical, and that his concepts could be implemented. Then, he conceived of how to break up a problem or need so it could be solved in a series of discrete steps – the program. To accomplish this, he and his group conceived of program steps, branching, logical choice, and the storage of information. The objective was to enter data only once, never to reenter intermediate results, and to have confidence that the machine was not erring. Pres Eckert concentrated on making the dream a reality with dependable counting and timing circuits operating in a controlled fashion to solve the problem. The steps in the solution were the program, which could be stored in the machine just as data would be stored.

A development that must be ranked as almost equal in magnitude to building the machine itself was the invention of branching or logical switching. John Mauchly told me he considered this a major breakthrough in information science. Eckert would later agree with that. There were many claimants for the invention of this concept. In private discussions with John Mauchly and with his widow, Kathleen McNulty Mauchly (Kay), and later Antonelli, the consensus was the team of which John was the leader and spark plug established branching with a major contribution from John in concept and leadership. The 'girls on ENIAC', who worked on programming long before they even saw the machine, certainly had some input into this development. Kay told me Betty Holberton was certainly one of those involved.

It is much simpler to build a machine that executes one instruction after another, as opposed to designing and building a machine that can switch its path of work automatically according to the logic of the situation. In the first case, what is developed is a special purpose machine; whereas in the second case it is possible to handle any type of problem - a general purpose computer. That distinguished ENIAC from everything that came before and set the stage for what came after. Branching allows the machine to jump control to a non sequential step and continue or even branch again and again, returning to the point of branch or not as the case warrants. That capability makes a system general purpose, and that capability makes the machine truly usable in complex operations. Eckert and Mauchly foresaw that need. Eckert built the control circuits to allow that capability called for by Mauchly's logical design.

The Importance of Branching

Some may ask why is branching so important? The concept of a program is that of a series of steps performed sequentially. The idea of branching is to perform the steps in a sequence determined by the results as they are found or calculated. For example, if temperature is a calculation, then the resultant actions must depend upon what that temperature reading is. For this reason, the actual steps performed will vary according to the intermediate findings as the process unfolds. That is the way we proceed logically. That is how the machines had to work – and how they work now. The first invention of this concept, as applied to digital computers, came with the ENIAC group. Some elements of this were implicit in the differential analyzer, but certainly not to the extent they were explicit within the ENIAC. The same is true for the ABC Computer, although, since it had no ability to do branching since all numbers had to be re-entered every step of the way, it is hard to say what it was capable of doing. The same is true of analog machines in general. Once again, however, with the knowledge of what is done in digital computers, it is possible to configure special purpose analog devices that will have some elements of conditional response and action. However, in analog devices, these elements will not be as all encompassing as is possible with digital computers.

If the reader will consider for a moment the ability to pre-establish diverse paths that are automatically selected in real time according to changing signals is the cornerstone of our modern on-demand information world. Both the machine and the program are needed. The program must include conditioned reaction. Therefore, the importance of the pioneering effort of the ENIAC team can never be underestimated. Faster, smaller, cheaper machines are available now, but they are essentially only perturbations of the "clunking test tube rack" that was ENIAC.

The ENIAC's memory consisted of the 18,000 tubes. Developments of acoustic delay lines, rotating drums, rotating discs, and chips all came later. ENIAC, as the product of the day, had a very limited storage for data, programs, registers, and locations for intermediate calculations. Hence, ENIAC did not have a large data storage capability necessary for storing programs and intermediate results.

In addition to limited memory, there was limited time. ENIAC was a wartime project with the capability of the machine urgently required by the Army. Furthermore, budget constraints also seriously curtailed the ability to incorporate all the features desired. Hence, the first version of ENIAC, as demonstrated in February of 1946, depended on a combination of internal and external instructions in order to function. The external instructions were plug board and rotary switches. As a result, the machine was extremely difficult and tedious to program. ENIAC initially was criticized as a machine without an internally stored program. Some charged that it was not a general purpose computer.

Mauchly and Eckert knew how to create the internally stored capability for ENIAC but had neither the funds nor time to accomplish this. It was done later when the machine was moved to Aberdeen, relying heavily on the work as outlined by the inventors. The stored program concept for ENIAC was created by adding acoustic delay lines to the original machine.[150]

That effort was the background for EDVAC, later BINAC, and ultimately UNIVAC. It most certainly was the cornerstone of the EDSAC developments in UK which sired the Manchester machines which challenged UNIVAC as the first commercially available general purpose digital computer.

Meanwhile, across the Atlantic, both Mauchly's old EDVAC project and his new BINAC initiative ran into obstacles.

Mauchly's Old and New Enterprises

After Mauchly and Eckert departed ENIAC/EDVAC, the engineers who remained struggled to finish what the former project leaders had started. Work on the EDVAC took place at Aberdeen's Computing Laboratory in Maryland. The stored-program or high-speed memory was to be made up of twin units having 64 lines with an 8-word memory. For use in arithmetic operations, there were also memory cabinets, each of which stored three lines of one-word memory. It was thought that a total memory capacity of 2,048 words would be too costly, so designers opted for a 1,024-word memory.

Progress on the EDVAC was slow. Installation was completed in August 1949, but the computer did not enter into use until October 1951, five years after its design. As Eckert recalled, "Other people tried to build the machine…and they managed to foul it up, and it never got really built decently."

One has to ask about the hubris exhibited by the Moore School administration to think that the EDVAC could be successfully built without the driving intellectual forces that had successfully produced the ENIAC.

Von Neumann and Goldstine went off to Princeton and recruited Burks and others from the ENIAC team. Mauchly, perhaps seen as an intellectual threat to von Neumann, was not invited to join them, and Eckert, the intellectually non-threatening engineering genius, turned von Neumann's offer down. The Institute for Advanced Study at Princeton produced no breakthrough technology. That was left to Eckert, Mauchly, and industry. The disagreements within the ENIAC group splintered a team that had worked wonders in a short period of time. It is unfortunate, except that the shift to industry probably accelerated growth as funding became more readily available.

The EDVAC project, though marked by delays and glitches, had a major claim to fame: it was the first computer designed that used a stored program. And that design was Mauchly and Eckert's.

In the meantime, they tackled their new project the UNIVAC or Universal Automatic Computer, to which I will return later. The UNIVAC was planned to incorporate the novel idea for a stored-program computer that creates enduring electronic memory that Eckert had used as a memory device in his childhood, which we noted in Chapter Three.

UNIVAC- Development efforts for the Universal Automatic Computer began to be plagued by Eckert and Mauchly's agreement to fixed-fee contracts that allowed no flexibility to establish contracts on a cost-plus fixed–fee basis to account for unforeseen events over which they had little or no control. Remember that these were developmental projects where the unknowns can destroy the best laid plans. As a startup firm, Eckert and Mauchly were to land several major government contracts, one involving the census. The federal government had long used advanced data automation techniques to help compile census data. For the 1890 U.S. census, inventor Herman Hollerith had used punch cards to tabulate data.[151] Mauchly and Eckert, to assist the compiling of information for the census, entered into a contract with the National Bureau of Standards, that was a sister agency at the Commerce Department that could issue contracts.[152] They were eager to get the contract, although they knew the contract would cost $400,000 but they were willing to settle for a $300,000 fixed-fee contract anyway. Although cost plus fixed-fee contracts were common in Washington, Stan Augarten notes that Eckert and Mauchly believed that such a contract would have given the National Bureau of Standards certain patent rights to the invention, and they were determined to avoid that situation. Unfortunately, that assumption was incorrect. Work began on the new UNIVAC based on their design for the EDVAC. From the beginning, however, this project was troubled by cost overruns and scheduling delays.[153] Furthermore, at the outset, George Stibitz of Bell Labs, who thought that government financing of the ENIAC was far too risky, was equally uncomplimentary to the Eckert and Mauchly proposal shown to him by the National Bureau of Standards. In that instance, Stibitz's advice was ignored.

In the case of the Census Bureau project, the National Bureau of Standards divided the contract into 2 parts; one part required developing the computer's internal memory, the mercury delay line and external memory, a magnetic tape drive. This effort was pegged at $75,000. The other part of the contract was for the development of the processor and the rest of the computer that eventually was delivered for $169,600. The government retained 15% of the contract price of $300,000 contract price for administrative overhead.

Later, a committee appointed by the National Research Council that included the overly cautious Stibitz, Harvard's Howard Aiken, who had missed the "technological boat" earlier and was currently focusing on automatic calculators that did not included a stored program, and Mauchly's nemesis, John von Neumann, would evaluate the UNIVAC unfavorably compared to the EDVAC and a computer being built by Raytheon, the Massachusetts electronics manufacturer.[154]

This pair of visionaries had to fight for their ideas every inch of the way- lukewarm to negative support from very cautious or jealous colleagues made it very difficult to directly obtain sought after government contracts. It did, however, lay the groundwork for the many future, practical applications of census data. Its challenges also set the stage for the notable BINAC that would end up being built as a smaller scale prototype of the UNIVAC machine to follow.

During this time of startup financial strain, Mauchly and Eckert's Electronic Control Company, soon dubbed the Eckert-Mauchly Computer Company, also took on a major, top-secret effort for the Air Force to build a small numeric computer, the BINAC or Binary Automatic Computer. The pair worked through the Northrop Aircraft Company to design a guidance computer for the Snark missile. The BINAC system contract was let on October 8, 1947 to be completed by May 15, 1948 for $100,000, $80,000 which was paid at the contract signing. The system was accepted as completed by Northrop at a demonstration in Philadelphia in September 1949, fifteen months behind schedule and $178,000 over budget. Thus, it is said that BINAC was actually the first stored-program electronic digital computer in the United States. Problems were encountered when the computer was disassembled and shipped to Northrop in California, and reassembled there by Northrop personnel. For example, the mercury and other parts of the system were said to have had deteriorated in transit. [155]

As you will see later, the EDSAC stored program computer built in the UK was operational a few months earlier in May 1949. Both the EDSAC and BINAC systems owe their birth to Eckert and Mauchly.

The BINAC system difficulties encountered later at Northrop have been traced to several causes and misunderstandings and it is fair to say that the quality of the machine suffered from its lower priority in the Eckert and Mauchly firm than the larger and costlier UNIVAC that Eckert and Mauchly had contracted to build for the US National Bureau of Standards.[156] Nonetheless, it created the dual serial processor approach that was designed to enable the two processors to run in tandem for processing redundancy and error-checking. The much smaller BINAC was but a fraction of the size of the ENIAC, with each of the two processors containing only 700 tubes. Each processor chassis measured only four feet long, five feet tall, and one foot wide. In addition, BINAC calculating speed was only 70% of the speed of the ENIAC but was three times quicker in multiplication tasks. Further, the mercury delay line could store 512 31 bit words.[157]

This BINAC project indicated just how rapidly technology was changing, especially in an area that would define the computer era: miniaturization. In a few short years, Mauchly and Eckert had gone from designing room-sized machines to ones that could fit inside a nose cone of a space vehicle. The eventual path to a supercomputer-on-a-chip had been established. This Air Force contract earned the fledgling outfit $100,000, with $80,000 of that up front, but it was a short term gain that could not thwart the continuing financial drain on the company.

Tarred by the Red Scare

In 1949, when Senator McCarthy was compiling his "list" that he introduced publicly in early 1950, the Eckert and Mauchly firm was working with the Air Force. Mauchly fell under the incongruous suspicion of being a Communist sympathizer. That the man who was in many ways the world's first computer entrepreneur was thought to be in league with Joseph Stalin seems ridiculous. For a time, his yeoman war-time labors to build the ENIAC for the U.S. Army would be ignored.

A secretary at Eckert-Mauchly, it was learned, had gone out with a man who some years before had attended a few meetings of the Communist Party. In a severe blow to an enterprise doing defense work, Mauchly, the firm's president, had his security clearance revoked.

Fortunately, a major investor in Eckert-Mauchly -- Robert Strauss -- had friends where it counted. Strauss was the president of American Totalizer, the race track par-mutual and odds-making board. Totalizer had poured $400,000 into the Eckert-Mauchly Computer Company, and wanted to protect its investment, according to Kay Mauchly Antonelli. When John Mauchly's clearance was cancelled, Strauss went to work on his friend -- all-powerful FBI director J. Edgar Hoover. He told Hoover, "This is ridiculous. You know how I have just bought into this company and this man [Mauchly] has no political allegiances whatsoever," recalled Kay Mauchly Antonelli. The investigation into Mauchly was dropped, and his clearance was restored.

Tragically, Strauss was killed in a plane crash in 1949. A while later, the charges against Mauchly were re-opened, with implications that were to dog him into his next enterprise. The second round of allegations seem, from today's perspective, to have been even more absurd. Mauchly was accused of membership in, not the Communist Party, but the Consumer's Union, the pro-consumer group, and of having attended, along with 900 other scientists, a meeting about the perils of the atomic bomb.

"John said the only reason he subscribed to the Consumer Union," remembered Kay Mauchly Antonelli, "was because it recommended which refrigerator was the best to buy." Two years of investigation ensued, during which the government determined, apparently, that a great number of leading scientists, and high-ranking officials, had belonged to Consumer Union. After a hearing in 1951, all charges against Mauchly were dropped. "It seemed absolutely ridiculous to hold up John's clearance for two years," said his widow, "because they could not even prove that he belonged to the Consumer's Union!"

In the years that have elapsed since the allegations, it has been proven that Mauchly was never a member of any subversive organization, and was guilty of no wrongdoing at all. "I have sent to the FBI and I have gotten a whole copy of his clearance hearings," said Kay Mauchly Antonelli. "They found absolutely nothing [implicating Mauchly] in the whole world. He was the victim of a witch hunt. In those years, she added, it seemed like John always got the worse side of everything." Some believe that enemies of Mauchly in the computer field might have been behind the bogus investigation.

The Winner of the Race

In the end, the BINAC, EDVAC, and Wilkes (UK) teams were edged out in the race to the first stored-program computer. While they labored, the Manchester "Baby" squad, with its TV screen technology, had edged ahead. On June 21, 1948, the research team at Manchester University attempted to run on its Baby a brief, 17-instruction program. The goal: find the highest factor of a number. It succeeded, calculating an 18-factor number, the highest yet discovered, taking a little over 50 minutes to plow through millions of variants.

Project leader Williams later described the experiment, which was executed on the instruction set stored on its CRT:

The spots on the display tube entered a mad dance. In early trials, it was a dance of death leading to no useful result, and what was even worse, without yielding any clue as to what was wrong. But that day it stopped, and there, shining brightly in the expected place, was the expected answer. It was a moment to remember.

Alan Turing was to serve as architect of the programming design for a bigger Baby built over the next several years at Manchester University, and installed there in February 1951. Called the Mark I, and made by the Ferranti Company, it was to be the "first commercially available computer" according to Manchester University. A total of ten Mark I units were sold in four different countries, one of them to Canada. There, as will be discussed in Chapter Five, I worked on a Ferranti Mark I as a very young programmer in a very new field.

Wilkes' EDSAC team trailed behind, with its machine's initial program executed in May 1949. However, the EDSAC proved more practical than the Manchester Baby. It went on to incorporate many subroutines now familiar in computers. By the early 1950s, the EDSAC had exponentiation, layout and print functions, floating-point numbering and logarithms, and repeating functions rather like the "for loops" of later programming. In 1951, it pushed the prime-number record to 79 numerals, and the following year it boasted a rudimentary computer game: the ability to play tic-tac-toe on its CRT.

Yet the Manchester Baby had won the race, beating EDSAC and beating the Eckert-Mauchly Computer Company. Outside of the ENIAC, it was the first stored program system that worked.

Conclusion

But Mauchly, and Eckert, could take considerable consolation. Their first test demonstration of stored-program computing, in March 1949, trailed the Manchester Baby by only nine months. Construction of their BINAC was completed that fall. Moreover, it was undeniable that they had fathered much of the theoretical and practical basis of the Manchester Baby, and the machines competing with it. Mauchly was a pivotal figure in touching off the fierce competition and relentless innovation -- with all the attendants benefits to mankind, and limitless future potentials -- that have typified the computer field ever since.

They began work on the new BINAC based on their design for the EDVAC. From the beginning, however, this project was troubled by cost overruns. It did, however, lay the groundwork for the many future, practical applications of census data. It also built the foundation for the notable machine to follow the BINAC – the UNIVAC, or Universal Automatic Computer.

Indeed, Mauchly's next project, the famed UNIVAC computer, was the first significant commercial-sector computer. As we shall see, it was in its own right a foundation stone of today's multi-trillion-dollar information technology industry.

Among other prominent early computers included EDSAC, BINAC, Whirlwind, SEAC, SAWC, UNIVAC, the IAS computer, and IBM 701. All of them, in one way or another, were part of the ENIAC legacy.

The Birth of UNIVAC

The UNIVAC was the culmination of all of the dreams and hard work of John Mauchly and Pres Eckert. More will be said about this machine in later chapters but for now, a few points will be made of how this was the total legacy of the ENIAC effort.

First and foremost, this machine was a radical departure from the past. It not only had a stored program to utilize magnetic tape for intermediate and mass storage, but used Eckert's acoustic delay line as the high-speed storage for the program and intermediate results.

From an engineering perspective, this machine encompassed many firsts. The acoustic delay line was an obvious one. This gave the machine greater speed and capability than its competitors and was a major factor in the first orders received in the late 40s and early 50s. Since dependability was an important moment for both men, redundant circuits were built into the computer so that calculations performed along two different paths and then the results were compared, with an automatic recycle in the event of an error. A minor point, but very important, was the incorporation of "buffers" permitting high speed throughput in this machine -- the buffers acting as collection points for the next lead of new data while data was currently being read by emptying the buffer.

The ability to use magnetic tape was dramatic in terms of the storage of vast amounts of information on magnetic tape instead of on decks of punched cards or punched paper tape. While the amount of data on a reel of tape was large for those days (slightly over a million characters), it is significant in these days when we have iPods with music that have 80 GB of data in a device even smaller than a credit card. These magnetic tapes were initially more of a nickel alloy and each tape weighed about 7 pounds. I still remember the day when I had three tapes in my briefcase handed to a doorman at the Mt. Royal Hotel in Montréal after I had left Sun Life Assurance Company where I had been working to install a Univac II System. The doorman assumed it was the normally light briefcase he usually encountered. As he took the briefcase from me he sagged perceptively and, looking at me, asked if I had bricks in my briefcase. He was even more mystified when I said they were magnetic tapes. Still chuckling as I recall this, I also recall a customs officer at the Canadian border wondering what I was carrying. I told him it was magnetic tape. He assumed it was music and still wondered why it was so heavy and large. I was afraid to tell him it was really data. The final humorous incident concerns the import of magnetic tapes into Canada where I was in charge of all of the Univac installations. Our customs brokers advised us that these metallic tapes had to come in as "plumbing fixtures" because there was no other possibility of importing them because of their composition.

And so it was in the early days. Naturally, in order to create input data for a machine that could only (supposedly) read magnetic tape, the Unityper was invented. This machine looked like a typewriter and on the top, a small reel of magnetic tape was mounted. The keystrokes were converted into magnetic impulses on the tape. This was far superior to the system that existed until then- i.e. using tabulating system key punching machines that would produce punched cards. Each of these cards could hold a maximum of 80 characters (IBM) or 90 characters (Remington Rand). To maintain compatibility, each Univac came equipped with a card reader and card punch capability.

The results were revolutionary. Despite the heavy competitive pressure from IBM, the Eckert Mauchly Corporation succeeded in selling a significant number of machines. The first of these was delivered to the Census Bureau in 1951 and created a sensation. Quite rapidly, machines were delivered to Metropolitan Life, Franklin life, the U.S. Army map service, the Franklin Institute, and the United States Air Force Air Material Command. A total of 45 to 50 Univac I machines were delivered before production was stopped in favor of the Univac II. Mauchly and Eckert had succeeded brilliantly. Financial straits made it necessary for them to sell the Eckert Mauchly Corporation to Remington Rand. The sad story of how this brilliant engineering and marketing success was squandered by mismanagement on the part of Remington Rand is recounted in later chapters.

Magnetic Tape

UNIVAC was the first machine to use Magnetic Tape as the mass storage medium. Until that development, punched cards had been the intermediate and mass storage medium.

John Mauchly credited the Census Bureau as delivering the first Univac, since it utilized the punch card as the storage medium. Ted Bonn was recognized as formulating the electrical properties for the coating of the magnetic tape of the Univac. Due to the fact that reels written by a Univac system could be interpreted among any other Univac system, a detailed analysis of the components of the Univac ensued. Ted Bonn retold the development of the magnetic tape, including the importance of metal tape for enduring storage. Since oxide coating was not entirely successful, Mauchly noted some electrical output occurred with it. This led Bonn to formulate the electroplating of a coating of nickel, cobalt, and phosphorous, which was used until it was replaced by Mylar tape in the '50s.

Albert Tonik, noted as a "minor computer pioneer", detailed an extensive summary of the components and dimensions of the Univac I magnetic tapes, including its retention for recording data and programs for processing by utilizing the punched paper tape. He indicated the process of the parallel bits of 7 characters, the Universo mechanism, and the implementation of an erase head before the read-write head so new information could be processed without errors appearing due to the old information. The impact of the Unityper's usefulness in comparison to human typing was emphasized.

The contributions of Ike Auerbach, "Mr. Binac", are also noted in a memorial speech, including his efforts to make Binac possible.

The Early Applications of UNIVAC

Some of the early applications of the Univac bear recounting for historic purposes. As in most cases of history, there is a repetitive cycle. Many of the first applications of Univac are current more than 60 years later. For example, as a humorous aside, Art Linkletter, who was famous in the early 50s, and later, for many radio and TV shows, used Univac for dating. There were a lot of loud laughs at the time but consider the size of that industry component today.

The election of 1952 utilized Univac for the presidential election. Even in those rudimentary days, our results of an Eisenhower victory were apparent quite soon in the evening but were never announced because of the fear on the part of the commentators that the machine was wrong. The machine was right! By 1956, there was more credibility and more daring on the part of the commentators in using the results forecast by the computer. I can still mentally hear the famous news commentator H.V. Kaltenborn exclaim over the airwaves, "The IBM Univac..." Of course IBM was thought to be the last word in computing capability even though the Univac was understood by everyone to be in the "giant brain". In 1960, we at Mauchly Associates had a contract for John to advise Chet Huntley and David Brinkley during their election coverage of the Kennedy-Nixon returns. The computers worked flawlessly and continuously predicted a Kennedy victory although the commentators did not make that claim until 3 a.m. They could have done so before midnight but wanted to be sure since the election was a cliffhanger.

Because of the ability of Univac to handle vast amounts of data, a necessary requisite for the contract with the Census Bureau, the statisticians at the Census Bureau thought they would develop newer techniques for handling economic data. Jules Shishkin, a mathematician and analyst for the Census Bureau, used the Univac for the first time ever and created moving average techniques which are a dominant factor in all economic activity today.

In those early days, we made proposals for the application of Univac to printing, publishing, advertising, product mix, operations research, and on and on. Everything was new, everything was dramatic, and a client list included a who's who of government and industry. The 50s were a heady time for innovation sparked by the ingenuity which led to ENIAC and then to Univac and onto the Information Age - the Cyber Age - which exists today.

CHAPTER FIVE

THE REST OF THE WORLD

No development as significant as that of the computer occurs in isolation. Many people pursue similar ideas, with or without knowledge of each other's work. Such research is often pressured by warfare and the demands for solutions needed for victory. World War II had a profound effect on the search for computing power in many parts of the world. Some succeeded, some failed, and some were pirated. The ENIAC was a pivotal development that most significantly benefited the UK and Canada.

The Modern History of Computing

In this paper, the Difference Engine of Charles Babbage was highlighted as a "special-purpose digital computing machine" of the 1800s. Babbage's Difference Engine No. 2 was produced from his templates in 1990. Babbage also proposed the Analytical Engine, which was to have a processing unit known as a mill and then absolutely to select among alternative actions. His work with Ada Lovelace is also noted, as she noted the ability to use the Analytical Machine for non-numerical data.

The importance of the early analog computers is analyzed, along with methods of representing numerical data, the output voltage, and the qualifications to be considered as analog. The foundation of analog computer was the mechanical wheel-and-disc integrator invented by James Thomson. Vannevar Bush's mechanical differential analyzer, known as the first large-scale analog computer, was invented in 1931.

Turing's stored-program concept served as the foundation for the universal Turing machine in 1936. Turing worked as a cryptanalyst at Bletchley Park, where he became acquainted with the work of Thomas Flowers, and contributed to the idea of machine intelligence during that time.

The electromechanical quality of the early computing machines dictated small basic components and electrical switches known as "relays." These were much slower as compared to the electronic computers, as they were built before and during WWII at Bletchley Park,

Princeton University, and by Konrad Zuse (Berlin). The replacement of relays with vacuum tubes contributed to high-speed quality, as contributed by Thomas Flowers.

John Atanasoff employed the use of vacuum tubes at Iowa State College. The Atanasoff-Berry Computer (ABC), an electronic digital machine, ensued in 1939. Work terminated in 1942 due to the inefficiency and errors found in the binary card-reader.

In regard to the Colossus, Max Newman suggested the automation of the decryption process in 1942. This was developed as the Heath Robinson, which utilized thyratron tubes. Upon Turing's advice, Newman turned to Flowers for advice, which was ultimately discouraged until the installation of the Colossus. Ten Colossi total were built, in which the later machines differed from the prototype due to a Special Attachment. This enabled wheel-setting and the decrypting of the German Lorenz. Unlike modern computers, the Colossus did not have internally stored programs and it was not a general-purpose machine. However, the contributions of the Colossus shortened the war by two years.

Turing's Automatic Computing Engine (ACE) differed from the U.S. EDVAC in that the ACE utilized distributed processing while the EDVAC contained a centralized structure. Although memory and speed were keys to the ACE, the actual progress of the ACE was slow. Harry Huskey ultimately used the designs for the ACE in the Bendix G15 computer, argued as the initial personal computer.

The Manchester Machine, "The Baby" was developed by F.C. Williams and Tom Kilburn, and was later enlarged as the Ferranti Mark 1. However, the Manchester Machine should also be attributed to Turing and especially Newman, since they contributed the fundamental logico-mathematical components.

The first U.S. electronic digital computer was produced by John Mauchly and J. Presper Eckert in 1945. Upon joining ENIAC, John von Neumann, influenced by Turing's 1936 paper, proposed an electronic stored-program general-purpose digital computer (EDVAC). This was a sore spot with Eckert and Mauchly all their lives, and the reason of their big falling out with von Neumann. Eckert and Mauchly had already designed the stored program before Von Neumann ever set foot in the place. Von Neumann listened and discussed their ideas with them, and then wrote them up. Goldstine made sure to publish Von Neumann's notes, and now the whole stored program concept is called Von Neumann's. It is doubtful that von Neumann could come in "cold" to the ENIAC project and suddenly conceive of a stored program machine. It is also doubtful that he even knew Turing even though they were both at Princeton at the same time in the mid '30s. It is more likely that von Neumann learned of the stored program concept from Eckert and Mauchly, as they always claimed, but was the first to write it down. There was significant acrimony over the years following von Neumann's publication under his sole name of a "Draft Report" that was, in reality, a set of notes and lectures delivered by Mauchly and Eckert. This is covered in more detail later.

Acoustic memory, utilized "delay lines" of mercury-filled tubes for internalized memory. Such capability was vital to meet the needs for an internally stored program computer. This is one of the motivations that Eckert had in perfecting the acoustic delay line storage system. This was later proposed for both the EDVAC and ACE. Turing organized instructions in relative positions to reduce waiting time, known as "optimum coding." Eckert's drum memories enabled the storage of large quantities of memory, and were utilized by the Manchester computer in 1949. The concept of magnetic core memory was furthered by Jay Forrester in his development of the superior ferrite core memory.

The Moore School Lectures

The Moore School Lectures and the British Lead in Stored Program Computer Development (1946 -1953

In 1946 between 8th July and 31st August the Moore School of Electrical Engineering at the University of Pennsylvania held a special course entitled "Theory and Techniques for Design of Electronic Digital Computers." The course was organized in response to interest generated by the school's public announcement of the ENIAC, and the publication of The First Draft of a Report on the EDVAC. 1945 by John von Neumann. Attendance was by invitation only and the "Students" were selected from the leading experts at the major institutions working on the development of computing devices in the US and UK. At the time of this event there were only three published designs for a stored program computer and it was expected that all those present were familiar with these documents.

- *First Draft of a Report on the EDVAC.* by John von Neumann. 1945
- *The Proposed Electronic Calculator.* by Alan Turing. 1945.
- *Preliminary report on the proposal for an IAS machine* by A.W. Burks, H.H. Goldstine and John von Neumann. June 1946

Within two years of these lectures the first stored program computer was operational; within 3 years there were 5 operational machines, and within 5 years stored program machines were commercially available. The Moore School Lectures, as they became known, were responsible for focusing all the leading developers of computing devices on a single problem:- How to design and build a stored program computer. It is interesting that despite being outnumbered and out-funded, the British took, and held, the lead in this development effort between 1946 and 1953. In some areas such as business applications the British held the lead for much longer. How they were able to do this is not directly explained in any of the historical material available online, which tends to focus on individual development efforts and not on the larger picture.

Moore School Lectures and Attendees:

The lecturers who delivered the course are listed below.

Lecturer	Organization
Aiken, Howard H.	Harvard University
Burks, Arthur W.	Institute for Advanced Study, Princeton
Chu, J. Chuan	Moore School
Crawford, Perry U., Jr.	Office of Research and Inventions, U.S. Navy
Curtis, John H.	National Bureau of Standards
Eckert, J. Presper, Jr.	Electronic Control Company
Goldstine, Herman H.	Institute for Advanced Study, Princeton

Lecturer	Organization
Hartree, Douglas R.	University of Manchester
Lehmer, Derrick II.	University of California, Berkeley
Mauchly, John W.	Electronic Control Company
Mooers, Calvin N.	Naval Ordnance Laboratory
Rademacher, Hans	University of Pennsylvania
Rajchman, Jan	RCA
Sharpless, T. Kite	Moore School
Sheppard,C. Bradford	Moore School
Stibitz, George	Independent consultant
Travis, Irven R.	Moore School
Von Neumann, John	Institute for Advanced Study, Princeton
Williams, Sam B.	Consultant, Moore School (Bell Telephone Laboratories)

40 lectures were delivered 5 days a week over 8 weeks. Most days a formal morning lecture lasting up to 3 hours was followed by an unstructured afternoon seminar.

The Lecture titles and the lecturer are listed below

	Lecturer	Lecture Title
1	George Stibitz	Introduction to the Course on Electronic Digital Computers
2	Irven Travis	The History of Computing Devices
3	J.W. Mauchly	Digital and Analog Computing Machines
4	D.H. Lehmer	Computing Machines for Pure Mathematics
5	D.R. Hartree	Some General Considerations in the Solutions of Problems in Applied Mathematics
6	H.H. Goldstine	Numerical Mathematical Methods I
7	H.H. Goldstine	Numerical Mathematical Methods II
8	A.W. Burks	Digital Machine Functions
9	J.W. Mauchly	The Use of Function Tables with Computing Machines

	Lecturer	Lecture Title
10	J.P. Eckert	A Preview of a Digital Computing Machine
11	C.B. Sheppard	Elements of a Complete Computing System
12	H.H. Goldstine	Numerical Mathematical Methods III
13	H.H. Aiken	The Automatic Sequence Controlled Calculator
14	H.H. Aiken	Electro-Mechanical Tables of the Elementary Functions
15	J.P. Eckert	Types of Circuit -- General
16	T.K. Sharpless	Switching and Coupling Circuits
17	A.W. Burks	Numerical Mathematical Methods IV
18	H.H. Goldstine	Numerical Mathematical Methods V
19	Hans Rademacher	On the Accumulation of Errors in Numerical Integration on the ENIAC
20	J.P. Eckert	Reliability of Parts
21	C.B. Sheppard	Memory Devices
22	J.W. Mauchly	Sorting and Collating
23	J.P. Eckert C.B. Sheppard	Adders
24	J.P. Eckert	Multipliers
25	J.W. Mauchly	Conversions between Binary and Decimal Number Systems
26	H.H. Goldstine	Numerical Mathematical Methods VI
27	Chuan Chu	Magnetic Recording
28	J.P. Eckert	Tapetypers and Printing Mechanisms
29	J.H. Curtiss	A Review of Government Requirements and Activities in the Field of Automatic Digital Computing Machinery
30	H.H. Goldstine	Numerical Mathematical Methods VII
31	A.W. Burks	Numerical Mathematical Methods VIII
32	Perry Crawford	Application of Digital Computation Involving Continuous Input and Output Variables
33	J.P. Eckert	Continuous Variable Input and Output Devices

	Lecturer	Lecture Title
34	S.B. Williams	Reliability and Checking in Digital Computing Systems
35	J.P. Eckert	Reliability and Checking
36	C.B. Sheppard	Code and Control -- I
37	J.W.Mauchly	Code and Control -- II Machine Design and Instruction Codes
38	C.B. Sheppard	Code and Control -- III
39	C.N. Mooers	Code and Control -- IV Examples of a Three-Address Code and the Use of 'Stop Order Tags'
40	John von Neumann	New Problems and Approaches
41	J.P. Eckert	Electrical Delay Lines
42	J.P. Eckert	A Parallel-Type EDVAC
43	Jan Rajchman	The Selectron
44	C.N. Mooers	Discussion of Ideas for the Naval Ordnance Laboratory Computing Machine
45	J.P. Eckert	A Parallel Channel Computing Machine
46	C.B. Sheppard	A Four-Channel Coded-Decimal Electrostatic Machine
47	T.K. Sharpless	Description of Serial Acoustic Binary EDVAC
48	J.W.Mauchly	Accumulation of Errors in Numerical Methods

The notes of the lectures published in <u>The Moore School Lectures (Charles Babbage Institute Reprint)</u> make the following observations about the lecturers.

Moore School Lecture "Students" are listed below. The term student is misleading as these people were the leading researchers in the field of computing.

Student	Organization
Alexander, Sam N.	National Bureau of Standards
Breiter, Mark	Office of the Chief of Ordnance, War Department
Brown, David R.	MIT Servomechanisms Laboratory
Cannon, Edward W.	National Bureau of Standards
Clark, Howard L.	General Electric Co.

Student	Organization
Curtis, Roger	National Bureau of Standards
Elbourne, R. D.	Naval Ordnance Laboratory
Everett, Robert, R.	MIT Servomechanisms Laboratory
Galman, Herbert	Frankford Arsenal
Gard, Orin P.	Armament Laboratory, Wright Field
Gluck, Simon E.	Moore School
Gridley, D. H.	Naval Research Laboratory
Hobbs, G. W.	General Electric Co.
Horton, Arthur, B.	MIT
Loud, Warren S.	MIT
Lubkin, Samuel	Ballistics Research Laboratory, Aberdeen Proving Ground
Pendergrass, J. T.	OP-20G CNO Navy Department
Rees, David	Manchester University, England
Rosenbloom, Joshua	Frankford Arsenal
Sayre, Albert	Army Security Agency
Shaffer, Philip A., Jr.	Naval Ordnance Testing Station Pasadena, California
Shannon, Claude E.	Bell Telephone Laboratory
Smith, Albert E.	Navy Office of Research and Investigations
Suss, Louis	Naval Research Laboratory
Verzuh, Frank M.	Rockerfeller Electronic Computer Project, MIT
Wilkes, Maurice V.	Cambridge University
Wilson, Lou D.	MIT
Zagor, H. I.	Reeves Instrument Company

Additional Attendees included:

Vistor	Organization
Cuthbert C. Hurd	IBM
Jay Forrester	MIT

Other people attended but no record complete was kept.

The Moore School Lectures in Perspective

There was significant effort in computing occurring in the rest of the world. Some predated the Moore School Lectures which exposed ENIAC and its concepts to the world; and a great deal followed, influenced to some extent by these findings. Such is the way of research. One idea leads to another until soon there is an avalanche. So it was and is with the development and creation of the Cyber Age. That is the story of People, Machines and Politics.

First, efforts and successes in the rest of the world up to the early post war period. The UK led the way followed by Canada, which benefited from the developments taking place in the UK.

UK Developments

Developments in the UK had three main sources. The first was tied to the wartime efforts in breaking the German codes – the ENIGMA efforts and the creation of the Colossus machines. Second, Alan Turing had a major part in this effort, dating back to his groundbreaking paper in the 1930s.

The third impetus to the UK developments was the availability of the *Draft Report* which von Neumann created based on the work of Eckert and Mauchly. While this report should have been classified, and of course should have attributed the concepts to Eckert and Mauchly, it was openly distributed by Herman Goldstine, and a copy of the *First Draft* made its way to Maurice Wilkes; who made immediate use of this in the ongoing efforts at Cambridge.

Maurice Wilkes, in his books and a couple of his quotes in my book, will show that he was well aware of the fact that the credit belonged to Eckert and Mauchly, and not to von Neumann.

The English Competition

A major competitor was a British group that drew on the ideas of Mauchly, as well as the computer's godfather, Alan Turing, and that built on the legendary work of the war-time Enigma code-cracking team.

Critical to the war effort, and credited with shortening the conflict by several years, was Britain's breaking of the German military's secret codes. The Germans ran their communications traffic through the Enigma machine, a mechanical rotary device which encrypted the messages. The Polish resistance had captured one of the German army's devices, and sent it to the British. Later, the British themselves, in a daring escapade, had snatched another Enigma from a U-boat that had been forced to the surface. They got on board, got the Enigma machine and then sunk the U-Boat while the Germans never found out that the British had the coding machine.

The Enigmas were complex gear boxes that looked much like a typewriter, so depending on how you set the gears (and there were settings for each day and for each operation), the gear boxes would convert the character you would type into the keyboard into something different. So it was a variation. It was not a straight replacement code. For instance, you did not have an "A" suddenly appearing as an "E" or a "G" or an "F". It would vary so that the frequency of a character in the encrypted code would not be a giveaway to what that code meant. The frequency was all over the place and that is how the Germans had solved it with a machine. Anyway, the British had the Enigma machine so that they could decode the traffic with the German Navy. They had no decoding machine for the Luftwaffe, the German Air Force. So in 1942, under Maurice Wilkes at Cambridge University, they started developing what they called the Colossus machine. They set up a very top-secret establishment at Bletchley Park, which was a manor house outside or close to Cambridge. They built this area up to top-secret and they built ten Colossus machines. These machines were used to decode the Luftwaffe traffic. Each Colossus machine had about 2000 tubes and while they were special purpose, they were digital computers. So, to the question, were the British using digital computers in the 40s, the answer is yes. They were special purpose for cryptanalysis. Were they stored program computers? No. They used punch paper tape; they did not use magnetic tape. They did not have vast amounts of internal storage of data; it was really in and out punch paper tape going in, punch paper tape coming out. These were the decodings of the Luftwaffe. They were quite effective

Possessing the machines was one step in solving the puzzle of German encryption. Another was the use of computing devices to sift through and decipher the immense number of coded messages transmitted by the Nazi command. Further, such apparatus might help decipher the messages of the Luftwaffe, the German Air Force whose Enigma-like machines the British had failed to capture. To break the codes, Britain set up near Cambridge University the super-secret and later famous Bletchley Park facility, where many of the country's best mathematicians and engineers, chess experts, amateur musicians, and actors labored around the clock. This brilliant, eccentric group brought a vast expertise on wiring and exotic algebra to bear on the deciphering problems they faced. By 1942, computer scientist Thomas (Tommy) Flowers had begun constructing the top-secret Colossus computer, and by December 1943 his crew had installed the first machine

Like the ENIAC, the aptly named Colossus was huge by today's standards. Each machine had between 1600 and 2400 vacuum tubes. In all, ten Colossi were built. The Colossus was a special-purpose device, geared to decryption, not a general-purpose machine like ENIAC. Nor was the Colossus a stored-program computer like the BINAC would be. It employed punched paper tape to enter data. As it lacked internally stored programs, its crew had to laboriously reconfigure its switches and plugs for each new task. Although crude, Flowers' brainchild did assist in deciphering the Luftwaffe's communications.

If we put aside for a moment Atanasoff's ABC machine and Colossus, both special purpose devices, then the first true general-purpose electronic computer was the electronic numerical integrator and computer (ENIAC).

Bletchley

As already stated, Colossus I was installed at Bletchley Park on the 8th of December 1943. In all, ten Colossi were built. Colossus I contained approximately 1600 vacuum tubes and each of the subsequent machine approximately 2400 vacuum tubes. Like the smaller ABC, Colossus lacked two important features of modern computers. First, it had no internally stored programs. To set it up for a new task, the operator had to alter the machine's physical wiring, using plugs and switches. Second, Colossus was not a general-purpose machine, being designed for a specific cryptanalytic task involving counting and Boolean operations.

The contributions of such figures as Thomas Flowers, Alan Turning, William Tutte, and Max Newman are addressed in an effort to understand the building of the Colossus. The Colossus was pivotal in decoding the encryptions of the German Tunny machine, not to be mistaken with the German Enigma machine. In examining the biographies of the above men, it is argued that Flowers was responsible for the Colossus even though history often credits Tunny, and alternately, Newman. Flowers himself stated, "I invented the Colossus. No one else was capable of doing it." Furthermore, although Tute's method of wheel setting, known as "the Statistical Method", was employed in the Colossus, it is often accredited to Turing. In reality, Turing developed a wheel breaking method using depths which was not utilized in the Colossus. The misattribution of credit underlies the history of the Colossus.

A wartime code-breaker known as the Colossus Mk2 is regarded as one of the first electronic computers. Hitler's Lorenz code was broken by using the Colossus at Bletchley, where it has been reconstructed in 1993. The Colossus, viewed as an expansion of the Mk1 of 1944, served as a prototype for electronic switching. The Colossus was notably different than other code-breakers since it was electronic and capable of scanning messages repeatedly and rapidly. Built by Dr. Tommy Flowers in London, the machine utilized thyratron rings, valve circuits, and over 1,500 valves to break the code. To prevent these valves from blowing up, the Colossus remained on until the war terminated.

Donald Michie and Jack Good served as contributors to the building of the Colossus. The Colossus decrypted "Fish" cipher text from the German Lorenz. The German cipher systems included the Enigma for tactical purposes and the Lorenz for "high-level strategic traffic." Michie and Good improved the Colossus to include the numbers two through ten which lead to breaking the Lorenz patterns, or "wheel-breaking." The Colossus 2, later developed in June 1944, was quickly replicated into eight others which increased the encryption of messages. The breaking of German codes was enabled by a mistake of the Germans; they were prohibited to retransmit a message without modifying the wheel setting. In August 30, 1941, a "Fish" intercept of 3, 976 characters was obtained with the exact same wheel settings. Michie was awarded the 2001 International Joint Conference on Artificial Intelligence research excellence award for his efforts.

Although the Colossus was built two years prior to the American Electronic Numerical Integrator and Computer (ENIAC), the ENIAC was viewed as the initiator since the Colossus was not revealed until the 1970s. The Colossus machines used in WWII cut ciphering time from weeks to hours and were utilized in the concluding strategies for D-Day. Overall, the decryption of 63 million German characters was possible through the Colossus.

The Colossus was not created "sui generis", for it sprang from earlier work and concepts developed by Alan Turing, who was perhaps Britain's foremost mathematician and worked at Bletchley Park. Turing had studied under Max Newman, who had previously proposed that any mathematical problem could probably be solved, by a fixed, purely mechanical process. Turing determined that "mechanical" implied, to him at least, automatic. This intriguing thought led Turing to turn his mind to the notion of an automatic calculator or computing machine, and in 1937 he authored a paper with sketches describing what such a device might look like. This hypothetical device has become known as The Turing Machine. The Turing Machine concept consisted of an endless tape made up of squares that would be either left blank or would contain symbols that would be written in binary code. The machine would read these symbols in serial fashion, moving the tape either forward or backward one space at a time.

While at Bletchley, Turing began to convert his ideas into working machines. It is known that one of the improvements of the Colossus was to create a parallel processing capability that speeded up the processing of data. The Colossus differed from its predecessor, the Heath Robinson machine and its cousins, in a number of respects, and one, which saved much time, was the mixing of data and program by message tapes, while using arrays of phone jacks and switches to arrange the programming.

Some of the work at Bletchley Park may still be considered a state secret. If so, it remains an open question as to the scope of Turing's contributions beyond the making of the electro-mechanical code-breaking machines called "Bombes" at Bletchley Park in the early 1940s. Owing to secrecy that was to persist for many years, perhaps to this day, Turing's full contributions still reside in the realm of speculation. However, he is believed to have contributed to the creation of an algorithm that speeded up the process of rapidly and accurately solving the German cipher by sorting through all the possible combinations of the Enigma's settings. This process did not actually perform the decoding of messages but determined the initial position of the German Enigma rotors. The intelligence these machines provided was code-named Ultra.

US General George Patton traveled with his own Ultra Intelligence field truck that quickly aided the deciphering of German messages transmitted to and from the German military on the ground.

Quite unlike these electro-mechanical Bombes, the Heath Robinson machine that preceded the Colossus was electronic, was built for speed more so than accuracy, and its output at Bletchley was small. What it did, however, was to prove that high speed electronic devices could be used for crypto analytic work

When Germany surrendered in 1945, the work on the Bombes and the Colossi machines at Bletchley came to a halt and these machines were dismantled and scattered. Only the British government may know exactly what became of these tools that proved so invaluable in the war effort.

Post World War II

As the war ended, the British began to work toward fully digital, stored-program devices of the type their American allies were keen to build. The third impetus for the early rapid British computer development effort came with the wide-spread dissemination of John Von Neumann's May 1945 paper on the EDVAC, the successor to the ENIAC that was to be built at Aberdeen. As noted above, the *First Draft of a Report on the EDVAC* was compiled from Mauchly and Eckert's ideas, although it went under Von Neumann's name. It contained information – essentially a conceptual blueprint for a working digital computer – that any other nation, friend or foe, would desperately want, and by all rights, should have been stamped ultra-secret. Yet von Neumann's colleague at Aberdeen, Herman Goldstine, had knowingly declined to classify it, and had sent it out to many other scientists, in the U.S. and abroad.

Britain's eminent Dr. Douglas Hartree, who would later give one of the Moore School Lectures in the summer of 1946, had previously interested both Maxwell Newman and Maurice Wilkes in the furthering knowledge of fast machine techniques. Newman was most interested in using the computer as a tool for heuristic investigations in areas of pure mathematics whose calculations exceeded human ability.

A few months after his arrival at Manchester, Newman wrote as follows to the Princeton mathematician John von Neumann (February 1946):

> With the development of fast machine techniques, mathematical analysis itself may take a new slant, apart from the developments that may be stimulated in symbolic logic and other topics not usually in the repertoire of engineers or computing experts; and that mathematical problems of an entirely different kind from those so far tackled by machines might be tried, e.g. testing out the 4-colour problems or various theorems on lattices, groups, etc., for the first few values of *n*.

As noted previously, at Cambridge University, Maurice Wilkes got his hands on a copy of the *First Draft Report on the EDVAC*. Wilkes was a remarkable figure who would serve as a professor emeritus at Cambridge into this century, and who had a hand in inventing timesharing and file servers. His account of the EDVAC makes clear the huge impact it had on his work:

> In the middle of May 1946, I had a visit from [astronomer and computer pioneer] L.J. Comrie who was just back from a trip to the United States. He put in my hands a document…entitled *First Draft Report on the EDVAC*. I sat up late into the night reading the report. In it, clearly laid out, were the principles on which the development of modern digital computer was to be based: the stored program with the same store for numbers and instructions, the serial execution of instructions and the use of binary switching circuits for computation and control. I recognized this at once as the real thing, and from that time on, never had any doubt as to the way computer development would go.

Wilkes applied key portions of the EDVAC paper, including an invention of Eckert's, the acoustic delay line, to the new EDSAC machine his team was developing at Cambridge's <u>Mathematical Laboratory</u>. (EDSAC stood for Electronic Delay Storage Automatic Calculator). In his later writings, Wilkes is quite open that he knew the ideas he appropriated were those of Mauchly and Eckert, not of von Neumann. In a trip to the United States, Wilkes also attended, in mid-1946, the Moore School's first-of-its-kind course on computers, whose content largely consisted of Mauchly and Eckert's innovations.

Wilkes was also aided by the insights of British math genius, Alan Turing, who, as noted above, had made important contributions at Bletchley Park. In late 1945, Turing crafted an important paper, "Proposal for Development in the Mathematics Division of an Automatic Computing Engine (ACE)". Turing's report contained a wealth of detail on building the ACE, including circuit designs, pieces of hardware, and an estimated construction price of eleven-thousand pounds. Like later computers, the ACE was to be a "distributed" device, with processing taking place in multiple areas, not in one centralized place. Turing even supplied sample software written in the "machine code" still employed today to make software more efficient.

Turing's "Proposal for Development in the Mathematics Division of an Automatic Computing Engine (ACE)" was the first relatively complete specification of an electronic stored-program general-purpose digital computer. An NPL file (now unfortunately destroyed) gave the date of Turing's proposal as 1945; Michael Woodger, Turing's assistant at NPL from May 1946, believes that the proposal was probably written between October and December 1945.

The first electronic stored-program digital computer to be proposed in the U.S. was the EDVAC (see below). The 'First Draft of a Report on the EDVAC' (May 1945), composed by von Neumann, contained little engineering detail, in particular concerning electronic hardware (owing to restrictions in the U.S.). Turing's proposal, on the other hand, supplied detailed circuit designs and specifications of hardware units, specimen programs in machine code, and even an estimate of the cost of building the machine (£11,200). ACE and EDVAC differed fundamentally from one another; for example, ACE employed distributed processing, while EDVAC had a centralized structure.

While Wilkes' team toiled on the EDSAC, more competition arose from the industrial north of England. This entailed a project whose key breakthrough involved the technology that became the basis of television. Engineering professor Frederic "Freddie" Williams had been a major force at Britain's Telecommunications Research Establishment (TRE), which under the lash of the German Blitz, had worked to develop radar. By autumn 1946, Williams was using an electron beam to store individual bits of data on a cathode ray tube, or CRT, that is, a TV screen. A bit was stored as a "1" or "0", and charged constantly to permanently keep the data. In December 1947 Williams, then working at the University of Manchester's Royal Society Computing Machine Laboratory, and colleague Tom Kilburn managed to store 2,048 bits of data on a 6-inch screen. It was named "The Williams Tube".

The Williams team next built a computer, the Small-Scale Experimental Machine (SSEM), to test the usefulness of CRT memory. The power of this "Manchester Baby" was small – just 32 words of memory – but its technique was novel, and powerful. It employed Random Access Memory (RAM) to store instructions, which would allow an operator to execute programs from the screen's keyboard, instead of laboriously flipping switches and swapping circuits.

I now want to review the succeeding developments in the UK and in Canada. In doing so, I would like to share some of my experiences in Canada in those early years that were made possible by the FERUT machine, a computer that stemmed from the UK developments made possible by the *First Draft EDVAC Report* blueprint.

As we have seen, owing to its wartime assembly of talent to decode German messages, the UK was best able to re-assemble the same individuals to produce the EDSAC stored program computer using the EDVAC "blueprint". This convergence of fortuitous circumstances yielded what appeared to place the UK in the technological lead in computer development.

Introduction to the Mark 1 [158]

The progression of the Small-Scale Experimental Machine (SSEM), or the "Baby", to the Manchester Mark 1 included the designs toward a more "useable" machine. The Baby was the foremost computer capable of retaining data along with any user program in the electronic memory form of Random Access Memory (RAM). Upon its first successful run on June 21, 1948, the aptitude of the Baby was realized and the more powerful Manchester Mark 1 ensued. With its magnetic drum for auxiliary storage, the Manchester Mark 1 became available as an Intermediary Version in April of 1949. By October, all the components of it were operational and were used at the University of Manchester, its place of creation, for scientific research.

The Ferranti Mark 1, whose building the government requested in October 1948, was similar to the Manchester Mark 1 but was ultimately faster. In February 1951, it served as the first commercial computer. An improved version was produced with a revised order code and the eradication of the anomalies of the Manchester 1.

The Ferranti Mark 1 [159]

A contract between the government and Ferranti Ltd., established in 1948, fostered an association between industry and the university, allowing the availability of the electronic computer to spread internationally. Its improvements from the Manchester Mark 1 included an "increased B-line, CRT, and magnetic drum stores, a much faster multiplier, and an increased range of instructions." These were contributed by members of Ferranti and Manchester University, namely Geoff Tootill and Alec Robinson. Robinson improved his multiplier, allowing its speed to double.

Although the Ferranti Mark 1 was comparable to the Manchester Mark 1, innovations included the return to only one page per CRT. An enhanced order code ensued, along with a reduction to two page display monitors and a single drum, in the revised version known as the Ferranti Mark 1*. Initial programming was painstaking, relying on the base 32. A comprehensive "Autocode" was produced by Tony Brooker in 1954 and was utilized by many despite its tendency to hinder the machine's speed.

"The Baby" [160]

The creation of "The Baby" was written and designed in 1948 by Tom Kilburn and F.C. (Freddie) Williams, respectively. In using a Cathode Ray Tube for digital storage, Williams began work at the Telecommunications Research Establishment (TRE) in 1946. He patented a bit memory system known as the "anticipation pulse method" and ultimately contributed to the process of "regeneration", still utilized to this day for RAMs. Kilburn, Williams, and another TRE member, Tootill, coupled their efforts at the University of Manchester. Since electronic storage was an impeding matter in the progression of the Electronic Digital Computers, Kilburn initiated the "defocus-focus" and "dot-dash" methods of the CRT. "Williams Tube" was termed for the CRT storage system, although Kilburn should have been included.

A computer built around the CRT memory, the Small Scale Experimental Machine, enabled running different programs to occur simply by resetting part of the memory. Kilburn and Tootill ordered most of the parts for "The Baby" from TRE. The first running of "The Baby" was successful in finding the highest factor of a number. Its main store was a 32*32 bit array and it relied on only seven instructions. "Within four months the Baby had been enhanced to a 4- instruction code, including A=S, A=A + S, and A=A & S. Improvements were made to later produce the Manchester Mark 1, followed by the Ferranti Mark 1.

Canada

My own experience with the earliest stored program computer produced in the UK altered the trajectory of my life in more ways than I can enumerate. Growing up in Canada, I had the advantage of seeing both the European and US influences on innovation. There was a heavy European influence, of course, in Canada and we were so close to the United States and I was attracted to the "get up and go" spirit there. I grew up in Toronto which is a "get up and go" city, as opposed to Canada as a whole which seems to be more European than American right now. It is still quite American but in my opinion, there is more of the traditional approach in Canada than there is in the United States. There is innovation in the United States and a certain amount of innovation in Canada, but to a lesser degree. In the time I was growing up, Canada was very advanced in aeronautics. The Canadian aeronautical industry had a very proud heritage. Many of the early developments in flight were Canadian. Many Canadian flyers during the First World War were great aces. Billy Bishop was a great one; he had 72 victories against Richtoven's 80. And Billy Bishop was still alive and we met him as kids. We went to the various airports where we met some of these earlier aces, but this proud tradition continued and at the University of Toronto in the late 40's, there was a great scientific push. That is why Toronto was one of the leaders of the computer age.

Continuing My Bleeding-Edge Work With Computers

The University of Toronto's interest in computers matched that at MIT, Penn, and other major universities in North America and Europe. It instilled in me a desire to learn more about these calculating machines – how to build them, use them, and employ them.

Canada is a British Commonwealth and many of the professors at the University of Toronto had trained at Cambridge or Oxford. As a result, instead of building its own computer, the faculty got the government of Canada to spend $250,000 to buy a computer that was in a warehouse in England. A British firm had drawn on the know-how of Robinson, who had drawn on the know-how of Mauchly and Eckert, to construct its state-of-the-art Ferranti Electric computer based on a design by Frederick Williams of the University of Manchester.

In 1952 it was installed at the University, and dubbed FERUT. This came as a deep disappointment to a solid group of researchers at the University who were well on their way to building UTEC – University of Toronto Electronic Computer. It was my good fortune to work closely with this group before and after the arrival of FERUT.

What is interesting is that the FERUT machine was the second of five machines built by Ferranti Electric, the first of which was in the University of Manchester. I am not certain where the other three wound up. The FERUT was contemporaneous with the BINAC and with the later UNIVAC. The machine I was to use in Toronto might very well have been the first stored program computer in the world – second model of it, but really the first stored program computer. Years later, when I went on to use UNIVAC I in New York, I found great similarities and great differences in the approach. FERUT for its day was a rather remarkable machine whose design in reality traces back to the work of Eckert and Mauchly.

The FERUT was, for its time, very powerful but also, compared to today, exceedingly tedious to use. Someone working on the machine had to do everything: write the program, run it, keep track of the accumulators, keep track of the storage addresses, etc. Thus I became very interested in the University's efforts to simplify the work of writing and operating programs.

Let me explain this a little more. At the time, the instructions were in the code of the machine. Everything was in binary, utilizing 20 binary bits (a bit is a zero or a one) per "word". For "clarity", the English Creed teletype code was used where 5 bits were used for a character. Hence the computer word consisted of 4 characters.

Each word consisted of an instruction code and an address upon which the instruction would perform a task. To say the least, writing the program to have the machine perform was extremely tedious and heavily prone to error.

Cally Gottlieb, Bea Worsely and Pat Hume embarked, in 1952, on a project to simplify the code by creating Transcode, an interpreter type of language that, instead of translating an instruction into detailed, arduous-to-program machine code, would allow programmers to write their instructions in a language very close to English and algebra, and have the computer running Transcode interpret the pseudo code into the operational code of the machine. For example, on seeing the term Add, the program would automatically look for the numbers to be added, and jump to a computer routine that would perform the addition. This saved a number of steps that would otherwise have to be performed with each instruction. It saved the programmer the boring task of keeping track of storage addresses. The way the interpreter avoided the labor of tracking addresses was a clever one. Each instruction code for the machine consisted of 20 bits, five bits for the instruction, such as Multiple, and other bits that contained the memory address. This was one of the first efforts anywhere of trying to simplify the methods of programming. John Mauchly and Grace Hopper in the United States were also working on Automatic Programming techniques, as they were called. The objective was to use the power of the machine to simplify the use of the machine.

Transcode swiftly spawned other innovations. It allowed a program to "loop": to continually examine a long series of values until an instruction was executed or the end of the series was reached. Further, if a useful routine like a loop did not exist, a programmer could readily develop it in Transcode. A library of such routines was put together. Libraries have been common in IT shops ever since.

I contributed my own small part to this nascent computer revolution. I developed a computer language on my own, called "Simple", for its simplicity of use. It bore a close resemblance to a later, very popular, and easy-to-use language, called Basic.

During this period, due to my computer connections, I was lucky enough to meet John Mauchly. I had joined the Association of Computing Machinery, whose president was the computer legend himself. He had succeeded Douglas, the Director of the U.S. Bureau of Standards, who had been forced to retire when it was found out he was gay. (Times have changed indeed.)

In October 1952, the Association held its national meeting in Toronto, and, naturally, I attended. I met Mauchly, and talked with many of the other 40 or so at the meeting, which included most of those who mattered in computing at the time.

The Manchester Machine

To surmise, two computers were built in England based on concepts presented in these two documents. Each predated similar computer systems built in the US.

Manchester's prototype Mark I was built and confirmed as a useful design in November 1948.

A small experimental machine (which was based on the EDVAC concept) consisting of 32 words of memory and a 5-instruction instruction set was operating at Manchester University, England, by June 1948.

The earliest general-purpose stored-program electronic digital computer to work was built in the Royal Society Computing Machine Laboratory at Manchester University. The Manchester "Baby", as it became known, was constructed by the engineers F.C. Williams and Tom Kilburn, and performed its first calculation on 21 June 1948. The tiny program, stored on the face of a cathode ray tube, was just seventeen instructions long. A much enlarged version of the machine, with a programming system designed by Turing, became the world's first commercially available computer, the Ferranti Mark I. The first to be completed was installed at Manchester University in February 1951; in all about ten were sold, in Britain, Canada, Holland and Italy.

The Winner of the Race

In the end, the BINAC, EDVAC, and Wilkes teams were edged out in the race to the first stored-program computer. While they labored, the Manchester "Baby" squad, with its TV screen technology, had edged ahead. On June 21, 1948, the research team at Manchester University attempted to run on its Baby a brief, 17-instruction program. The goal: find the highest factor of a number. It succeeded, calculating an 18-factor number, the highest yet discovered, taking a little over 50 minutes to plow through millions of [variants]

At the National Physics Laboratory (NPL), Alan Turing of Bletchley Park was leading efforts to build a computer of his own design called the Pilot ACE. Both Max Neumann and Alan Turing tried to recruit Tommy Flowers to help with development in 1946. Both failed; sadly, he stayed at the Post Office. Alan Turing continued to use the Post Office research center at Dollis Hill to build mercury delay lines but Flowers and W. M. Combs, another Bletchley man, were being pulled onto other "more important" work and progress was delayed. Eventually, Turing was persuaded to go to Manchester by Max Neuman. The Pilot ACE was constructed without him and was operational in 1951.

Wilkes' EDSAC team trailed behind, while its machine's initial program executed in May 1949. However, the EDSAC proved more practical than the Manchester Baby. It went on to incorporate many subroutines now familiar in computers. By the early 1950s, the EDSAC had exponentiation, layout and print functions, floating-point numbering and logarithms, and repeating functions rather like the "for loops" of later programming. In 1951, it pushed the prime-number record to 79 numerals, and the following year it boasted a rudimentary computer game: the ability to play tic-tac-toe on its CRT.

Yet the Manchester Baby had won the race, beating EDSAC and beating the Eckert-Mauchly Computer Company. It had the first stored program that worked.

Analysis and Speculation

What follows is mostly speculation. I would be interested in evidence that supports or refutes these ideas

I suspect the British were able to take the lead in computing in 1946 because the main challenge had become the rapid construction of a machine while solving the one remaining major technical problem - storing a program in memory. This problem was well understood in concept but the practical solution was more challenging than it appeared. As a result of their experience in the war, the British were approximately 2 to 3 years in advance of the Americans in the crucial area of rapid prototyping and evolution of complex electronic devices. It was this ability that enabled them to take the early lead from America

During the War, the British had developed the effective use of RADAR further than any of the other combatants. This work occurred in secret at the Telecommunication Research Establishment TRE in Malvern

Meanwhile at Bletchley Park, they had secretly built and operated 10 Colossus Mk II code breaking machines. These machines were complex special purpose computing devices. They matched ENIAC in complexity and capability, if not in size and generality. At the end of the war, Britain had the largest concentration of electronic computing devices in the world and a significant number of engineers with practical skills in rapidly building complex electronics. The British centers of electrical engineering excellence, which included Bletchley Park, the Telecommunications Research Establishment (TRE) at Malvern, and The General Post Office Research Station at Dollis Hill, had all been driven by desperation to work with great speed and had each developed similar evolutionary prototyping approaches. The Colossus Mk I, and Mk II were constructed by Tommy Flowers in a matter of months at Dollis Hill, and the development of RADAR at the TRE had been similarly rapid. Americas leading center of excellence in the field of electronic computing - The Moore School had become used to working around the clock. It was faster than expected but not as fast as hoped for. From an empty room in 1943, ENIAC was created in three years. The team worked night and day. Kay Mauchly told me that she and Pres, who both separately lived in Chestnut Hill, would often take the last train.

In 1946 the Moore School's leading experts left the school and went to other institutions. John von Neumann went with Herman Goldstine to the Institute for Advanced Study in Princeton and Mauchly and Eckert also left to setup their own company which was later purchased by Remington Rand. Both these groups lost valuable time in these reorganizations; however, this was not the cause of the lead in computing passing to the UK. Similar reorganizations had happened already in the UK and other countries, as military programs were wound down and research expertise returned to civilian institutions

By 1946 the conceptual architecture for a stored program computer was well understood by those interested in the field of electronic computing. Both John von Neumann and Alan Turing had developed and published designs. While these designs were revolutionary, they were not particularly complex conceptually. As has been pointed out elsewhere, a competent electrical engineer can grasp the main features of von Neumann's' design in a day. Maurice Wilkes was famously given only one night to read the *First Draft* and decided there and then that this was the correct approach and that he would develop a machine along these lines - the EDSAC - generally accepted as the second operational stored program computer and the first machine to actually perform useful work. By the time the Moore School lectures had finished, there were many people who understood exactly what needed to be done

Two basic types of stored memory were under investigation, Serial Access Memory (SAM) and Random Access Memory (RAM). SAM could only be read in the order it was written, while RAM was much faster as it could be read in any order. SAM devices in the form of <u>mercury acoustic delay lines</u> were already available as a result of RADAR development, which needed memory devices to improve image quality. RAM devices such as the Selectron were still under development but at the time of the Moore School Lectures, they were expected to be ready within a year.

In the UK, all three centers of computer development hired people from either TRE Malvern, Bletchley Park or both to fill Senior positions. These men combined their expertise and rapidly developed plans for building stored program computers.

At Manchester University, Max Neumann, who had directed efforts to break the Lorenz Cypher at Bletchley Park, became Fielden Professor of Pure Mathematics. He recruited I.J. Good and D. Rees both from Bletchley. Meanwhile, the Electrical Engineering Department recruited Freddie Williams from the TRE Malvern. Williams brought Tom Kilburn and later Geoff Tootill also from TRE to continue the development of a memory device based on the Cathode Ray Tubes CRT. Once at Manchester, Williams and Kilburn rapidly perfected a working RAM based on the cathode ray tube and installed in "The Baby", the first stored program computer that was operational in 1948. The speed of this development must be compared with the ill-fated development of the Selectron, electrostatic storage tube, which was running into difficulty in the US and was still not operational in the middle of 1948 when The Baby became operational. It was not used in a computer until the Johniac, named after Johnny von Neumann, and built by the Rand Corporation in California in 1954.

The IAS team led by von Neumann at Princeton was struggling with the RCA Selectron tube for electrostatic storage and switched to the Williams-Kilburn tube soon after the Manchester team announced the Baby.

There is some dispute over who actually led the effort to build the Baby at Manchester: the mathematics department or the Electrical Engineering departments. But what is clear is that men from TRE Malvern were able to solve the technical problems that were slowing efforts elsewhere and by employing a rapid evolutionary prototyping approach, the Manchester University team was able to beat all the other teams in the UK and US to build a working stored program computer. The Baby ran its first successful program on June 21, 1948

At Cambridge University, Maurice Wilkes, who had also been involved in Radar Development at TRE Malvern, took a different approach. He chose to build a machine of modest capabilities from stock parts, or as near to stock as he could get - he chose mercury delay lines for the memory. The machine was called <u>EDSAC</u>. It was the second operational stored program computer after the Baby in Manchester and ran its first successful program on the 6th May 1949. Wilkes was funded in part by the J. Lyons Company, a forward thinking British teashop chain similar to today's Starbucks. Lyons decided to build a computer of its own based on the EDSAC design. Lyons hired John Pinkerton also of TRE who seconded two of his staff to Wilkes to help build EDSAC. In 1951 Lyons built their machine and called it LEO. It was the first business computer ever used and was rapidly commercialized. IBM's first computer, the Defense Calculator, was not available until March 1953.

Williams' great contribution was the storage on the face of the CRT as fast storage. As a student, that drove me crazy because that was part of the fast storage capabilities of the FERUT; the other storage of course was the drum. And the mean free time between hours to me was 20 seconds.

It was very unreliable but it worked, and I could not have done what I did without that machine. I would do things twice to make sure that they agreed and then I would do it three times and sometimes I would have to do it five or six times and I would get five or six answers, but that is beside the point. Kay Mauchly Antonelli's understanding was that ultimately Von Neumann did not like it either.

With 50+ year hindsight and knowledge of the secret British activities at TRE Malvern and Bletchley Park, the Moore school lectures can be seen in a different light - one that raises many questions. To what extent did the hosts at the Moore School know about their British guests experience and skills? Had they known the truth, would they have been so open with their information? What would have happened if the British had been able to share their knowledge?

One fact seems undeniable: only four stored program computers were operational before 1950 and three of these were built by people who had worked at TRE Malvern during the Second World War. The one exception, Eckert and Mauchly's BINAC, worked for 48 hours and was then dismantled, never to work again. There is some controversy over this.

At the beginning of 1950, there were three working stored program computers in the world and none of them were in America. The expertise developed at Telecommunications Research Establishment (TRE) Malvern placed its engineers two to three years ahead of anyone else. How the British lost this lead is much less clear. The post war austerity measures contributed and the failure of the UK government to make adequate investments may have been a factor. There was no direct equivalent to the US ARPA and the agencies that did exist were not well funded. Industry and universities failed to partner well in the way J. Lyons and Cambridge University had done. Whatever the case, between 1950 and 1960, the British lost a 2 to 3 years lead in computing to America. But it may be fairer to say that the Americans took the lead back from the British.

Finally, consider the case of David Rees of Manchester University. He must have had a uniquely interesting and frustrating experience at the Moore school in 1946. He had been sent by Max Neumann from Manchester University to the lectures as a "student" and yet he was the only person present who had first-hand knowledge of Bletchley Park - the largest computing facility in the world, but, in the interests of British national security, he was not allowed to talk about it.

Elsewhere in the World:

Germany

Work on computers in Germany never got off the ground under the Nazis. While they espoused weapons and technology, they had no real strategy until the rocket program began in 1942 and 1943. Until then, their senior scientists were often given menial assignments. I met one world famous scientist in 1952 who told me he served as an assistant truck driver on the Russian Front until he was summoned to work at Peenemunde – the German V1 and V2 development site. He was Fritz Ebor.

Germany had a very talented group of scientists and engineers but when the war ended, these individuals had no supporting organization to focus their efforts and the US attracted many of the top talent in rocketry to provide the necessary leadership to create an early capability to explore space.

Other than the impressive efforts of Konrad Zuse, who built several relay calculator devices during the war that tested remote controlled rockets, Germany did not become a major factor in the development of the computer industry. Zuse had been working on calculating machines from 1938 to 1941 and produced the Z1-Z3 series during that period.

The Z3, built in 1941, could be considered a general purpose program controlled calculator. It was fast but it could not execute conditional jumps, as that idea never occurred to Zuse. While there was no interest in a general purpose machine, Zuse was excited by its promise and set out to create a larger version, the Z4. Allied bombing, destroyed the Z3 and caused him to have to move the Z4 several times in 1944. This machine journeyed to the Bavarian Alps and was later set up in 1950 at a technical institute in Zurich. It was said to be the only mathematical calculator of any consequence in continental Europe for several years.

"The Z3 included the ability to perform arithmetic exception handling. Konrad Zuse implemented this exception handling because he wanted to be sure that the Z3 would calculate numbers correctly, even when it was working without a supervisor."

Konrad Zuse followed a minimal design principle in the construction of his computers, because his goal was to build a powerful computing machine with minimal effort and cost. He really did not have any other choice, because his parents were not rich and he did not have much money. As far as he was concerned, the Z3 was the last in a series of trial machines (Z1-Z3) that were intended to pave the way to a machine that would be able to solve the mathematical problems of engineers and scientists.

Konrad Zuse was convinced that his computer could calculate all mathematical problems. In 1941 he told his friends that his machine was capable of playing chess, but he could not prove that this was the case. In fact, it was not until 1998 (three years after Konrad's death) that Raul Rojas formulated the proof that the Z3 was a truly universal computer in the sense of a Turing machine.

Konrad Zuse's Z3, built in Berlin from 1938 to 1941, was destroyed during World War II. The reconstruction project started in 1994. A functional replica was built and unveiled at a conference commemorating the 60th anniversary of the public presentation of the original machine in 2001. The reconstruction project includes several Java simulations of components of the whole machine and a 3D functional simulation of the Z3 and its user console.

Japan

As with Germany, the same might be said of Japan. For example, in 1943, the Japanese knew of the importance of computers and built an analog computer to solve systems of linear equations. Subsequently, a committee on electrical computing machines was established that encouraged the use of differential analyzers that were built between 1944 and 1952. Herman Goldstine reported that one of these machines employed electronic techniques. In 1952, Japan's Electrotechnical Laboratory in Tokyo built a relay computer, the ETL Mark I. This was followed in 1955 by the ETL Mark II of the same type. Goldstine noted that in 1957, only two years later, the Japanese were producing further iterations of the Mark series that were fully transistorized.

Australia

In Australia, yet another alumnus of TRE Malvern was having more luck. Trevor Pearcey had moved from the UK to Australia in 1945 where he decided to design and build a computer. In 1948 he visited England and confirmed the soundness of his design. By November 1949, the CSIR Mk I was operational.

Israel

After the war, Israel became very interested in the field of computing and sent the head of applied mathematical work at the Weizmann Institute of Science to the US. Chaim Pekeris wanted to have an electronic computer at the Institute. Gerald Estrin took a leave from the Institute for Advanced Study (IAS) at Princeton in 1954 to build the WEIZAC for the Institute. This machine was tested in 1955 and conformed to the types of computers being developed at the IAS.[161]

While many computer scientists were Jewish, work in Israel never became a factor until the late 1950s and into the 1960s. They were busy building a state. For a more exhaustive listing of other nations' interest in computing in the earlier days, the reader can refer to the appendix in Goldstine's Book, The Computer from Pascal to von Neumann[162].

The Soviet Union

The Soviet Union, for its part, certainly had talented scientists and engineers on hand. While they may have had access to the *First Draft EDVAC Report* "blueprint" and a centralized economy that might have directed these resources to begin the effort to build to the blueprint, they were operating from a lower base of computational analysis so their efforts did not receive the kick-start that took place in the UK, Canada, and elsewhere. This is not to say they did not appreciate the importance of the computer for weapons and for espionage. It is rumored that the first machine they built in the 1950s was an exact duplicate of the UNIVAC Scientific 1101, the only machine that was known to have classified commands used in decryption and telecommunication monitoring by the NSA.

The Politics of Fear and Economic Survival Driving Forward Technological Thinking in the US

By attracting the top talent in Germany to the US, several purposes were served. By working in behalf of the US, these talented individuals had an outlet for their appetite that had been whetted by their successes in German rocketry. For the US, this movement of intellectual resources kept the same talent from falling into the hands of the Soviet Union that was emerging as a new threat to world peace.

The importance of providing a creative outlet for professional technical talent, as was successfully done in the US in terms of the German rocket experts, was brought home to me years later. Almost ten years ago, I was invited to create a curriculum for the Kurchatov Institute for the purpose of re-training Russian engineers to find productive outlets for their enormous talents. Originally known as Laboratory No. 2 of the USSR Academy of Sciences, the Kurchatov Institute was founded in 1943 to develop nuclear weapons. Therefore, their expertise was developed mainly through the Soviet Union's Nuclear Weapons Programs but upon the collapse of the Soviet regime, this cadre of talent ceased to have a productive outlet.

When it becomes a matter of economic survival, the real fear, then and now, was that this talent and intimate knowledge of these technologies would find a market elsewhere, and that the results of such re-direction might easily flow to unfriendly lands or non-state movements.

Conclusion

As noted previously, Eckert and Mauchly's first test demonstration in March 1949 of stored-program computing, in the BINAC computer, trailed the Manchester Baby by only nine months. Construction of their BINAC was completed that fall. Moreover, it was undeniable that they had fathered much of the theoretical and practical basis of the Manchester Baby, and the machines competing with it. Mauchly was a pivotal figure in touching off the fierce competition and relentless innovation -- with all the attendant benefits to mankind, and limitless future potential -- that have typified the computer field ever since.

The work of Mauchly and Eckert truly laid the foundations for the development on a global basis of the computer and information industry as we know it today. Their innovative efforts, opposed by many, copied by many, and for which they were often denied credit, provided the genesis of what we have today.

CHAPTER SIX

THE EARLY WORLD OF
THE ELECTRONIC COMPUTER

What were the early days like? Who embraced change, who opposed it, and who sought to benefit from it? How were programs written, entered in the machines of the day, and tested? The initial trial-and-error approaches gave birth to techniques of using the machines themselves to write the programs. Automatic programming was a gear shift change in the move from early invention to the wide-ranging acceptance of today. Included are some humorous aspects of the early applications and the popular and professional reactions. This chapter contains a number of firsthand observations of the art, the science, and the people.

Remington Rand UNIVAC ends the vacuum tube era. A Thrilling Career Start with War-Time Legends

I had always dreamed of aerospace, but I had also been bitten by the computer bug. I wanted to do both. One company stood out. It came about by pure chance.

Back in the winter of 1944, when I was in high school and a World War still raged, I had attended a Saturday night lecture on science at the University of Toronto. The Royal Canadian Institute sponsored such talks on advanced topics. Prior to the lecture, the University awarded the speaker, a man with an unusual last name of Watson-Watt, with an honorary doctorate. There was no real reason given except for his contributions to the advancement of science. It all seemed pretty bland to me. His lecture was on wave propagation.

In retrospect, he was talking around the subject of radar, which was new and very top-secret, and his degree was for his contributions to the war effort. That man was Sir Robert Watson-Watt, the inventor of radar, that was devised during the 1930s and the Second

World War. His creation had allowed the Royal Air Force to turn back the German Luftwaffe during the Battle of Britain.[163]

Born in Angus, Scotland, Sir Robert had served in Britain's wartime cabinet under Winston Churchill. In daring missions, Sir Robert had been deposited on the shores of occupied France to investigate the radar antennae of the Germans, shimmying up poles to inspect their gear, noting how far advanced the enemy devices were, then slipping back to the beach for pickup by motor boat.

Robert Watson-Watt was descended from James Watt, the inventor of the steam engine and the progenitor of the Industrial Revolution, which is now drawing to a close due to electronic breakthroughs by the likes of Watson-Watt.

Sir Robert was also the creator of operations research. This is the method, much used by business and the military, where a model of an "operation" of some sort – a business, the assault of an armored division, an investment strategy – incorporates such factors as risk or change. These models help decision makers compare and predict the outcomes of differing strategies or controls. During the war, in an early example of operations research, Sir Robert's team was ordered to develop a means of sweeping "acoustic" mines that exploded from the noise of ship engines.

The solution seemed obvious – drag a big noise emitter, say a jackhammer – a thousand yards behind a minesweeper, and watch the mines blow up. However, when the research team took a jackhammer and put it in a steel sphere, they found it did not fit. Then they took off the handle, and it fit but did not work. Apparently, jackhammers had been designed in an ad-hoc fashion until they functioned. The Royal Navy minesweeping unit totally redesigned the jackhammer to work with or without a handle. This kind of constant tinkering is common in operations research; in fact, the field is often referred to as reengineering, or systems engineering.

Operations research is usually a very serious business, but there are occasions of humor. One of my classmates in Math and Physics, Peter Wade, who went on to a distinguished professorship in Montreal, started his working career in operations research at the Aluminum Company of Canada in Kingston, Ontario. Peter was assigned the task of finding out why the firm was using so much toilet paper. He devised a system of numbering the sheets on a roll, checking on the number of sheets used through direct monitoring of each use of a toilet, and accumulating statistics. He determined the number of sheets used for each operation varied from one to over two hundred. His solution was to crimp the roll holder tighter to make smooth flowing of the roll impossible. To this day, I do not know if Peter told me the truth, or pulled my chain. However, from personal observation of many operations research jobs, many were just as ridiculous.

Still, some had great merit. One of the earliest operations research concepts was that of optimum product mix. This was very important in refineries and manufacturing operations where there was potential for some kind of bottleneck. With the aid of some mathematical formulae, the most profitable mix of product was found through observations of a limited production facility. Imperial Oil of Canada, part of the Esso (now Exxon) group, pioneered this concept, and crunched its numbers with the Ferranti machine at the University of Toronto.

Operations research became a real science which swept the business and military world from the 40s through the 70s. Then systems engineering caught on, and operations research went out of vogue. Sir Robert told me the best personnel in operations research, at the start of a project and often throughout, were biologists, because they were very adept at designing experiments. The heart of operations research was observation, followed by analysis and leading, hopefully, to improvement. Systems engineering, on the other hand, concentrates more on the potential gains of rearranging the elements of a system.

In systems engineering, a system can be defined as groups of elements connected in some fashion, all directed to some purpose. The manner of rearranging the components or parts can result in a startling improvement in capability, even to the point of adding additional capability.

Let me provide a very simple version of systems engineering. A radio carries sound from a distance to the point of use, while television carries sight and sound. Yet the components of both are identical except for the viewing screens of the TV set. Oscilloscopes, which are really television screens or CRTs, had been known for years before TV: hence, combining CRTs with radio and rearranging their parts created TV and video. Simply adding a viewing screen can touch off a technological and societal revolution.

Returning to the start of my career, in the midst of my job search, I had a chance meeting with Sir Robert at a cocktail party. He asked what I was currently working on. I told him I had just completed my doctoral work and was waiting for the official degree. In the meantime, I was looking for a job. He offered me one on the spot after he learned of my computer experience and my work in astrophysics. The firm was Adalia. The more he talked, the more interested I became, due to the famous, intriguing characters in the firm and its client firms. The founder of Adalia was Sir Robert himself. He offered me the chance to be a systems engineer, a big step up from the mundane jobs of problem solver I had been offered. I leapt at the chance. I also enjoyed his company: the good-natured scientist had a grand sense of humor.

I learned from Sir Robert that several ironic developments had befallen radar's inventor. In the early 1950s, he was pulled over by Toronto police who had caught him in a new spin-off from his creation – the radar-based speed trap. He knew that he had not been speeding, but also knew there was no point in telling the authorities that radar could malfunction; hoisted on one's own petard indeed.

More seriously, Sir Robert had to fight in the British courts to establish the patent rights to his own invention. It is interesting that I have worked with the man who invented radar, and the man who invented the computer, and that both of them were assailed by frauds who sought to grab for themselves the renown due these remarkable men.

Adalia was a company with intriguing clients and projects. As a young Ph.D. of 25 years, I was fascinated by the work and the world figures whom I came to know and labor with. Sir Robert always had a circle of interesting people.

One of Adalia's major clients was Logistics Research, a California-based computer firm, which was manufacturing an early minicomputer, the ALWAC, at that time. Logistics Research was one of many firms owned by Axel Wennergren[164], a legend in the world of espionage. Sir Robert's firm had the contract to manage this business, with my role being computer applications.

Axel owned Electrolux, the appliance company that today holds the Frigidaire and Westinghouse brands. He also owned the ALWEG Corporation, owner of the patents for the monorail, and later the builder of monorail systems at Disneyland, the Seattle World Fair, and many other places in the world.

Axel was also a major owner of the Swedish steel industry, then one of the world's largest, which had very profitably supplied Nazi Germany with much of the wherewithal for its war machine. A Hitler sympathizer, he had donated significant sums of money to the Nazi Party and supported it throughout the Second World War.

Axel Wennergren held title to a fair chunk of South America's real estate, and among his holdings were well-known Caribbean isles. Two of these were Andros Island and Pig Island, across the harbor from Nassau and Grand Bahama. The reader may know them by their contemporary name of Paradise Island. Axel had built port and refueling facilities on Pig Island and during the war, he put them at the disposal of German U-Boats preying on British and American ships.

During this period, the Duke of Windsor -- who had shocked the world by abdicating as King Edward VIII to marry the American Wallis Simpson -- was the Governor General of the Bahamas for the British Crown. So, on one side of the Bay was the former King of Britain, and on the other side were German submarines at war with Britain. One of the great mysteries of the war is the extent to which Windsor sympathized with the Nazis' cause. Whatever the truth of his loyalties, it is true that the Duke of Windsor took no actions for or against the military maneuvers going on underneath his formerly royal nose.

Another key associate of Sir Robert was Eddie Leon. Eddie, of the prominent New York law firm of Leon, Weill and Mahoney, had been a member of the OSS -- the Office of Strategic Services -- the CIA's precursor. He had operated in Europe, spying on the Nazis.

I found that business, like politics, makes for strange bedfellows. What is even stranger is the manner in which one-time foes can come together in commerce after a war. They may have been on different sides, even to the extent of trying to kill each other, but their former differences were put aside and, in the interests of profit and fellowship, they proceeded as if nothing had happened.

In October 1955, during one of my New York stays, I got to witness, and comment on, an important event in the global revolution in electronics. Sir Robert and I attended a special breakfast at the Waldorf in New York. We were there to observe the very first transatlantic fax transmission. John Diebold [165], the young Harvard grad who had coined the phrase "automation" and written the influential book of the same name, was there. The conversation leapt to the future of global communications.

As a former student of Marshall McLuhan, who was then formulating his Global Village philosophy, I advanced the theory that the world would become smaller and smaller in terms of immediacy of travel and information, but would never become a completely flat playing field. As I recall, we all ended up agreeing. The next year, I saw the first modems in breadboard form at both AT&T and Western Union in New York. For me, actually, globalization started in the 1950s.

Axel asked me to spearhead the computer applications of Logistics Research, Axel Wennergren's LA-based computer firm, the manufacturer of the ALWAC Computer. I was to go with Bob Johnston of Adalia to Redondo Beach to check on the design and progress of the ALWAC, and the newer design, the ALWAC IIIE.

For its day, the ALWAC was a powerful mini-computer, almost as powerful as FERUT, but one tenth its size and cost. Its total capability, however, was less than the processors in today's cell phones.

Axel wanted us to check on this machine since he had invested an additional five million dollars in the company, a significant sum even then, considering the value of a dollar has since fallen about tenfold.

This assignment led to some experiences that proved technically interesting, and to others that were outright glamorous.

Bob Johnston and I set up shop in offices at Redondo Beach, which in 1956 was just that -- a beach, with a pier. In very small offices down the way, Fletcher Jones[166] had started a computer services firm, called Computer Sciences Corporation, today 78,000 employees strong. Fletch, with his lean, handsome looks, was known informally as the Gregory Peck[167] of the computer business. He had convinced Remington Rand UNIVAC to give him an 1107 computer to use for development work for its benefit. In 1972, he was tragically killed in a plane crash flying his own plane in the hills around Los Angeles.

Our main accomplishment at Logistics Research was a means of increasing the mass storage capacity of computers.

In those days, the mid-1950s, storage was on rotating cylinders called drums. Magnetic spots in lanes around the drums held the data. These data were "read" or "written" with magnetic heads that moved up and down the drum. The time spent in finding and changing the lane or track was called latency, and it was a neat trick to spread data along tracks along the drum to minimize this time delay.

Our forward-looking conception was the Magnus drum, a cylinder that could store about a million characters of data, then a great amount. But we dubbed it "Magnus", as in big, because it was a foot-and-a-half across and two feet long. Now, my grandson's little iPod holds far more data.

An interesting sidelight of the ALWAC trip occurred on the way out to California. We flew from New York into Denver, and visited United Airlines at its then-headquarters in Stapleton Airport. Bob had worked with Trans Canada Airlines, now Air Canada, in developing an airline reservations system. We sought to add United as a client.

Airline reservations then were pathetic. The phone operators had strips of paper for each flight. These were taped to the wall above the desk where the operator sat. When a call came in, it was routed to a particular operator for a particular flight. This person then penciled in the information on the strip of paper, and then taped it back to the wall. When I saw this, I burst out laughing, until Bob shut me up. Even in 1955, it was an antiquated method. I could visualize how it could be done, as we do it now.

United told us they did not need a new system. Their executives were just too far behind the curve, I suppose.

A Path Finder in the World of Early Aerospace

In 1955, the United States and Canada were very concerned about the Soviet Union launching an attack across the Arctic with long-range bombers equipped with nuclear bombs. Thus, the two nations built the Distant Early Warning system, or DEW line, a series of radar posts across northern Canada that served as a tripwire against hostile aircraft. The radar sites had to be precisely positioned, and I worked on the complex calculations required to place them in their right locations. The project also demanded precise mapping, and modified P-38 fighter aircraft from the war were used for aerial photography of the Arctic tundra and ice. We also used Mosquito bombers and the P-51 Mustang. The Mosquito was a very interesting aircraft. The wings and fuselage were made of plywood. The plane was very fast, and had a high cruising altitude. The same was especially true of the twin-boomed P-38. The P-51 Mustang was a gem of an airplane, fast, easy to fly, and capable of extended high-altitude performance; it was famous for flying long-range protection for bombers.

Finding planes was not as easy as one would imagine. Joe Richards, the Executive VP of Adalia, would often spend hours and days scouring the world for aircraft. Without the

Internet, and with the airline industry far less logistically developed, all he, and we, had was the telephone and a grapevine of contacts and intelligence.

Some years later, after the Cold War adversaries had developed nuclear-tipped ballistic missiles, we worked on the creation of BMEWS[168], the Ballistic Missile Early Warning System. This was done at a significantly higher cost than the DEW line because of the great speed of the missiles: the computers had to analyze the tracking data in very short timelines.

Once, the BMEWS radar sites picked up what appeared to be a covey of missiles headed towards North America. In fact, the outposts had misinterpreted radar signals that had bounced off the Moon. Happily, the Deputy Commander of the North American Aerospace Defense Command, or NORAD, urged caution before any retaliatory strike was launched. One of the great, yet little known, crises of the Cold War passed on.

I was also heavily involved, in the civilian sector, in computerizing air navigation systems. One of these was for the Decca Navigator Company, the same Decca whose music label recorded Patsy Cline's "Crazy" and Bing Crosby's "White Christmas". Decca owned the rights to the Navigator system, and wanted to explore its usefulness for trans-Atlantic flight.

In the mid-50's, before satellites and long before GPS, it was impossible for a pilot to pinpoint his aircraft's exact location. As in the days of Magellan, aviators still made use of star sightings and compasses to find their way. Compass headings were sometimes unreliable because of anomalies from the varying gravitational pull of the magnetic North Pole. Gyrocompasses[169] were therefore devised: because they are unaffected by metal, they can find true North. Still, even they left an amount of doubt as to the aircraft's actual position. For the Decca Navigator, my team did a host of computer calculations on positioning and distance measuring.

The winter of 1955 entailed heady and heavy work formulating the mathematical calculations to make the Decca navigation system work accurately. It called for a master ground station and three satellites at a distance surrounding it, each at an arc of 120 degrees to one another. The satellites were called red, green, and purple. All would transmit a signal.

The red satellite, for instance, would communicate with the master station and create a series of red signals categorized by numeric values. The same happened for the green and purple satellites. An aircraft would know its position from two coordinates. A position was calculated, therefore, by the red and green coordinates, or green and purple, or purple and red.

The fly in the ointment was the variation of the speed of electromagnetic propagation of the signals over land or sea. That was my job. I had to correlate the findings to predict accuracy over both land and sea to keep the plane on course.

The same principles, with variations, were used with the US Navy Tactical Air Navigation System, or TACAN, and later with the commercial Long Range Navigation system, LORAN, heavily used for recreational and commercial boating until the advent of GPS.

GPS, or Global Positioning System, works in much the same way with triangulation, where signals from different points form a triangle whose angles and distances can be readily calculated through well-known geometrical formulae. By using satellites, however, GPS avoids the problems of speed of propagation over land and sea since the signals come directly to the device from space.

For all this labor, my travel load was heavy. I was assigned to work with Joe Reid and train him in computers. Joe was a Rhodes Scholar with many friends in government service. He was a joy to work with, and soon got the hand of using FERUT, especially its Transcode application. I also trained a colleague in heavy calculations, especially for the arcane systems of Bessel Functions, often used in wave propagation, which were a beast. This led to a detailed publication of calculation of speed of propagation of radio waves by Ray and me. Sir Robert was pleased.

We negotiated with Burroughs and acquired a Burroughs minicomputer with about the same capability as the ALWAC. We tried to get an ALWAC from Axel, but he wanted full price. Burroughs was much more flexible. We established a data center for our own use and for the sale of extra computer time to other companies.

One of the major structures in Montréal at that time was the 24-story Sun Life building. It was the largest office building in the British Commonwealth; it has since been demoted to seventeenth in height within bustling Montréal itself. During the Second World War, for safekeeping, the edifice held England's Crown Jewels and the Bank of England's gold reserves.

Jumping Jobs to the Young Computer Industry's Leading Innovator

I was walking along a street in Toronto when I bumped into Cally Gottlieb, the computer science instructor from my grad student days. He asked how I was doing at Adalia and I told him I wanted more challenge. He told me the UNIVAC division of Remington Rand was organizing an effort in Canada, and that I should call Jesse Greenlief, its director. I had an appointment with IBM, and after that I went to see Jesse.

The contrast between both interviews was remarkable. Two of my classmates were at IBM, one from Math and Physics, Walter Smuk, and one from Engineering, John Aitchison. At IBM, I was told I would have to punch a time clock, "because IBM makes them." At Remington Rand, Jesse laughed his head off when I asked if they had time clocks.

I decided then and there to choose UNIVAC.

It had the kind of free-wheeling—albeit hardworking—style that evoked Bletchley Park and Mauchly's ENIAC project, and presaged the software firms of the future, with their emphasis on creativity, not rules for regulation's sake.

Jesse had me meet his boss, Ed White, who was a Vice President of Sales for Canada of Remington Rand UNIVAC, the Canadian subsidiary. Jesse was its sales manager. I was surprised at Jesse's knowledge of the entire company worldwide, until he told me that he had just been transferred from New York. Then, I wondered why someone with 20 years experience running a major part of a company would suddenly be transferred to a startup in another country. I did not wonder why for long, as Jesse just looked at me and said, "I had an argument with Marcel Rand." That said it all. Butting heads with top management does not often pay dividends.

Still, I was full of enthusiasm. I knew that I would be working for a pro in helping develop a full-blown organization for Remington Rand UNIVAC in Canada. Jesse said, "Come to work tomorrow", and that was the way I was hired.

The next day, June 1, 1956, was my first day of work and Jesse handed me a set of manuals. He told me that I was scheduled to go to New York for an intensive six-week training program on UNIVAC beginning the middle of July. It was actually a 12-week course, but Jesse said I would only need the last six weeks since he assumed that I would be able to grasp all the written material before traveling to New York.

Those were still the early days of the computer, despite the fact that I had been involved quite heavily with the machines for seven years. When people asked what I did, I told them I was Technical Director of UNIVAC of Canada. I figured there was hardly any point in confusing the issue since the word "computer" was not popularly understood at the time. What a difference today, when every newspaper and every newscast are filled with references to computers.

Perhaps due to the public's fuzzy understanding of computers, there were many attempts during the summer of 1956 to publicize UNIVAC in particular and computing in general. For instance, an arrangement was made with Art Linkletter, on his TV program, People are Funny, to use the UNIVAC in an early version of computer dating. This resulted in a very humorous TV episode. That year, on Linkletter's show, the UNIVAC compiled a 32-item questionnaire for a prospective couple. That pair wound up marrying, and Linkletter paid for their Paris honeymoon. However, because a large-scale computer was used, it was tedious to enter the data and the choices of participants.

In fact, for all the mainframe machines, the UNIVAC I was the first commercially available computer. The user entered data via punched cards or magnetic tape. This was always a "batch operation" – to use an old IT term meaning a job taking a very long time to process -- and obviously lacked any real-time interaction. The inability to provide immediacy dramatically inhibited the tension associated with a radio or TV program – or a prospective date -- and could not retain audience interest. Computer dating did not become the rage: E-Harmony.com and Match.com would have to wait another 45 years.

Again, a computer industry veteran is staggered by the contrast with today. The proliferation of personal devices -- PCs, cell phones, PDAs, and hand-held machines, all linked to the Web -- makes it possible for anyone to enter his or her personal information into a major pool of data and have a matching process take place. And, of course, all this happens practically instantaneously.

It is necessary to put such things in a historical perspective. We had the right idea from the very beginning, but we lacked the vitally important element of mass participation in real-time.

Another interesting thing that we did in the summer of 1956 was a publication of a computerized Bible Concordance. A "Concordance" Bible is one that hews as closely as possible to the original language of the Scriptures, while also presenting it in contemporary English. This document was received with wide acclaim since scholars could much more easily find passages in the Scriptures associated with their research or writings.

The Bible Concordance was produced as a printout, since the ability to search a large database did not then exist. In fact, we did not have enough storage to have the entire report online. The Bible was produced by placing the text on reels of magnetic tape which were then searched back-and-forth, setting streams of data to a number of other tape units, and then gradually merging all of the information into the final product.

Electronic data processing, circa 1956, was mainly associated with sorting and dispersing data onto a number of tape units, merging streams of data, and hopefully coming up with the desired result. Much of the work was "input-output bound", as the time required to move data in and out of the machine far exceeded the amount of time required to manipulate the data.

Here, too, there were a number of striking contrasts between then and now. The most obvious, of course, is the ability to find anything immediately. We even had a saying that, "If you couldn't find it in a couple of days, then do it over". In this context, it was no surprise that I spent time writing a means of retrieval to search an entire reel of magnetic tape for particular data in question. Then came the "technological fix": the development of disk storage, which I saw demonstrated for the first time in October 1958 in New York with the IBM RAMAC 305. This remarkable machine, rudimentary but revolutionary compared to what we had, changed the whole face of electronic data processing.

As mentioned, I began work with Remington Rand UNIVAC in the summer of 1956 by spending six weeks in the advanced training program for UNIVAC. The objectives were to learn the overall, logical design of the machine, and how to program it. Our final exam, as such, was to write a program to merge two reels of tape onto one, and to have the data on that tape stored in an ascending sequence.

In those early days, there were two basic schools of thought on the construction and application of computer systems. In both cases the objective was the same: to stay on top of new business while playing catch-up by getting all the records from existing business onto the machines.

One approach was to tackle each category of business records one at a time; for example, group life, annuities, whole life, and so forth. The other approach was to compile and store records by date: storing and maintaining records by working backwards from the most recent to the oldest, regardless of business type. For a company the size of MetLife, the task was horrendous. And for a newer, but rapidly growing firm, such as Franklin Life, in Springfield, Illinois, the new business alone was enough to suck up all available resources. I immersed myself in these matters, as I knew that our Canadian division, to which I would soon return, had ordered a UNIVAC II for its SunLife client. And Jesse told me that he felt the odds were excellent for signing LondonLife as well. The more the merrier!

There was and is no simple solution to such problems. It became a matter of specifics, of the devil in the details, and sizing up the degree to which new business was being created as well as the degree to which current information on the old systems was correct. The notion of "accurate information" became almost oxymoronic, even though companies must have accurate records in order to function. We were startled to find that records were often wrong, incomplete, or misfiled, and, just as often, missing. After all, a major advantage of converting from manual or punched-card systems to computers was supposed to be the creation of accurate records that would be much more difficult to misfile or to lose. Note the emphasis on "much more difficult", as opposed to "impossible".

I have a sign over my desk that reads, "Humans make errors; computers create chaos." Based on my experience with computer projects, it might be amended to say, "Humans make errors, but when a human programs computers, and makes errors, he or she creates an unbelievable mess".

In addition to slogging it out in the trenches, I took pains to follow some of the important technical developments then going on in computer design, at my firm and in the computer world at large.

The UNIVAC's inventors, John Mauchly and Pres Eckert, were then still at Remington Rand. While Mauchly came up with one great innovation after another, his great partner Eckert matched his inventiveness, and at Remington Rand he continued to demonstrate why. The latter had a group in Philadelphia developing the LARC, the

Livermore Atomic Research Computer, built for the Lawrence Livermore National Lab. In 1956, Eckert and Mauchly began a multi-year project that culminated in this new machine.

Nuclear energy calculations are complex in the extreme, requiring great internal speed and manipulation of vast amounts of data. So Eckert invented a new box; actually, two boxes.

This machine was the first "client/server" ever built. It consisted of a front-end or client machine to input and set up the data, and a back-end, server machine to process the data. The latter machine did the calculations; the former did the input, output, and setup and controls. For this breakthrough device, Eckert devised the concept of parallel programming[170]. This greatly boosted the machine's efficiency, or throughput. It also anticipated the networked computers of the 1980s and today's client-server Internet world, so to say the LARC was ahead of its time is the grossest understatement. In typical Eckert fashion, it had built-in redundancy to ensure the accuracy of the results.

At the same time, operating systems were being developed to lessen the "input-output bound", or data traffic jam, mentioned above. In one approach, the operating system kept track of the computer instruction being performed while looking at the next one to be performed to determine the optimal way to process it. Say the next instruction was an input or output function that could not be performed since the input output circuits were already in use. In the meantime, the current instruction was handled and disposed of internally, freeing up the processor for another instruction. The operating system would then search for another instruction that could be performed internally. In other words, the operating system would keep the computing power of the machine busy with those functions that could be currently performed, resulting in greater system throughput, or efficiency. The computer's own "down time", if you will, be it the internal processor or the input-output, was lessened.

This approach gave rise to the concept of having multiple programs running at the same time all under the control of the operating system. This would theoretically improve throughput even though the "overhead" of the operating system, the number of machine cycles required for it to track multiple instructions and multiple programs, would increase. Indeed, the initial application of multiprogramming led to significant gains which were rapidly dissipated and lost as the operating system ate up more and more resources. In fact, within 10 to 15 years, more than half of the operating cycles of a computer were consumed by the operating system and not by the working programs. The first wave of PCs eliminated that burden, until the PCs themselves were burdened by more and more requirements imposed by complex operating systems. Currently, cell phones and PDAs, which are really more modern, miniaturized versions of the earlier PCs, do not suffer, as yet, from that burden.

The alternative approach to running multiple programs under one operating system was to build numerous machines under one system umbrella. This one computer would run multiple programs that simultaneously shared data stored on tape and, later, on disk. Honeywell was a forerunner of this concept with its 800 series machine. The Tandem, and later the Stratus companies, went on to dominate this field. I will cover this topic later in the discussion on redundant, "fail-safe" computing in a following chapter.

Remington Rand UNIVAC Ends the Vacuum Tube Era

Following the training program in New York, I was sent on a tour of the UNIVAC facilities in Philadelphia and in Minnesota, at Minneapolis and St. Paul.

The Philadelphia operations were an outgrowth of the Eckert Mauchly Corp. I traveled there to spend time with the development group, and went on to Minnesota to meet the engineering group. The two groups were headed, respectively, by John Mauchly and Grace Hopper.. They were working on the associated fields of automatic programming and generalized programming, which I will delve into in a bit.

In my final hour with John, he told me of their development work on a construction scheduling process still in its infancy, not much more than an idea. This became the basis of the Critical Path Method, a basis of modern project planning, and a cornerstone of the work of Mauchly Associates.

I spent one whole day in Philadelphia before going on to Minneapolis and the Engineering Research Associates (ERA) division of Remington Rand UNIVAC. There, I toured the plants and met Bill Norris, the general manager of the division. He had been president of ERA before its acquisition by Remington Rand. This was the home of the UNIVAC scientific systems and also a division involved in military work, especially for the U.S. Navy. ERA had many assorted computers under development at the time. Ironically, ERA had undertaken a contract for the design and prototype of a minicomputer for IBM. This was to become the IBM 650, which provided the income and market penetration for IBM to establish ascendancy in the computer field, wresting dominance from Remington Rand UNIVAC. This was not to be the only time my company showed little strategic sense vis-à-vis "Big Blue".

The success of the IBM 650 was to cause consternation in our sales force, which rightly demanded an equivalent machine. However, Minneapolis totally ignored the work it had done for the Navy on a swell minicomputer, the M-460. Instead, it plunged ahead with new development on the UNIVAC File Computer. That machine was, in my opinion, the camel of the day. Ultimately, some were built, two years late, but they never achieved commercial success. When attention returned to the excellent minicomputer technology sitting in the lab, work began on the Solid State 80. Solid state in this sense means no moving parts. This was a superbly designed and superbly performing machine. It and its ilk, which were built with solid-state transistors, meant the end of the vacuum tube era.

However, as often happens with computer manufacturers run by perfectionists with little understanding of market demand, its introduction was continually delayed by engineers who wanted to make it even better. The Solid State 80 finally started deliveries in 1958. By that time, market-savvy IBM had made its dominance of the field bullet-proof with the success of its 1400 series.

A Fly-on-the-Wall: Watching the IBM/Remington Rand Brawl for Supremacy of the Computer World

As technical director of UNIVAC's Canadian operations, I had landed right in the center of a battle for dominance of the computer industry. This position was to provide me with a fly-on-the-wall's view of the epic battle between Remington Rand and IBM for that control. To some extent I was able to help forestall UNIVAC's loss of its number one position, but found it impossible to stem the tide.

Some background about my new firm is in order. Remington Rand's breakthrough UNIVAC machine, the first general-purpose business computer, was based on Mauchly and Eckert's design for the EDVAC computer. Remington Rand was the firm that had acquired the Eckert-Mauchly Computer Corp. in 1950.

Jimmy Rand, Remington Rand's boss, had been persuaded to buy the Eckert-Mauchly Corporation, which was deeply in debt. Rand and his partners offered the company $100,000, and took over $400,000 in obligations that Mauchly and Eckert owed Totalizator, the racetrack tote board firm that had bankrolled them.

In fact, Eckert and Mauchly had first gone to Tom Watson, Sr., the president of IBM, to see if he might buy them out, and Watson turned them down. Mauchly once told me that Watson informed him, "I can't buy your company because it would open me up to anti-trust." And in fact, the Justice Department then was considering action against IBM. Subsequently, the government did sue IBM for unfair trade practices, which ultimately led to a 1956 consent decree where IBM agreed to a $10 million payment to Sperry Rand, Remington Rand's successor company.

From Jimmy Rand, John Mauchly and Pres Eckert each received $34,000, and had to hand over their crown jewels: their patents and the contracts for their machines. For some years, as I have described, they both stayed on with the company as prominent innovators, but they no longer ran it.

For a while, on the strength of Mauchly and Eckert's designs, Remington Rand was the leading computer company in the world. As we saw in chapter four, through 1955, the firm sold 45 units of the UNIVAC I- an impressive volume. But by the time I arrived, it was hearing footsteps from IBM.

The latter developed the IBM 701 and IBM 702, for crunching numbers and data, respectively. These were inferior to the UNIVAC, but as Remington Rand dallied in getting out the UNIVAC II, IBM came out with the 704 and 705. These it marketed relentlessly.

IBM had focus, while Remington Rand was all over the map. With 50 years of industry experience, IBM's owner -- Thomas Watson, Sr. -- understood data processing in his core. His was by and large an information processing company. Remington Rand was not.

Remington Rand made computers, but it also made electric shavers, and typewriters, and much else. (IBM also made various products including typewriters, clocks, and even time clocks which it "requested" all its employees to use.) The Remington Rand sales force was dominated by punch card salesmen, who did not seem to understand the UNIVAC and by engineers who were not market-driven. Its speed-to-market was torturously slow. Instead of continuing production of the UNIVAC I, it stopped producing it when it started building UNIVAC II. This development project took two-and-a-half years. For two-and-a half years we were totally out of production while IBM kept chugging out the new versions of its machines! The hare was to pass the tortoise.

Remington's strategy of canceling the production of the UNIVAC I in the midst of strong demand was bizarre. It is mindful of another Aesop fable, where a dog holding a bone is smiling at its image in a pond. It drops the bone in reaching for the image in the water.

One interesting sidelight is that even in the midst of the spurt to get the UNIVAC II machines to the market, a total of only 19 men and women were assigned to this vital project. Furthermore, the design, development, and production of the UNIVAC II moved to Minneapolis, which was a fatal blunder. Many aspects of the UNIVAC system were unknown to the ERA personnel in Minneapolis. This led to the critical mistake of incompatibility between the two systems. The Philadelphia team under the Eckert-Mauchly division of the firm had the knowledge to make the UNIVAC II work, but it was assigned to the new LARC system. Had that talent pool been assigned to the UNIVAC II, perhaps the story would have ended differently.

<u>Observing Mauchly and Eckert, and Grace Hopper, Up Close at Remington Rand</u>

In 1956, as IBM was catching up, I was appointed, as noted, technical director of Remington Rand's Toronto office. My task was to interview and hire what would become the company's Canadian staff. That year, I took Mauchly's company course on the UNIVAC, and came to know him well. His background in academia and his free-spirited approach to learning were fully evident. Mauchly's stimulating class was more like a grad school seminar than a corporate training room. It was full of bright young men and women, who eagerly exchanged views with their instructor.

Although no longer running the company, Mauchly and Eckert were engrossed in several leading-edge projects. With his application research group, Mauchly developed, as mentioned, what became known as the important technique of Generalized Programming. He also worked on his long-time dream of devising techniques to forecast the weather.

The UNIVAC I was the work of the Mauchly and Eckert combo. Eckert's no-fault design was remarkable for any age. It was the first computer that checked itself. In demanding a machine of precision, Pres Eckert stated, "Any machine leaving my lab is going to run accurately. No circuit is going to function by chance; we're going to know if it functions properly."

So Eckert duplexed, that is, duplicated, all of the circuits that performed the calculations. He was ahead of the technology curve by at least two decades. Not until the 1970's did companies like Tandem develop what are called redundant, disaster-tolerant computers. The operating systems of those machines had program controls that check functionality to maintain continuous operation. Yet the UNIVAC was more "elegant" from an engineering perspective.

A Tandem device, you see, was actually two computers. Each computer checked the operation of the other, and when one was "down", the other, without a pause, took over its functions. The UNIVAC, in contrast, required just one computer. It had had two sets of circuits that checked each other within one machine. The UNIVAC I, and the UNIVAC II that followed, had this redundant, self-checking capability. As we saw in chapter Four, Eckert conceived of the Tandem innovation in 1947-48 in the BINAC and designed the principle of redundancy and self-checking into the UNIVAC in 1949. In this, as in other technical areas, the UNIVAC was far ahead of IBM's machines.

Even more vital than the duplex design was Eckert's invention of the acoustic delay line as the high-speed memory for UNIVAC. It made storage faster, and did not have to strictly rely on tubes for storage like the ENIAC. The major component was a container of mercury. Timing pulses were impressed upon a carrier wave in the mercury. The waves received varying pulses that represented the zeros and ones of digital data

For the UNIVAC I, Mauchly and Eckert also invented one of the computer's key accessories – magnetic tape. In this, they brought to life the notion of a mass storage device. In this, they broke the barrier of record size, formerly constrained to 80 or 90 columns of data entered via punched cards or punched paper tape. Along with the hard disk, "mag" tape is still the major means of storing large amounts of data.

John Mauchly must be credited with the concept for this technology breakthrough, and Pres Eckert with the ability to make it happen.

Mauchly's interest in magnetic storage owed to his father's work at the Bureau of Standards, which devised the standards for magnetic recording. At Remington Rand,

Mauchly and Eckert came up with the Unityper, the UNIVAC version of a typewriter. Onto a little cartridge atop the writing device, it produced a magnetic tape of the input. It also produced, like a regular typewriter, a paper or "hard" copy of the data.

Their work on the invention was typical of the way they operated. Mauchly conceived of magnetic tape as an "on the fly" storage device, reading and writing data as the tape rolled. Skeptics said this was impossible. Then Eckert took Mauchly's notion and made it a reality.

An interesting sidelight of their invention was the decision to use a ferro-magnetic alloy rather than plastic. Plastic tape at the time was not very reliable. It was paper-based and had a tendency to flake and disintegrate. Later, this problem was corrected with the Mylar tape. During the early 1950s, however, Mylar was not available and the decision was made by Eckert and Mauchly to use the metal tape. This medium was not foolproof. Holes would get punched in areas of imperfection, and the tape reader/writer would skip over those portions.

Data was so much less compressed back then. In 1958, for installing the UNIVAC II system at Sun Life in Montréal, I would lug around three magnetic tapes in my briefcase. These weighed about 8-1/2 pounds each. Twenty years later, I would often travel with a 5-MB Wang disk about 18 inches in diameter. Today, I carry a 5-GB chip with the size and weight of a pocket pen.

In crisscrossing the Canada-U.S. border, I often took the tapes with me. Customs officers would ask me to show them "what was on" a tape. I was tempted to suggest I sprinkle a tape with iron filings, to reveal the stored data's magnetic outline, but managed to curtail my sense of humor and say with a straight face that it was a recording tape. When they pressed harder I would say things such as, "Like Music!" One way or another, thankfully, I always got through customs.

That same year of 1958, I was setting up a UNIVAC II for the data center in Toronto. For this purpose, we had to import a large number of magnetic tapes. Because the tapes were made of an iron alloy, they were ultimately brought into the country as "plumbing products", according to the customs brokers. I took their statement at face value.

In this age of terror and talk of regulating the Web, it is interesting to imagine the problems all of us would encounter if we had to get a permit for each bunch of information we wanted to carry across a border. Such a proposal was made numerous times in the '50s and '60s for the U.S.-Canada boundary. Some even raised the possibility of taxing the movement of data across territorial limits. Today, some call for taxing the Internet. Thankfully, these public musings have so far amounted to idle speculation only, but they should be remembered as a warning. Currently, in my opinion, there is too much talk of sealing our borders and taxing the free commerce of the Internet, as well as controlling its content. I am willing to trust the authorities for fighting terror and to trust the people for determining the content of the Web. Let freedom reign.

Another important initiative of Mauchly's, which I touched on above, was helping to come up with what we now call critical path analysis. Akin to PERT[171] and Gantt charts[172], and now routinely used in business, critical path analysis is a method of scheduling all the tasks and resources for a business project. Mauchly and others developed the technique to manage large, unwieldy projects, such as the radar defense and missile programs of the time.

Yet another of Remington Rand's technical assets was legendary computer developer Grace Murray Hopper. She was the first person to write a program for the Mark I computer that IBM built in the 1940s at Harvard. Long after her breakthrough work on developing computer compilers, she retired as a Rear Admiral and the Navy's oldest serving officer, at age 84. But she is best known for popularizing the computer terms "bug" and "debug".

As I briefly mentioned in an earlier chapter, when she was working on the Mark II, her co-workers noticed that a moth stuck in a relay had interfered with the computer's operation. In her log book, Hopper wrote that they were "debugging" the machine, and the term gained wide currency. The log books, and the moth's remains, are now at the Smithsonian.

Grace Hopper was Remington Rand's Vice President for Programming Applications, with the responsibility for creating better programming techniques. John Mauchly had hired her in 1949, back when he was still president of Eckert-Mauchly, before it became Remington Rand.

Grace's group was developing what is called Automatic Programming[173], and it is in this area that she did some of her famous work in developing compilers. A programmer could write statements in English, and from them, the compiler would create actual programming code. Starting around 1952 and beginning to peak in 1956, there was great interest in getting a computer to generate its own code.

Automatic Programming consists of various attempts to simplify the development of the code that runs the computer. Every computer has its own unique real code or operation code. These are abstruse characters or a combination of characters. Computers also have to function with data that is stored in specific locations. Early programmers had to know, among other things, the addresses and sizes of the data. So writing real code for a machine becomes very complex. Computer compilers are an attempt to deal with this problem.

There are three kinds of compilers: interpreters, assemblers, and the true compilers. The programming language is built around "pseudo code". Pseudo code has a great resemblance to natural, English-like language, and thus is relatively easy to write, and to use.

With interpreters, the program interprets, or processes, each instruction of the pseudo code in turn. This is slow, since there is a constant back-and-forth between a pseudo code and the block of real code that runs the particular instruction.

Transcode was the epitome of an interpreter. Very fast, it ran rings around what the A series of Grace Hopper or the FORTRAN series of IBM could do. In Toronto, I had worked with its creators, Pat Hume and Bea Worsley. They never received much credit or acclaim, which they really deserved for their very advanced, and very fast, application. Transcode literally ran rings around later, related applications of the Defense Department and of IBM.

Assemblers are more direct and faster than interpreters. The real code is replaced with a mnemonic code; that is, one relatively easy to remember and manipulate. An assembler uses symbolic addresses with a tag pointing to the real address, which the assembler then assigns. This saves a lot of work updating addresses. Assemblers are much faster to operate, but their programmatic assembly code is harder to write. IBM was concentrating on its Autocoder assembler for business applications.

The true compiler takes a pseudo code instruction and converts it into the real code of the machine. The real code is then used to process the application. More advanced versions optimize the generated code to make the code "tight" and run as fast as possible.

In this vein, the work of Grace Hopper and her Philadelphia-based, automatic programming research group involved computer compilers. It was divided in the so-called A-track or series, the A standing for arithmetic, or scientifically oriented, automatic programming, and the B series, standing for business automatic programming. Grace had begun her operations in this field for Remington Rand around 1952, about the same time as the University of Toronto was doing its own related work with Transcode.

The A series were an early forerunner of FORTRAN, for Formula Translator -- an early, important programming language that became a standard in scientific enterprises. IBM, by 1956, was heavily involved with making FORTRAN a practical application. The B series became a forerunner of COBOL, for decades the major programming language of business.

In my post, I figured we could use this for a client, Ontario Hydro. I began corresponding with Grace, and learned many lessons from her group on how to write effective code for compilers. Over time, we trained about a hundred people on creating pseudo code for the compiler's use.

Meanwhile, I found that John Mauchly and his advanced projects group were concentrating on a related field, the components of programs, specifically, plugs of code and "objects" -- the building stones of programs. Here again Mauchly was a visionary: object-oriented coding dominated development by the 1980s. He was, in effect, creating subroutines; the extension of the concept he had for the ENIAC and the core building blocks of modern programs. His area was named "G. P.", for Generalized Programming. John's UNIVAC Applications Research Center was blessed with brilliant Associates, like Nat Turansky and Tolley Holt.

However, tragedy struck when Nat was killed when, while walking down a sidewalk, a car jumped the curb, knocking him down. He appeared to be alright, but an hour after the incident he collapsed, and later died in the hospital. Whenever John talked about this, I could see tears in his eyes; his young associates were almost sons to him.

I ran a parallel effort using Mauchly's novel G.P. capability. It was fascinating to compare the results of Mauchly's object-oriented approach with Grace's B series. Writing pseudo code was faster using Hopper's technique, but the programs produced by GP proved faster and better. I well realized that these inconsistencies would be muted if not eliminated with time, as indeed they were. I also began considering alternatives. I wrote two papers at the time, the summer of 1958.

The first of these I called "Shorthand for Computers." I laid out an approach for a system that I called SOC, standing for System Organization Compiler. While I concluded that pseudo code could be written to produce computer code in various ways – for an interpreter, assembler, or compiler - I concentrated on the creation of pseudo code to describe the computer system. I laid out the manner in which such a system-oriented approach would work. It actually set the standard for much of my work in years to come.

The other paper was a comparison of the relative merits of the object-oriented approach of John Mauchly's G.P. versus the compiler approach of Grace Hopper's. I delivered this in Chicago at a meeting of the Life Insurance Institute. I was followed on the platform by my good friend John Acheson of IBM, who, in the interest of corporate rivalry, totally ignored everything I said and talked about IBM's developments, which were years behind. I detail this below.

I believe the work we did at the Ontario Hydro was the forerunner of natural language systems, the languages the great majority of programmers use today, which was a very important thing. Those experiences set the stage for the United States Department of Defense to establish the Codasyl Committee. Codasyl was the acronym for Conference on Data Systems Languages. This committee oversaw the creation of COBOL. By the mid-60s,

COBOL, besides being paramount as a business application, was the most widely used programming language.

Grace was a member of the Codasyl Committee, but despite the fact that I had more experience with these matters than just about anyone else, I was never invited to share my experiences with the committee, much less be invited to join the committee. By that time, in the 1960s, I was busy with Mauchly Associates anyway, especially with making CPM, my Critical Path Method of project scheduling and management, a universally employed term in business. As far as I can remember, Grace never said thank you.

She and I remained friends over the years, sharing experiences and ideas, but Grace Hopper was not given to devoting time to mundane matters such as gratitude. Grace was a brilliant woman, but one might say she was rather direct in getting what she wanted, and somewhat of a showboat. Trained in math, Grace Hopper lived one of Euclid's precepts: the shortest path between points is a straight line!

Remington Fumbles Away Its Lead

While Eckert, Mauchly, and Grace Hopper focused on their various projects, Remington Rand's main emphasis – due to its rivalry with IBM -- was of necessity on the UNIVAC II. Like many computer companies since, Remington showed it had excellent technology and engineers but awful marketing and management sense. This was unfortunate, for it was taking on a competitor that, from its inception, had taken a ruthless approach to any rival.

I was caught in the middle of the terrible delay in rolling out the UNIVAC II. For over two long years, we waited for the UNIVAC II to be delivered while our clients cried out for it and while the production of the UNIVAC I had been suspended. I think the adage about not leaving one's job until a new one is lined up, generally applies to products as well.

Remington Rand had the engineering expertise to roll out the UNIVAC II quickly enough. However, top management did not put enough people on the project. And some ancillary, but important, items like the Unityper – Mauchly's magnetic tape device -- proved incompatible between the two machines.

The Unityper of the UNIVAC II could not function with the UNIVAC I's Unityper. Different companies had manufactured the two kinds of tapes, with the reel of one tape twice the size of the other. Nobody in management had anticipated this problem. Until this was fixed, none of our existing clients, those who had used the UNIVAC I, could restore their existing data on the UNIVAC II.

IBM's Aggressive Style

Remington Rand managed to grasp defeat from the jaws of victory. While our management bumbled, our marketing team was unable to keep up with IBM's bruising approach.

IBM's Competitive Roots

From its start, IBM reflected the ferociously competitive nature of its founder, Thomas Watson, Sr. It is instructive, from the standpoint of what to do and not to do to succeed in the business of technology, to briefly look at the firm's history.

In 1895, at age 21, Watson, Sr. joined the National Cash Register Company (NCR), which was owned by John H. Patterson. NCR was already dominant in its field, but it faced more than 50 competitors. The ruthless John Patterson brought in Tom Watson to establish a secret operation to smash his rivals, according to the book Electronic Brains[174] by Michael Hally.

Watson and the "Cash", as NCR was called, threatened its rivals, slandered their managers, and sabotaged their factories. With a million dollars in funds supplied by Patterson, Watson would wreck the finances of a firm, and then buy it on the cheap. Ironically, one problem for NCR was the high quality of its cash registers: they lasted for years, undercutting sales, and boosting the sales of used cash register companies. Explains Hally:

> So, in 1903, Patterson drafted Watson to run an elaborate scam. After ostensibly resigning from the company, Watson set up a chain of used cash register stores that was secretly backed by National Cash Register. By paying more for secondhand machines and selling them for less, Watson drove virtually all of Patterson's competitors out of business.[175]

Due to public outrage at the unfair business practices of firms like NCR, and of John D. Rockefeller's Standard Oil, Congress had previously passed the Sherman Anti-Trust Act[176]. In 1912, the U.S. Department of Justice indicted Watson and Patterson for violating the Act. After a trial exposed their vile practices, they each received a one-year jail term and were hit with major fines.

Fortunately for NCR, a great flood then hit Dayton, Ohio. Rather like Wal-Mart did in the wake of Hurricane Katrina, Patterson and Watson won the public's regard by employing NCR's personnel and other resources to help in recovery efforts. Moreover, the First World War loomed, and the federal government, instead of wanting to break up big business, needed it for the war effort. President Wilson pardoned Patterson and Watson.

Watson's relationship with Patterson eventually soured, and he left NCR for the Computer Tabulating and Research Company. It had been established by information processing wizard Herman Hollerith, the inventor of a punch-card mechanical tabulator used in the 1890 census. Watson was appointed the firm's general manager, and he changed its name in 1924 to the International Business Machines Corporation.

Under Watson's watch, IBM formed its distinctive corporate culture. A benevolent despot, he treated his workers well – if they bent to his will. During the depression of the 1930s, Watson kept most folks on the payroll. Yet conformity was the rule. Although it seems odd in the informal IT world of today, employees had to wear blue suits and knotted ties. The reader may have seen, perhaps in the *New Yorker* magazine, those popular cartoons of an office, with the sign "Think" above employees' desks. Such signs were originally posted by Tom Watson, Sr. at IBM, and widely imitated by other firms.

Watson's dealings abroad were as dubious as his NCR work had been at home. In search of overseas sales, he visited Nazi Germany, believing he could convince Hitler that international trade would guarantee the peace. Finding him a compliant tool, *Der Fuhrer* presented Watson with the Order of Merit of the German Eagle. IBM set up a German subsidiary and, as related in the book IBM and the Holocaust[177] by Edwin Black, the Nazis used the company's punch cards to keep track of Jews sent to the death camps. During the war years, IBM reaped substantial profits from sales to enemy countries.

At home during the war, IBM acted decisively, behind the scenes, to preserve a deserved reputation for making significant investments in cutting-edge IT. IBM had poured $500,000 into the Mark I computer, the souped-up differential analyzer built at Harvard University by computer pioneer Professor Howard Aiken. However, Aiken tried to claim all the credit for the Mark I, according to Mike Hally's book

Electronic Brains

In August 1944, Harvard, with much fanfare, scheduled a ceremony to unveil the Mark I, but Tom Watson, Sr. got wind that speakers at the dedication, such as Aiken, were not going to even mention IBM. So the day before the ceremony, Watson telephoned James Conant, Harvard's president. No doubt he "reminded" Conant of his company's flush bankrolling of the Mark I. At the dedication, Conant waxed eloquent about the tremendous contribution of IBM. Big Blue never missed a marketing opportunity.

This was the beginning of IBM's historic role with the computer. Its desire to dominate the field was stoked by the undeniable fact that the ENIAC and UNIVAC were initially superior to its machines. In the late 1940s, the Census Bureau decided that IBM's tabulators were outdated, and bought UNIVAC machines in their place for the 1950 census. As Hally puts it, "IBM could have foundered in the 1950's, holding onto its monopoly of a technology that was
becoming obsolete while failing to get to grips with the electronic computers that were threatening to replace its mechanical calculators."[178]

Instead, the company labored double-quick to roll out its digital IBM 701 in 1951, and then the 704. The following January, Tom Watson, Jr. succeeded his father as IBM's president. Later that year, the younger Watson faced a big setback of his own when the UNIVAC correctly predicted Dwight Eisenhower as the winner of the 1952 presidential election. The publicity was considerable: people began to speak, mistakenly, about the "IBM UNIVAC", which enraged Watson.

But IBM did not throw in the towel. It got tougher, and put out the IBM 702 and 705. Watson, Jr. replaced his manager of engineering, and hired hundreds of electronic engineers. By 1954 Remington Rand still had more computers in the field, but IBM was exceeding it fourfold in new orders. It did not take long after that for IBM to take the lead, and keep it.

Keep it, that is, until it concentrated so hard on the eventually outdated technology of the large mainframe machines that it lost out to the young upstart minicomputer firms of the 1970s, a tale I cover in a later chapter.

IBM always had superb intelligence about competitive moves. As the ENIAC was developed at the University of Pennsylvania, a senior IBM account executive eyed its progress carefully, aware of the competitive impact the machine could cause for IBM if it succeeded.[179] During this period, IBM was supporting the Mark 1 efforts at Harvard.

IBM was also very much aware of the patent controversy concerning ENIAC ongoing at the University of Pennsylvania. There is speculation that IBM might have been involved on the periphery. At the time, there were rumors that IBM offered $10 million to the University of Pennsylvania as a down payment of royalties should the University ultimately gain sole rights to the ENIAC's marketing and patent rights.

There was another important side to IBM. It demanded and received absolute loyalty from its employees. IBM was the blue suit and white shirt brigade. It maintained country clubs for its employees, was very liberal in benefits, and high paying. It was equally ruthless with those who did not meet quotas or, God forbid, lost an account.

To give some credit to the great scientific achievements and advances of UNIVAC, it should be mentioned that the leading organization at the beginning of a new industry is not always the one that benefits the most in the end. For example, while RCA established television, it was later Zenith, and now the Japanese and Koreans, who are benefiting most from that invention.

Big Blue was becoming big indeed, but unlike many large successful companies it retained the key ability to quickly respond to changing markets and technologies – up to a point!

Remington Rand's management and marketing were very frustrating. I greatly admired the company's know-how, and I enjoyed my own work, but it was hard to sit back and watch IBM beat our brains in. Further, I was ready as ever for a new challenge and work experience. So when I got a call in June 1959 from my long-time hero, John Mauchly, I was primed to make a leap.

The phone call touched off a period of consulting work with Mauchly Associates, and later with Olin Matheson. It was also a time where I helped establish a major expansion of Ontario's university system, with an emphasis on the sciences. Further, I was engrossed in systems engineering, artificial intelligence, and defense work, as well as early computer games. I became the target of vicious corporate backstabbing. Most importantly, during this time, I courted and married my wife.

Conspiring with John Mauchly To Start Anew

The telephone call should have come as a shock, but it did not, really. I was at my office as Director of Data Centers at Remington Rand when John Mauchly called. As I have related, after being bought out as president of the firm he co-founded with Pres Eckert, he had tried to develop various cutting-edge technologies for Remington Rand.

John told me his Advanced Research Group had been "de-budgeted," that is, cancelled. Overnight the inventor of ENIAC, and the inventor of UNIVAC—the company's foundation product—was out of work. Remington Rand had practically fired him. He told me he was being transferred to work for the sales manager in New York, or "kicked downstairs" as it were.

Having labored with UNIVAC for three years, I already thought poorly of its company's management, so I was not that surprised. But I was angry. To think that a man of Mauchly's accomplishments was in effect being shown the door!

Leaning against the filing cabinet outside my office, I repressed a strong urge to curse the managers of the firm. "John," I said, "You should quit."

He answered, "But how am I going to earn a living?"

The fact of the matter was the father of the computer had no money. He had put his modest amount of settlement funds from Remington Rand into his house at Little Linden Farm, a spread of 50 acres or so in Ambler, Pennsylvania.

I told him, "Here you are, practically the inventor of this whole darn place, and you're being treated like this!"

I continued, "John, why don't we start our own company?"

As Kay Mauchly later put it, "John didn't need much motivation. He was already fed up with Remington in so many ways."

John agreed with my notion. On July 1, 1959, I joined Mauchly Associates as a partner to my friend and mentor.

This is a fitting time in the book to probe into the greatest accomplishment of Mauchly, and perhaps the greatest harbinger of our modern technological world – his co-invention of the digital computer and the decisions and indecisions by others that hurt him very deeply.

I will always remember the days at Mauchly Associates when John would recount stories about the ENIAC, and the *First Draft of a Report on the EDVAC* and von Neumann and Herman Goldstine's attempts to diminish the roles of Eckert and Mauchly in developing the forerunner systems to even the modern computers of those days. The methods employed were a variety of techniques. Some were of the subtle kind like "damning with faint praise" and failing to disavow certain credit for the computer's features that the public came to incorrectly attribute to others, as for example reference to the "von Neumann machine". Some were more overtly hostile, such as the attempt in 1947 to patent certain features of the stored program computer that Goldstine and von Neumann insisted was being done to insure that the scientific community would properly benefit from these discoveries and the public interest would be served. The claim overlooked the fact that the original agreement between Eckert and Mauchly, the inventors of the ENIAC, granted the University of Pennsylvania the right to sub license this technology to any other educational institution. That right would have enabled the academic scientific community complete access to the technology disclosed in the patent application.

The next chapter tells the epic story of how this travesty of injustice transpired and was given the unfortunate imprimatur of the US legal system.

CHAPTER SEVEN

The Intellectual Property Rights
Trial of the Century:
The Honeywell v. Sperry-Rand Court Battle

Was justice blinded in this case? It is often said that the best defense is to attack vigorously. This was the case in 1972, when Honeywell launched a countersuit on Sperry Rand in an attempt to avoid paying significant royalties based on the ENIAC patents assigned to Sperry Rand by Eckert and Mauchly. Through a series of strange convolutions, the trial was moved to Minnesota, a state where Honeywell was one of the largest employers. The ten-month trial was heard in Federal Court without a jury by Judge Earl R. Larson, who had no knowledge of computers and who apparently asked no questions during the proceedings. The ruling astounded many. Judge Larson declared John Atanasoff the inventor of the computer, invalidated the Sperry Patents, and dismissed Honeywell's complaint against Sperry for unfair trade practices. The byproducts were unsettling to many and a total surprise. The background and the impact of these decisions are covered in this chapter.

An Infamous Trial

Honeywell Incorporated filed a suit against Sperry Rand Corporation and a subsidiary Illinois Scientific Developments, incorporated on May 26, 1967 in the 4th Division of the Minnesota U.S. District Court (No. 4-67-Civ. 138), on the grounds of anti-trust violations and unjustified claims to the automatic general purpose electronic computer. On that same day, only minutes later, Sperry Rand Corporation filed a suit against Honeywell Corporation for patent infringement in the US District Court for the District of Columbia. The case was referred to Minneapolis by Judge John Sirica, Chief Judge of the District of Columbia, who reasoned that the Washington, D. C. District Court could not adequately adjudicate such a case that would likely require an extended period of time. In Minneapolis, Judge Earl R. Larson would preside over the case whose trial phase extended from June 1, 1971 to March 13, 1972, but whose case timeline exceeded five years.

A trial is essentially a contest between two or more parties, the plaintiff or accuser on one side, and the defendant on the other. This particular trial was a juxtaposition of the fact that Honeywell had been willfully infringing a patent held by the Sperry Rand Corporation and had been refusing to pay royalties on their invention. Honeywell seized the initiative and launched its suit before Sperry could carry out its threats to sue Honeywell for infringement. Honeywell went on the offensive, adding restraint of trade to the suit in an attempt to cloud the original issue of willful infringement by them which could carry significant damages. Their strategy was well conceived and well executed and secured every advantage possible.

As plaintiff rather than defendant, and as the largest employer in the State of Minnesota, Honeywell could present itself as the seriously aggrieved party before a judge who would look beyond the law for factors more in the line of his notion of "justice" than in the letter of the law. In that regard, Honeywell opted for a strategy of characterizing itself as the hapless victim of a blatant attempt at monopoly by Sperry Rand. This allegation cited an earlier cross-licensing agreement between Sperry and IBM as a conspiracy to control the fledgling industry. Honeywell further opted for a strategy of inundating the court with a myriad of documents that would both smother Sperry's documents and inhibit the ability to extract the truth from the avalanche of material. The company's strategy succeeded in a bizarre twist that saved them millions of dollars. One byproduct of Honeywell's victory was the unfortunate pall cast upon invention that has affected the computer industry to this day.

The trial essentially concerned itself with the following issues:

1. Derivation of ideas from another,
2. Prior publication and public use of concepts such as would deny the patentability of an invention, and
3. Violation of the Sherman Antitrust Act Section involving Restraint of Trade.

This chapter questions the basis of the findings in this trial primarily from the point of view of properly assigning credit for the invention of the first electronic automatic digital general purpose computer - the ENIAC.

So far as is known, Judge Earl Larson was neither a patent lawyer nor a technologist. He is said to have engaged some technical support but we have no idea what agenda such individuals may have had in assisting in the formation of Judge Larson's technical understandings. (As the sole decider who said next to nothing and posed no questions to the numerous expert witnesses testifying throughout the trial, he was charged with evaluating the veritable mountain of testimony and voluminous legal briefs presented to him. This put him, in my judgment, in an impossible situation to reach conclusions that, in hindsight, did not produce the measure of justice we expect from our legal system.)

Judge Larson was presented with over 32,000 exhibits, some of which contained several hundred pages. The trial transcript was over 20,000 pages.

The results of all this were disastrous to some, and very beneficial to others. Further, in my judgment, the computer's true inventors were pilloried by the Judge. Within the large context of invention and the proper protection of Intellectual Property, his findings may have helped to convey a sense that "anything goes" in the realm of invention and that the inventor's right to intellectual property may become increasingly difficult for the resource-constrained solitary inventor to sustain in the marketplace.

As an inventor myself, I think this is so, and I want to challenge certain findings of Judge Larson because the creation and protection of intellectual property is simply too important an issue for our economy to let it pass.

Intellectual Property protection is a national resource that may well prove to be America's most valuable asset in a global economy that no longer favors American manufacturing. In an age which is dominated by the large corporate interests that are typically burdened by bureaucratic procedures that generally represent a drag on creativity, the miscarriage of justice that took place in 1973 needs to be challenged. Injustices such as these can easily attenuate the creative spark that fires the mind of the individual inventor. Having confidence in the legal protection of unique concepts, inventors of any stripe are free to give free rein to their imagination and conceive ground-breaking advances in a particular field.

Recognition due to an individual may or may not be an important motivator for invention for some. However, the public denial of it and, in the Honeywell vs. Sperry Rand case, the suggestions that the inventors' ideas were not their own but were derived from someone else, surely must give would-be inventors pause when they consider that the economic and/or psychological fruits of their labors may well be denied them and awarded to an undeserving party. It is not "just", and that fact alone helps to further erode confidence in our legal system and may diminish this country's ability to maximize the leverage of what is its most valuable economic asset.

Cynical people within and without the legal profession are sometimes heard to say that our justice system is less about justice than it is about winning. In 1973, Judge Earl Larson, after expending over a year digesting material - depositions, court testimony, cross examination, exhibits and demonstrations, issued a set of rulings that produced winners.... and therefore losers in a VERY high stakes episode that altered more than legal Intellectual Property history.

From Judge Larson's perspective, his rulings were intended to be accepted as representing a balanced and highly reasoned assessment of the information presented to him. Judge Larson was not an engineer, yet as the sole decision maker, he was required to understand a massive volume of highly technical information, presented by attorneys whose objective was to win the case for their client.

Since winning is the goal, attorneys representing the plaintiff selected the information to be presented that, in the context of an overall legal strategy, was designed to win.

In the case of Honeywell vs. Sperry Rand, that strategy was initiated when Sperry naively notified Honeywell of its intention to file a lawsuit charging that Honeywell products in the marketplace constituted infringement of the US 3,120,606 patent, the ENIAC patent.

Once alerted that Sperry Rand was proceeding to file a lawsuit against them, Honeywell quickly rushed to enter a countersuit response, claiming that the ENIAC patent was invalid, fraudulently obtained, and that Sperry Rand was engaged in Restraint of Trade in the industry. U.S. Judge John Sirica, the Chief Judge of the District of Columbia and the renowned judge who later presided over President Nixon's impeachment trial, concluded and declared that Honeywell had beaten Sperry to the courts by only a few minutes. Judge Sirica continued saying that due to the time required and nature of this case, the overcrowded federal court dockets in the District of Columbia would not be able to give the case the time it merited.   Therefore, Judge John Sirica ruled that the jurisdiction should be placed in Minnesota, where Honeywell happened to be the largest employer in the state. As a result of this ruling, Sperry was immediately put on the defensive and thus, Honeywell made it appear as though Sperry Rand was the one at fault, unfairly turning the favor towards itself. Honeywell's action set in motion a series of other initiatives over the nine month trial from June 1971 to March 1972.

The roots of this trial can be traced back to those early days at the Moore School. After Mauchly and Eckert left Penn for being unfairly treated regarding who could claim rights to the ENIAC patent, the duo formed their own company, the Electronic Control Company, later renamed the Eckert-Mauchly Computer Corporation. In 1947, they filed (and years later, in 1964, were ultimately granted) a patent for the ENIAC. A few years after founding the Eckert-Mauchly Corporation, the founders of the first commercial computer company ran into financial difficulties and the company was sold to Remington Rand, along with the rights to the eventual patent.   Remington Rand later merged with the Sperry Corporation in 1955, creating Sperry Rand. In 1962 Bell Telephone Laboratories and Sperry were engaged in Interference regarding priority of Sperry's claims and Sperry was sustained. Bell, seeking to invalidate Sperry's claims, appealed on one issue, that of prior public use, regarding the ENIAC patent.   The allegation was not sustained as Bell failed to produce adequate evidence, according to Federal Judge Archie Dawson, thereby sustaining the legality of the patents. Accordingly, any case thereafter upsetting Dawson's ruling was believed to be a difficult task. After years of pretrial litigation and depositions, the trial finally began on June 1, 1971 in Minneapolis before Judge Earl R. Larson.   Dually representing the plaintiff, Honeywell Inc, were the Minneapolis firm of Dorsey, Marquart, Windhorst, West and Halladay and the Chicago firm Molinar, Allegretti, Newitt and Witcoff. On the other side, the defendants, Sperry Rand Corporation and its subsidiary Illinois Scientific Developments, Inc., were represented by the firm of Dechert, Price and Rhoads.

As stated in the University of Pennsylvania's archives:

"The plaintiff's counsel presented its case on a number of points that would show the groundlessness of Sperry Rand's claims to the exclusive patent rights and control of the electronic data processing field. The main points that they presented were generally confined to five areas:

1) a discussion of the work and developments in the field of electronics at the Moore School of Electrical Engineering at the University of Pennsylvania between 1930 and 1947 as the result of "complex team effort"

2) a presentation of the state of research in the field of electronic digital computers undertaken at other institutions and companies during the 1930s and early 1940s

3) an explanation of the attempted domination of the electronic data processing industry by Eckert and Mauchly, and later Sperry Rand Corporation, through numerous patent applications based upon dubious claims, the defects of which were knowingly concealed from the patent office

4) a demonstration of Sperry Rand's "pattern of prosecuting patent applications from which they knew no valid patents should issue"

5) an exposition of Sperry Rand's plan to dominate the computer industry through the vigorous assertions of its patents and patent application "portfolio" which it had amassed through cross license agreements with IBM, AT&T, and Western Electric Company, Inc. (both in 1965).

The plaintiffs also argued that through its cross-license agreement with IBM in 1956 and settlements with a number of other large computer companies, Sperry Rand had effectively eliminated any threat of a careful investigation and analysis of the ENIAC patent claims. It was from this position of immense strength, Honeywell contended, that smaller companies would be powerless to fight." [180]

For Honeywell's part, they were to discover a key witness in the person of John V. Atanasoff. It seems that Honeywell's attorneys were made aware of John V. Atanasoff and used him successfully as part of their legal strategy to invalidate the ENIAC patent and by extension, the 30A package of additional Eckert-Mauchly patents that Sperry had acquired; thus removing themselves from the obligation to pay license fees for use of a technology they had no proprietary right to use.

However, Larson was mostly interested in Honeywell's claim of premature public disclosure. They asserted that the concepts used within the ENIAC originated in Atanasoff's machine, also stating Mauchly incorporated these ideas as a result of his 1941 trip to visit Atanasoff in Iowa. Furthermore, Honeywell claimed prior publication, citing Von Neumann's June 30, 1945 *EDVAC Report* which Goldstine failed to classify and the Moore School lectures of July and August 1946.

From 1967, when the lawsuits were entered, until 1972, the hard case dragged on. When the trial finally began in 1972, there was an expectation of a major examination of the nature of patentability and the rights of invention. Rumors persist to this day that Honeywell sought to settle the case for three and a half million dollars, and indeed had a check ready to be tendered. Sperry wanted five million. The deadlock was not resolved, and the trial began.

The courtroom heard oral testimonies by seventy-seven witnesses and an additional eighty witnesses were presented by deposition transcripts. Moreover, as plaintiff, Honeywell introduced 25,686 exhibits and Sperry Rand introduced an additional 6,968 exhibits. Many of these exhibits were extremely voluminous—comprised of, for example, a 496 page book on the 19th century and Babbage, to a file cabinet of documents regarding the ENIAC patent. When it was finished, the transcript of the trial exceeded 20,000 pages. Finally, on October 19, 1973, Judge Larson introduced the document that would frame his ruling: *Findings of Fact, Conclusions of Law and Order for Judgment.*

Larson's ruling is very long, exceeding one-hundred pages. Hence, a summary is beyond the scope of this examination. Perhaps in a future book, a summary can be introduced and dissected. For now, however, a summary of the major points, just the facts, is presented.

Essentially, Larson concluded that Mauchly had been "broadly interested in electrical analog calculating devices, but had neither conceived nor built any electronic digital calculating device" prior to his 1941 visit to Atanasoff in Ames, Iowa. This is not true. Mauchly had built digital circuits directed towards a general-purpose computer in the thirties, and these models were still in existence. They were not introduced in the trial. Furthermore, it was Atanasoff who sought out Mauchly following a presentation by Mauchly on his work at a meeting of the American Association for the Advancement of Science in December of

1940. It was Atanasoff who invited Mauchly to visit because of his ability to reduce the cost of storage of data to two dollars a bit. It was the economic factor that interested Mauchly, rather than the technology.

Furthermore, Larson stated that Atanasoff's work was very important to Mauchly, implying that Mauchly's creation of the concept of a general purpose computer was based on what he learned from Atanasoff. This seems rather farfetched since Atanasoff was working on a special purpose device for solving simultaneous equations, a device that he never reduced to practice or to a patent application. Atanasoff wrote a detailed 35-page description of how to build the device; this was intended to be used for his patent application which was never filed. It was also the basis for building the replica in 1971. The device just never worked. It could not run a program or do anything automatically.

In any event, Larson stated that shortly after, Mauchly joined the faculty at the Moore School at Penn, took a "crash course" in electronics and began applying the concepts which Atanasoff "taught him." This is somewhat farfetched since Mauchly had been a Professor of Physics for years, had created circuits in the 30's, had stirred interest at Penn, and had taken the course to learn any new techniques that might be available. Knowing John Mauchly as I did, I doubt that John even attended many of the lectures or classes. At the very least, he did meet Eckert there, thus he attended the Labs.

The most damaging evidence for Larson was correspondence between Mauchly and Atanasoff. On September 30, 1941, Mauchly wrote to Atanasoff:

> "A number of different ideas have come to me recently about computing circuits - some of which are more or less hybrids, combining your methods with other things, and some of which are nothing like your machine. The question in my mind is this: Is there any objection, from your point of view, to my building some sort of computer which incorporates some of the features of your machine? For the time being, of course, I shall be lucky to find time and material to do more than merely make exploratory tests of some of my different ideas, with the hope of getting something very speedy, not too costly, etc.
>
> Ultimately a second question might come up, of course, and that is, in the event that your present design were to hold the field against all challengers, and I got the Moore School interested in having something of the sort, would the way be open for us to build an 'Atanasoff Calculator' (a la Bush analyzer) here?"

Atanasoff replied stating he had no issues with the idea, however wished not to disclose anything to the public until he had sufficient patent protection procedures in place.

Larson continues saying that the ENIAC contract, W-670-ORD-4926, did reference Atanasoff's work, but did not identify it specifically. On the other hand, Eckert and Mauchly "filed patent applications involving subject matters stemming from Atanasoff's work" and made no reference to Atanasoff in the patent nor did they inform their patent lawyers of Atanasoff's work. The patent office would have had records of such work had Atanasoff continued his patent application in 1942 and 1943—which he did not pursue for some unknown reason. There is a story circulating the he was dependent upon Iowa State to file the patents, but this seems rather unlikely. As the owner of a number of patents myself, I can aver that securing a patent is a tedious, all-consuming process that must be directed at all times by the inventor. Patent attorneys formulate the inventor's ideas into legal language.

Without the spirited and dedicated attention and input of the inventor, no university and no patent attorney can in reality secure a patent, much less develop an effective patent application. It is more likely that Atanasoff did not pursue a patent since he had either been told or come to realize that success was unlikely.

> "What should be disclosed to the Patent Office as possible sources of invention, prior art or derivation must, in some degree, be left to the judgment and conscience of the applicant. Mauchly may, in good faith, have believed that he did not derive the subject matter claimed in the ENIAC patent from Atanasoff. In September 1944, he wrote a summary of the situation as he then saw it: 'I (thought) his (Atanasoff's) machine was very ingenious, but since it was in part mechanical (involving rotating commutators for switching) it was not by any means what I had in mind.'" Additionally, "Atanasoff saw the ENIAC machine as it existed on October 26, 1945, and in early 1946 extensive publicity was given to the ENIAC project, acknowledging Eckert and Mauchly as the inventors, but Atanasoff did not assert that the ENIAC machine included anything of his until two decades later."

Larson credited Atanasoff with invention that Atanasoff never claimed, never acknowledged, and never wrote about. Atanasoff was concerned with building a digital special purpose calculator for solving simultaneous equations. Such a machine would be a decided improvement on the Bush Differential Analyzer. In no way would it be a general purpose digital computer as envisioned by Eckert and Mauchly. This is clarified later in this chapter in an analysis in Eckert's own words of what these differences were, and what the major impact was of the Eckert-Mauchly invention. All of this was lost on Larson. Was it due to his lack of technical expertise, the deluge of documents, or bias? Why didn't he ask questions during the trial?

Larson's opinion was obviously based on ignorance of the fine points of computer technology. Perhaps an analogy to aircraft will explain the point. Consider the situation with aircraft before the invention of the jet engine. Assume that someone was working on a new way to increase lift of the aircraft through redesign of the wing. Along comes Francis Whittle, who secured a patent for a jet engine in the 1930s. The idea of James Watt with a steam kettle was not considered prior art. Nor was the work of Fulton with his steam engine. Whittle was granted a patent for a jet engine that would propel an aircraft at greater speeds than previously achieved, and without necessarily having a propeller. The shape of the wing, while important, was not a critical factor in creating a faster aircraft. If Larson has been the patent examiner, he might have rejected the patent because of prior art associated with creating faster aircraft, and might have awarded the accolade for the jet engine to James Watt or Robert Fulton because of their work.

There is a world of difference between a special purpose calculator and a general purpose electronic computer. While both generate numbers, the methodology is vastly different. It is surprising that Larson ignored that difference. Was he ignorant of the difference, misinformed, or indifferent? Were the facts of no consequence in his decision process, or were they clouded by the barrage of documents and other smoke screens generated by the attorneys, especially those representing Honeywell? If so, why didn't Larson ask questions, seek more experts to advise him, or take more time? In fact, why didn't Sperry insist on a jury trial or a hearing before more than one judge?

"What if" is a game that can be played forever. The tragedy lies in the results of this miscarriage of justice.

Eckert and Mauchly maintained that they were the sole inventors of the ENIAC and signed sworn oaths to that effect on July 19, 1947, and again on September 11, 1963. By August 1945, without prior consent from the University of Pennsylvania, both Eckert and Mauchly informed the Army Ordnance Patent lawyers that they were the solve inventors of all inventions rising out of the 4926 contract. However, in September 1944, again without authorization from the Moore School, they sent letters to the rest of the ENIAC team members "asking each man to identify any features of the ENIAC machine to which he claimed inventorship." Two men, T. Kite Sharpless and Robert F. Shaw wrote Eckert back claiming inventorship to some of the features of ENIAC and EDVAC. Even so, Eckert and Mauchly stood firm in their position that they were the sole inventors. Both Sharpless and Shaw were deceased at the time of the trial. All that said, point 13.29.1 of Larson's ruling states:

"Honeywell has not proven that there were any inventors or co-inventors, other than Eckert and Mauchly, of the subject matter claimed in the ENIAC patent."

"Honeywell has not proven by clear and convincing evidence that Eckert and Mauchly, their attorneys, successors or assigns, committed willful and intentional fraud on the Patent Office in connection with any alleged co-inventors of the subject matter claimed in the ENIAC patent."

However Larson did state that Eckert and Mauchly had, in fact, derived the technologies described in patent no. 2,629,827, referred to as the revolver patent, that related to the EDVAC's memory system, from Atanasoff's work in Iowa.

"In one embodiment of the EM-1 application, information is stored in a coded sequence of pulses, the pulses being temporarily recorded on a rotating carrier as electrostatic charges, carried by rotation to another station where they give rise to electrical potential pulses which are handled through an external feedback circuit for replacement or reinforcement of the pulses on the carrier. This subject matter as claimed in the '827 patent was anticipated by the disclosure contained in the Atanasoff manuscript disclosed to Mauchly." Furthermore, "Atanasoff's concept of the recirculating or regenerative memory was used in the EDVAC program, with Atanasoff's rotating electrostatic charge carrier being replaced by the recirculation of pulses through an electrical delay line; this delay line version of a recirculating memory was disclosed in the [2,629,827] application as an embodiment of Eckert and Mauchly's invention."

The 2,629,827 patent was issued in October 1953, into Sperry's hands. Accordingly, in 1964, Sperry Rand began its infringement cases, charging the Control Data Company, Potter Instrument Company, and brought attention to other companies such as Honeywell.

Prior art seemed to have been a stumbling block for Larson. He ignored basic patent law, the work of the patent examiners, and rulings of the United States Supreme Court. Larson asserted Von Neumann's *First Draft Report* was prior publication. In patent law, as stated on the United States Patent Office's website:

"If the invention has been described in a printed publication anywhere, or has been in public use or on sale in this country more than one year before the date on which an application for patent is filed in this country, a patent cannot be obtained. In this connection, it is immaterial when the invention was made, or whether the printed publication or public use was by the inventor himself/herself or by someone else."

In other words, in order to have preserved rights to a patent on any of the ENIAC technology, Eckert and Mauchly must have begun the patent application process within one year of the initial publication date. Accordingly, Larson considered the *First Draft Report* of June 30, 1945 credited solely to John Von Neumann (which fell short of being classified), as prior publication—barring the ENIAC patent filed on June 26, 1947. Moreover, Eckert and Mauchly allegedly were made aware of this at the April 8, 1947 meeting with Von Neumann, Goldstine and Army Ordinance patent attorneys in attendance. Church and Libman, two of the patent attorneys later stated, "It is our firm belief from the facts that we now have that this report of yours dated June 30, 1945, is a publication. ...That the report was unclassified taken together with widespread distribution there seems to be very little doubt about it." Eckert agreed: "The publication makes what is in the report public property." However, because neither Eckert nor Mauchly wrote the *First Draft*, Mauchly felt as though they should claim whatever they could.

Now let us take a look at the actual "Findings of Fact and Rulings" Judge Larson issued and see if the evidence presented supports them.

A brief prepared by the attorneys representing Sperry Rand covers the legal precedents as outlined by the United States Supreme Court on this matter. It was intended to clarify the issue of Derivation for presiding Judge Earl Larson. There is no evidence that Judge Larson ever read it. In this brief, the following is included:

"Careful attention to the description of the invention and the claims of the patent will enable the parties interested to comprehend the exact nature of the issue involved in the first defense presented by the respondents.....

The settled rule of law is, that whoever first perfects a machine is entitled to the patent, and is the real inventor, although others may have previously had the idea and made some experiments toward putting it into practice. He is the inventor and is entitled to the patent who first brought the machine to perfection and made it capable of useful operation.

Suggestions from another, made during the progress of such experiments, in order that they may be sufficient to defeat a patent subsequently issued, must have embraced the plan of the improvement, and must have furnished such information to the person to whom the communication was made that it would have enabled an ordinary mechanic, without the exercise of any ingenuity and special skill on his part, to construct and put the improvement in successful operation."

US Supreme Court- Agawam Company v. Jordan, supra

In view of this "settled rule of law" previously enunciated by the US Supreme Court, it is most troubling to read Judge Earl Larson's "Finding of Fact, Conclusions of Law and Order for Judgment on the question of Derivation" that are presented below. Judge Larson's position appears to fly in the face of settled rule of law. It must be left to the reader to determine whether one of the grossest injustices to a brilliant physicist, inventor and engineer was committed. If so, we are left to speculate as to why this could have taken place.

First, we should look at the conclusions Judge Larson asks us to accept based on the evidence presented. Where appropriate, I will provide my responses based on the evidence presented by the Sperry Attorneys that cites court testimony that does not support Judge Larson's conclusions, information provided at a later time that John Mauchly was not able to offer as testimony, as well as my own views as a computer technologist whose career spans almost the entire history of the modern computer genesis.

Judge Larson's "Findings and rulings with regard to Derivation" and my comments are as follows:

3.1.1 The subject matter of one or more claims of the ENIAC was derived from Atanasoff, and the invention claimed in the ENIAC was derived from Atanasoff.

Author's Comment: *There was no proof of this assertion advanced in the trial.*

Only two claims, 88 and 89 in the ENIAC patent, were presented as evidence by the Plaintiff Honeywell that the key elements of the ENIAC were derived from the ideas of John V. Atanasoff.

The brief submitted to Judge Larson singles out the testimony of Honeywell's own witnesses in their attempt to make their case.

The Sperry Attorneys' brief reads as follows:

"In its posture of infringing the '606 patent, Honeywell has alleged that Mauchly derived the invention disclosed and claimed in the '606 patent from Atanasoff. (par. 12 of amended complaint, Honeywell Brief section 408.27, Tr. lIS).

Honeywell had the burden of going forward to prove its case on derivation as set down by the Supreme Court in upholding the patent in issue in the similar case of <u>Aqawam Company v. Jordan,</u> 74 U.S. 592, 597 (1868):

"viewed in any light the proposition amounts to the charge that the invention was made by the person therein mentioned, and not by the assignor of the complainant, and the burden to prove it is on the respondents, not only because they make the charge, but because the presumption arising from the letters patent is the other way."

To sustain the charge of derivation the proofs must show:

(1) That Atanasoff had a complete conception of the claimed invention and
(2) That this complete conception was disclosed to Mauchly.

Honeywell introduced testimony from 11 witnesses relating to Atanasoff's attempted ABC machine[181]. Their testimony required 20 of the plaintiff's 80 trial days but totally failed to make out a case of derivation as the law requires.

In the early case of Agawam Company v. Jordan, supra, the Supreme Court further stated:

"Careful attention to the description of the invention and the claims of the patent will enable the parties interested to comprehend the exact nature of the issue involved in the first defense presented by the respondents. The settled rule of law is, that whoever first perfects a machine is entitled to the patent, and is the real inventor, although others may have previously had the idea and made some experiments toward putting it in practice. He is the inventor and is entitled to the patent who first brought the machine to perfection and made it capable of useful operation."

"Suggestions from another, made during the progress of such experiments; in order that they may be sufficient to defeat a patent subsequently issued, must have embraced the plan of the improvement, and must have furnished such information to the person to whom the communication was made that it would have enabled an ordinary mechanic, without the exercise of any ingenuity and special skill on his part, to construct and put the improvement in successful operation."

"What was actually done by the person who, as alleged by the respondents, was the real inventor of what is described in the reissued letters patent? They do not pretend that he invented or even suggested the entire invention, nor all of the several elements embraced in any one of the separate combinations, as expressed in the claims of the patent; and if they did, it could not for a moment be sustained, as it finds no support whatever in the evidence." (Emphasis added)

In the recent (to 1972) case of In re Whittle, 454 F.2d 1193 (CCPA 1972) the Court said, at page 1196:

"[I]t would appear incontrovertible that there can be no derivation of an invention or its description without possession of a conception of the critical features of that invention by the party alleging derivation prior to the time of the asserted derivation."

"Thus, to prove derivation, it must be shown that the party alleging derivation had, prior to the time of the alleged derivation, a complete conception of an operative embodiment of the patented invention, and this was disclosed to the named inventor. The authorities cited by the plaintiff on the issue of derivation in no way contradict the foregoing, and if fact, do not prove helpful at all."

Plaintiff cites Interstate Bakeries v. General Baking Company, 84 f. Supp. 92 (D. Kansas, 1948). In that case, documentary evidence clearly indicated that the inventor named on the patent signed an agreement, prior to filing his application, admitting that a working machine was conceived and built by another. The court found the prior machine worked "in substantially the same manner as described in the …patent" and that the inventor named in the patent testified that when the earlier machine was explained to him " I knew immediately that my problem was solved".(84 F. Supp. At 112)

From the foregoing recitation of facts, it is clear plaintiff's authority is inapposite to the present facts, i.e. Atanasoff's to complete his attempted conception even of his electromechanical single-purpose machine and his inability to find how to use flip-flops and gates.

In King v. Burner, 90 F.2d 343 (CCPA 1937), the invention at issue related to a dump car and the appellant asserted he disclosed the invention to the assignee of the appellee's application prior to the conception of the invention by the appellee and urged the court to find that the knowledge of his conception must be imputed to the appellee. In the course of its opinion, the Court stated, at pages 346-7:

"It should be thoroughly understood throughout the consideration of the issues in this case that the involved invention is not the 'Achilles lever' mechanism, but consists rather of a combination of elements, including the Achilles lever' mechanism, in such relation to each other as to make an operable dump car."

Accordingly, the first question presented for our consideration is whether appellant disclosed such a combination of elements to the Western Company [assignee of appellee's application] in 1925. If he did, the question of originality will need to be considered. If, on the contrary, he did not disclose such a combination, it will then be necessary to determine whether, from what he did disclose, the involved invention would be obvious to one skilled in the art."

The Court concluded, at page 348:

"We think it is clear from the record that appellant did not have a full and complete conception of the invention in issue, prior to appellee's conception and reduction of it to practice in 1927, and that, therefore, he could not have disclosed it to appellee's assignee the Western Company either in 1925 or 1926."

As shown above, all that the law allows as relevant is what Atanasoff specifically disclosed to Mauchly. For simplicity, it will be shown that had Atanasoff disclosed everything he had or had planned in June 1941, or ever, it would still amount to nothing of consequence in the invention of ENIAC and of the general purpose digital electronic computer.

The entire case is a "dilemma wrapped in a conundrum". The facts so evident today were just as evident during the trial. How the ruling could have been derived from the evidence presented is highly questionable.

The fallout from the verdict was appalling. John Mauchly's picture was removed from the Smithsonian at the insistence of a senator from Iowa. Atanasoff's children wrote scathing articles and books about how their father had been cheated of his rightful reward as the inventor of the general purpose digital computer. Mauchly was disgraced. Eckert was assumed to be a dupe of Mauchly. What was totally ignored is that the ENIAC worked, and kept working for ten years. What were ignored were John Mauchly's circuits built years before meeting Atanasoff. What was ignored were prior rulings of the United States Supreme Court.

Larson did his work well. There were no appeals. There were certainly plenty of grounds for appeal. In fact, Larson commented on this in his rulings. However, he carefully crafted his rulings to appeal to both sides to avoid any danger of an appeal. As will be shown later in his rulings, he dismissed the restraint of trade charge, which satisfied Sperry. He dismissed the charge against Honeywell for royalties, which satisfied Honeywell. Neither side had much to gain from an appeal. The reputations of John Mauchly and Pres Eckert were not factors in the decision of either company. Mauchly and Eckert did not have the funds to launch an appeal.

John Mauchly's wife told me how bitter John became at this turn of events. He felt soiled by the unfair treatment he received, and the virtual muzzling by the Sperry lawyers who denied him any opportunity to show his work from the thirties. In addition, he was ill through most of the trial, with off-hours battles and ultimatums that he acceded to sharing credit with associates or they would be sure that his reputation would be destroyed.

These points will be commented on further after additional elements of the Larson opinion are covered.

3.1   The subject matter of one or more claims of the ENIAC was derived from Atanasoff, and the invention claimed in the ENIAC was derived from Atanasoff.

3.1.1   Sperry Rand and Illinois Scientific Developments (ISD) are bound by their representation in support of   the counterclaim herein that the invention claimed in the ENIAC patent is broadly "the invention of the Automatic Electronic Digital Computer."

Author's Comment: *This is an accurate premise.*

3.1.2 Eckert and Mauchly did not themselves "first invent" the automatic electronic digital computer, but instead derived that subject matter from one Dr. John Vincent Atanasoff.

Author's Comment: *Here Judge Larson seems to employ Aristotelian syllogistic logic to make his point. (premise + premise = conclusion). While his first premise in 3.1.1 above is supportable as the Sperry attorneys framed their argument, the conclusion Judge Larson reached in 3.1 is based on the premise in 3.1.2 that the ABC machine was both "invented" and was a fully automatic computer. A computer is a working system of many components working together to achieve a result. While some parts of the ABC were shown to work, the entire system disclosed to Mauchly did not work. Nor had Atanasoff solved the vital issue of control. Therefore, it could not be said that the machine was fully automatic. Thus premise 3.1.1 + false premise 3.1.2 = false conclusion 3.1*

3.1.3 Although not necessary to the finding of derivation of "the invention" of the ENIAC patent, Honeywell has proved that the claimed subject matter of the ENIAC patent relied on in support of the counterclaim herein is not patentable over the subject matter of detailed claims 88 and 89 of the ENIAC patent corresponds to the work of Atanasoff which was known to Mauchly before any effort pertinent to the ENAIC machine or patent began.

Author's Comment: *The Dority-Green Brief presented to Judge Larson amply demonstrates from the direct testimony of Honeywell's own witnesses that Honeywell did NOT provide convincing testimony to support Judge Larson's conclusion. Whether or not Judge Larson ever read the brief, he was still present at the trial.*

3.1.4 Between 1937 and 1942, Atanasoff, then a professor of physics and mathematics at Iowa State College, Ames, Iowa, developed and built an automatic electronic digital computer for solving large systems of simultaneous linear algebraic equations.

Author's Comment: *This is an outrageous conclusion that is not supported in either legal terms or in fact, as the machine never actually worked and Atanasoff could not solve the control problem which he himself admitted; nor could the machine reconstructed in 1972 with subsequent knowledge solve these problems even then. The machine just did not work. This was a direct violation of the Supreme Court's ruling on what constituted invention.*

3.1.5 In December, 1939, Atanasoff completed and reduced to practice his basic conception in the form of an operating breadboard model of a computing machine.

Author's Comment: *Atanasoff's computer could not be built from his manuscript or his patent attorney would not have said that he could not file the patent application without additional information from Atanasoff that was never provided. Thus, no patent was ever filed by Atanasoff – therefore, he did not complete and reduce to practice anything, ever. If he had a complete understanding of the basic principles required to build a working computer, it necessarily follows that the fully funded assignment by the Navy Ordnance Lab enabled Atanasoff to finally realize his dream for an automatic computer. Instead, he did nothing with the funding and it was ultimately withdrawn by the Navy. The article in the Annals if the IEEE History of Computing speaks volumes on this subject.*[182]

3.1.6 This breadboard model machine, constructed with the assistance of a graduate student, Clifford Berry, permitted the various components of the machine to be tested under actual operating conditions.

Author's Comment: *The "so-called fully automatic computer" (system) never worked. Thirty years later, Honeywell paid to have a machine built for the trial. It is not known whether it was built to the description that Atanasoff showed to Mauchly in Iowa in 1941. It is known that Atanasoff could not solve the control problem in '41, so what could the Honeywell funded machine really demonstrate? Again see Calvin Moore's article*[183] *regarding Atanasoff's avoidance of talking about his ABC computer or even building one for the Navy that the Navy had ordered. If Atanasoff could demonstrate certain components of the electro-mechanical ABC but not the entire concept, that does not qualify as reducing the invention to practice. An invention of a computer implies that the computer works as a whole system. The ABC machine never did, nor was it automatic.*

3.1.7 The breadboard model established the soundness of the basic principles of design, and Atanasoff and Berry began the construction of a prototype or pilot model, capable of solving with a high degree of accuracy a system as many as 29 simultaneous equations having 29 unknowns.

Author's Comment: *The ABC was always viewed as a "special purpose" machine and it was electro-mechanical. It also was no faster than a human could feed it, for it had no branching capability whatsoever. Mauchly and Eckert designed a very fast automatic general purpose electronic digital computer and it solved a variety of problem types for 10 years.*

3.1.8 By August, 1940, in connection with efforts at further funding, Atanasoff prepared a comprehensive manuscript which fully described the principles of his machine, including detail design features.

Author's Comment: *Here again we have the premise + premise = conclusion approach. His machine was not an automatic general purpose computer*

3.1.9 By the time the manuscript was prepared in August 1940, construction of the machine, destined to be termed in this litigation the Atanasoff-Berry computer or "ABC," was already far advanced.

Author's Comment: *Judge Larson ruled in 3.2.5 above that it had been reduced to practice. That being said, the patent attorney for Atanasoff should have been able to submit a patent application. But he could not without additional information from Atanasoff.*

3.1.10 The description contained in the manuscript was adequate to enable one of ordinary skill in electronics at that time to make and use an ABC computer.

Author's Comment: *How is it that Atanasoff's patent attorney did not think that was so as to make it a patentable system? If it was not patentable, by whose definition was it even an invention? Judge Larson acts as his own lexicographer here, ignoring the settled rule of law.*

3.1.11 The manuscript was studied by experts in the art of aids to mathematical computation, who recommended its financial support, and these recommendations resulted in a grant of funds by Research Corporation for the ABC's continued construction.

Author's Comment: *What experts? What was it they were recommending funding to support? Atanasoff was building an electro-mechanical special purpose machine that might be an improvement on the extant Bush Differential Analyzer then in use at a few universities. What Atanasoff dreamed of building could not have fathered the modern computing industry of today. What Mauchly and Eckert were proposing was an entirely new approach to create a general purpose computer such as we have in use today. Judge Larson's framing of a statement of fact assumes, incorrectly, that the design was complete- all that was needed were the funds to construct a system from the design. The design was not complete as Atanasoff clearly admitted that he had not solved the vital problem of control.*

3.1.12 In December, 1940, Atanasoff first met Mauchly while attending a meeting of the American Association for the Advancement of Science in Philadelphia, and generally informed Mauchly about the computing machine which was under construction at Iowa State College. Because of Mauchly's expression of interest in the machine and its principles, Atanasoff invited Mauchly to come to Ames, Iowa, to learn more about the computer.

Author's Comment: *We know that Mauchly was led to believe that Atanasoff was building an electronic computer that could function at a cost of $2/digit. He arrived at Ames Iowa, saw what Atanasoff had, and was disappointed in that it had nothing much to do with what he envisioned or expected to see, although he did comment to Atanasoff that there were a couple of ideas that might be useful. Referring to the definition of Derivation by the US Supreme Court, we can cut through the various opinions about what this statement referred to, like a slight improvement to the Bush Analyzer, and conclude, as the Sperry attorneys properly did, that this statement in no way supports the claim of Derivation*

3.1.13 After correspondence on the subject with Atanasoff, Mauchly went to Ames, Iowa, as a houseguest of Atanasoff for several days, where he discussed the ABC as well as other ideas of Atanasoff's relating to the computing art.

Author's Comment: *Once again, it was a mutual exchange of ideas between two physicists that proves nothing of Derivation, as required by law.*

3.1.14 Mauchly was given an opportunity to read, and did read, but was not permitted to take with him, a copy of the comprehensive manuscript which Atanasoff had prepared in August, 1940.

Author's Comment: *This fact, like the finding in 3.1.13 above is irrelevant to the issue of Derivation.*

3.1.15 At the time of Mauchly's visit, although the ABC was not entirely complete, its construction was sufficiently well advanced so that the principles of its operation, including detail design features, was explained and demonstrated to Mauchly.

Author's Comment: *This may be factually true, but irrelevant, nonetheless. This irrelevance was due to the fact that the principles of operation of the ABC were entirely different than those of ENIAC.*

3.1.16 The discussions Mauchly had with both Atanasoff and Berry while at Ames were free and open and no significant information concerning the machine's theory, design, construction, use or operation was withheld.

Author's Comment: *See author comment 3.1.15 above.*

3.1.17 Prior to his visit to Ames, Iowa, Mauchly had been broadly interested in electrical analog calculating devices, but had not conceived an automatic electronic digital computer.

Author's Comment: *This is not a statement of fact. As John Mauchly's wife, Kay, reports in an article written for The Annals, "After Mauchly's death in1980, while I was assembling the papers to be given to the Van Pelt Library, I came across a letter file from the Ursinus period. This box had been sealed for nearly 40 years, and its contents had not been known at the time of the 1973 Honeywell-Sperry trial in Minneapolis. In the file were carbons of letters showing that Mauchly had been actively working on a computer at Ursinus -something he had claimed all along. Besides these paper items, we have the physical components of the electronic computer that Mauchly was building during the time he was teaching at Ursinus College. These components also are evidence that Mauchly's concept of an electronic 'computer calculator' predated any association with John V. Atanasoff and led directly to the design of the ENIAC".*

Further, Mauchly wanted counters that could count beyond zero and one, so he joined ten of his flip-flops together in a ring to make a "decade counter" that could count to ten. He also had plans to build flip-flops using condensers instead of bulbs or tubes. A few years later, Mauchly would use such a device to help build one of the most famous computers of all time.[some time in 1936]

Before November 1940, Mauchly had successfully tested certain components of his proposed computer and convinced himself that it was possible to build a cheap, reliable digital device using only electronic elements. He was now ready to build...His students at Ursinus well remember his scrounging for tubes and other components that would produce a machine "with no moving parts."

3.1.18 As a result of this visit, the discussions of Mauchly with Atanasoff and Berry, the demonstrations, and the review of manuscript, Mauchly derived from the ABC "the invention of the automatic electronic digital computer" claimed in the ENIAC patent.

Author's Comment: *Here Judge Larson becomes his own lexicographer by simply ignoring the settled rule of law articulated by the US Supreme Court. In my judgment, the ABC was a machine, but it was not a computer. In an interview with me in 2005, Kay Mauchly Antonelli asserted, "I don't think that he ever thought that he had designed the computer. And it was only when Honeywell came to him and said you know we have discovered that you have actually done this stuff at Iowa State College. Where is that machine? Well, it had long since been destroyed, there was nothing* *existing left of it at all. Oh, we'll rebuild one for you, which they did. And then the nice thing was they told him that if they won the suit they would pay him $300,000."*

In the same discussion, I said, "There is really no difference between that concept and the concept of a rotary calculator, where you have disks and rotors and as a matter of fact, a more advanced concept was the Enigma machine where you had rotors and drums that were used for encoding and decoding. So, just looking at it, I can't see how – I'll be brutal, that the fiction was propagated that this man invented the computer. He didn't. He couldn't."

Furthermore, as noted in Alice Burk's Who Invented the Computer?: The Legal Battle That Changed History, Atanasoff's wife further emphasizes that Mauchly had his own computer ideas, different from her husband's:

"According to Mrs. Lura Atanasoff, Atanasoff, referring to Mauchly, says...'I don't think his [machine] will work.' "[184]

This makes it clear that Mauchly communicated his computer designs to Atanasoff, who did not believe they would work. This was overlooked by Larson. Therefore, Mauchly's ideas were not Atanasoff's ABC ideas. Rather, Mauchly's ideas were those that formed the ENIAC.

A further indication of this may be found in Saul Rosen's "The   Origins of Modern Computing.. In this objective and even-handed   treatment, Rosen says, "The importance of the possibility that   Mauchly 'was inspired at least in part by his meeting Atanasoff')the quotation is from the Burks book) has been blown up out of all proportion."[185]

3.1.19 The Court has heard the testimony at trial of both Atanasoff and Mauchly, and finds the testimony of Atanasoff with respect to the knowledge and information derived by Mauchly to be credible.

Author's Comment: *With this statement, the Judge presents himself as an objective witness to testimony while at the same time ignoring the settled rule of law on the matter of Derivation. It is my view, in light of what the testimony of these and other witnesses provided, that Judge Larson was highly selective of the information he chose to consider that would enable him to erroneously arrive at the conclusions above.*

Judge Larson himself notes that Mauchly, along with Eckert, were the real inventors of the ENIAC. Alice Burks has argued that this comment by Judge Larson only referred to the question of whether others at the Moore School, such as her husband, should have been identified as co-inventors on the ENIAC patent application. As we know, Judge Larson did not say that Atanasoff invented the ENIAC, but that Eckert and Mauchly did. The Judge allows that the ENIAC is an automatic, electronic digital computer and seeks to make his case that the ABC, Atanasoff's hoped-for computer, was reduced to practice in that it contained all the necessary working elements and descriptive material so as to enable a person normally skilled in the art to build such a working automatic, electronic, digital computer system. This, however, ignores the proof of Derivation set forth previously by the US Supreme Court, thereby rendering this finding irrelevant as it in no way meets the legal test. The Dority-Green Brief, which may be found in the University of Pennsylvania's archives, argues that the ENIAC would have been created if Atanasoff or his dream machine had not existed. Judge Larson also seems to use different standards when applying his own concept of Derivation. In the case of Arthur Burks, T. Kite Sharpless and Robert Shaw, three members of the ENIAC team, they argued through their attorney, twenty years after the fact, that Judge Larson should order the Commissioner of Patents to issue a certificate adding them as joint inventors of ENIAC. The Judge acknowledged that they "had made inventive contributions" but that Honeywell did not establish that assertion based on the ENIAC patent claims. Larson further ruled that none of these three individuals "asserted any inventive contribution to the inventive subject matter claimed in the ENIAC patent for some twenty years, so their assertions are not sustainable".[186]

John Atanasoff was shown the ENIAC working at the Moore School and had even brought John Mauchly in as an occasional consultant at the Naval Ordnance Laboratory where Atanasoff was employed by the Navy to build a working computer that presumably would be automatic, electronic and digital. For all his alleged "ideas" for such a machine, he could not do it, and funds were withdrawn due to the absence of progress on that project.[187] It is curious that Judge Larson did not apply the same reasoning to Atanasoff that he applied to the claim made by Burks, Sharpless and Shaw; not that, as I have tried to show, they would have had any relevance in meeting the legal requirement to sustain Derivation in any case.

Now, we look at the essential breakthrough concepts of the ENIAC identified by Pres Eckert years later in a speech in Japan (REF). His remarks pinpoint the obvious fact that whatever Atanasoff's contributions might have been, they hardly meet or even approach the legal standard required to support a finding of Derivation, nor did any of his work approach the completeness of the ENIAC design and concept. It is inexplicable to me how a man possessing a full and complete understanding of an automatic electronic digital computer in 1941, as Judge Larson found, could fail to reduce the concept to practice, thereby substantiating the assertion that he had invented a system at all. Atanasoff was given the opportunity and the necessary funds and staff to do it just four years later at the Naval Ordnance Laboratory, yet he produced, not an ENIAC, but nothing at all.

The following are excerpts from Eckert's speech delivered at the 10th anniversary of the Eckert Research International Corporation (ERIC) April 15, 1991, in Tokyo, Japan.[188]

Eckert's thoughts are what he believed were the most important firsts that came about through the development of the ENIAC:

1. The most important in the ENIAC was control of the sub-routines in programming. This idea was first proposed to me by Mauchly and it became immediately clear that it was absolutely essential to the design and construction of the ENIAC

2. The second important idea in the ENIAC was the idea of a general purpose register which could be used for many purposes and which could be read into and out of, at electronic speed. ENIAC ideas are the origin of our modern Random Access Memory or /RAM

3. The concept of rerouting the sequencing process by examining the value or sign of a particular number and then choosing an appropriate subroutine as a result allowed the ENIAC to make decisions based on numbers it had calculated and this feature gave it both great programming power and flexibility

4. The concept of nesting and interloping subroutines to produce complex results with comparatively little program switch equipment was intrinsic in the design of the ENIAC program system

5. ENIAC had the ability to stop the process after each pulse time, after each addition or data transfer period, or at special points introduced in the subroutine process and in accord with some set of conditions or rules. The purpose of this was to facilitate troubleshooting of both the hardware and the software and to allow for human intervention in the problem-solving or decision-resolving processes being investigated

6. ENIAC had the ability to provide automatic input, on demand from the process, from a stack of punched cards placed in a suitable machine

7. ENIAC also had a similar output ability and could punch cards from data in the machine. These output cards could be sent to the tabulator for printing and for certain types of data checking, which otherwise would have tied up the ENIAC itself

8. Each register of the machine had its own program control system built into it. This allowed each unit to be tested without too much dependence on other units. But it also allowed operation of several sections of the machine at one time. The ENIAC allowed for parallel operation of several processes at the same time

9. There were also banks of buffer relays between the punch card machines and the rest of the ENIAC which allowed data to be put in and data to be taken out, and data processing to occur; all three at the same time in order to save time

10. The ENIAC's forty main panels and seven power supply panels for servicing and manufacturing reasons. These were plug-in units with special handles for forcing the units into or out of the back panels. No screwdriver to disconnect wiring from wiring terminals was ever required. Today's printed circuit cards that plug into motherboards are direct descendants of this idea, an idea not really exploited in electronic equipment before ENIAC

11. The idea of testing parts and then designing to tolerate the variations in economically produced parts is still a part of the computer business today and this approach really did not adequately exist to any great extent in consumer electronics before ENIAC

12. ENIAC accomplished all of the above goals at speeds much in excess of all past human experience for devices which carried out complex sequential processes.

Most of the above 12 items are still found in "astronomically improved" form in today's computers.

Pres Eckert went on:

"Mauchly's big idea, in my mind, was the sub-routine control concept.

My big idea was the idea of the stored-instruction sequence or program, using a single fast memory for both data and instruction, with no distinction between registers used for many purposes."

True, Judge Larson said that Mauchly and Eckert invented the ENIAC, an automatic, electronic digital computer. It is not true that Atanasoff described or was in the possession of an automatic electronic digital computer. What components he had worked on did not work as a whole system, was not automatic, was electro-mechanical, and was conceived as a special-purpose device.

Perhaps Atanasoff had an idea about regenerative memory but, as we have seen in the tests prescribed by the Supreme Court, it would have meant nothing. Perhaps, Charles Babbage had a concept that, had Eckert and Mauchly known about, might have helped them. In either case, it would have been irrelevant in support of a charge of Derivation as required by law.

In addition to Honeywell, Control Data, also a Minnesota company, was involved in a series of suits over payment of royalties, and countersuits
for restraint of trade. There were reports at the time, that Judge Larson had a standing 9 a.m. Sunday morning tee time with William Norris, Chairman of the Board at Control Data. It appears that Judge Larson was more interested in solving the case to the advantage of his old golf buddy than in finding the truth. He handed a huge victory to his friend Norris and incidentally to fellow Minnesotans at Minneapolis Honeywell. And he did it in such a way that an appeal was unlikely.

When I began to think about this chapter, a series of questions emerged in my mind and I set out to find the answers to them.

The questions were the following:

Did John Mauchly really derive his ideas about the ENIAC from John V. Atanasoff as Judge Larson found?

Since I am convinced that no one in human history could honestly say that something they invented emerged as whole cloth, without any reference to anything that had preceded it, what does the term "derive" mean in the context of ideas that result in invention? In our society governed by laws, it seems that we must turn to the law to seek a definition of such a term that can only be dealt with in a court of law.

Further, what is invention, if not what the same legal system has defined it to be?

What was the basis on which Judge Larson determined that the ABC manuscript, or the ABC machine on which it was based, described an Automatic Electronic Digital Computer system?

Judge Larson had no qualifications to define patent law. A key attorney involved in this case doubted that Larson could have reached any conclusion about the ABC since he never demonstrated any understanding about the ABC, either at the trial or in his subsequent opinion.[189]

Was Judge Larson, founder of the Minnesota ACLU, as noted in his biographical information[190], desperate to stretch legal definitions in order to create a loophole? Did he hope to achieve a result that would avoid what he may have perceived to be a recipe for eliminating competition in an emerging field whose broad growth would best serve the public interest? Or did he view this case as nothing more than a commercial dispute involving a locally based firm with a human dimension that resonated with his larger concerns?

Secondarily, what constitutes a prior publication and "public use" of an invention that, if evident more than twelve months before a patent application, would serve to deny the patentability of an invention?

Finally, what is meant by engaging in Restraint of Trade as a violation of the Sherman Antitrust Act?

In my judgment, this trial that pitted two powerful litigants against each other, concerned the most provocative and far-ranging issues surrounding Intellectual Property Rights that occurred throughout the 20th century. As Dennis Byron has written, the reasoning "why the ENIAC patent was voided is vital to understanding all the 2006 legal action. The case illustrates two of the three types of typical law suits we see in the IT industry today: patent and anti-trust."

The basic issue with respect to "derivation" comes down to whether the subject matter of the ENIAC patent "claims" could be attributed to John Atanasoff and connected to the ABC machine he designed. It was Honeywell's requirement to prove the connection to this subject matter and they failed to do so. That should have been the only criterion for determining "derivation" of any of Atanasoff's ideas.[191]

More in-depth answers to these questions would require a book in itself. In this chapter, however, I have tried to show that Judge Larson, having no known professional qualifications to define patent law, or demonstrated competence to even attempt such, took unreasonable liberties to stretch definitions beyond the settled rule of law and to interpret actions and inactions, in the case of Atanasoff's years of silence, in a manner that enabled him to arrive at a conclusion that ignored the rights of an inventor in favor of achieving what he thought was a larger public good, as McCartney has suggested[192]. While it should have been irrelevant anyway, why was Judge Larson so blatantly inconsistent in applying a statute of limitations on the claim to "inventive contribution" of the ENIAC by several members of the Moore School team for failing to raise their claim much earlier for co-invention? John Atanasoff failed to claim any rights to the ENIAC invention for the same period of time, but Judge Larson recognized no comparable statute of limitations with respect to Honeywell's allegation.

An objective review of the trial must leave one deeply troubled with Judge Larson's handling of the case and his crafting of the rulings that discouraged any appeal by either party.

This book is concerned with helping to provide a roadmap to aid in the creation and support of paths that lead to continued and vital innovation to remain competitive in a global economy. In the context of a free market economy that the US seeks to maintain, and indeed export to other political entities, great care must be taken to achieve the equitable balance necessary to recognize and reward individual achievement, lest the underpinnings of the entire economic enterprise stagnate and succumb to mediocrity.

To recall Pres Eckert's observation upon his visit to the Futuristic World's Fair in 1939, "If somebody makes an improvement, then somebody who remains the same is going to go down." In other words, constant innovation and technological improvement is crucial to staying ahead.

As for the issue of "prior publication" of the *First Draft of the EDVAC Report*, Judge Larson ruled that it was an "enabling disclosure" in spite of the fact that it did not disclose the working of the ENIAC's hardware equipment and in spite of the fact that it was distributed inappropriately, if not illegally, since both the ENIAC and the somewhat concurrent EDVAC projects were classified military projects in wartime.

As for Restraint of Trade, this allegation was previously raised by AT&T in New York and the New York Federal District Appellate Court ruled that Sperry was not guilty of Restraint of Trade. In view of that ruling and the fact that Honeywell could properly compete with Sperry by simply obtaining a license to do so, the unanswered question is why Honeywell even made the allegation in the first place. Would Honeywell have gone to such lengths to try to make their case if the issue were to be settled in a jurisdiction that did not provide them with a home field advantage?

It is interesting to note that Pres Eckert, the ENIAC's co-inventor and Sperry executive at the time that the technology cross license between IBM and Sperry was negotiated, did not support the arrangement since he believed that Sperry was getting no useful technology from IBM in the bargain. From what I have described earlier, IBM was intent on besting Sperry in the marketplace and did so. This was taking place before the ENIAC trial, so it is difficult to successfully frame the issue of restraint of trade in terms of a monopolistic agreement forged by IBM and Sperry.

In summary, for over fifty years now, the image I retain of John Mauchly is that of a kind, brilliant, dreamer, teacher and doer whom I knew so well and so admired. This image, does not "compute", if you will, with the negative image of a perpetrator of fraud that Judge Larson tried to paint through his interpretation of events and statements made in the trial. The trial called into question the issues about invention, innovation, and intellectual property rights associated with these pursuits.

I knew that John Mauchly was ill when he was on the stand being grilled by the Honeywell attorneys whose mission was not to learn from him but to destroy him. Knowing John as I did, I knew he thought and spoke in shorthand about ideas and that in an adversarial situation, he could be made to appear, to someone who had had never experienced the endlessly patient consummate teacher that was John Mauchly, as somewhat abrupt, if not arrogant. Illness can have that effect on anyone's behavior under similar conditions.

Until I began to look into the larger circumstances that surrounded the trial that produced what I consider to have been the supreme injustice to this honorable man, I had no idea how and to what extent these circumstances could have impacted the trial's outcome. From what I have been able to learn, it was short-sighted of Sperry management and most unfortunate that Sperry Corporation allowed itself to become the defendant rather than the plaintiff in the case. This fact and a heavy case load in the Washington, DC Federal District Court, ultimately resulted in the venue chosen for this most important trial to be the home field of Honeywell, and that any and all home field advantages that Honeywell could accrue could affect the outcome. In my judgment, they did. For example, as a homegrown Minnesotan, Judge Larson and his attitudes about certain issues would have been well known to Honeywell and their attorneys who, as the Plaintiff's representatives, would have shaped the issues to their client Honeywell's greatest psychological advantage. In this case, there was no jury, Judge Larson was both jury and Judge. This fact made the job of the Honeywell team to win the case for their client, at any cost, that much easier. We are not talking about justice here, only winning, at whatever cost. Collateral damage, for either Honeywell or Sperry would be simply an acceptable cost.

To me, it seems likely that Judge Larson, however fair-minded he made himself appear in his findings and rulings, was pre-disposed to favor the Honeywell home team by ignoring the settled rule of law on Derivation established by the US Supreme Court.

For Sperry Corporation's part, losing the ENIAC patent was an acceptable cost, if it meant dodging the much more economically lethal bullet, that is, being judged guilty of violating the Sherman Antitrust Act in Restraint of Trade. -. For Sperry, an appeal of Judge Larson's verdict would elevate the risk of greater economic consequences and most certainly the cost of litigation. Thus, the reputation of one of the 20th century's greatest scientists and inventors was left "twisting slowly, slowly in the wind" as acceptable triage by Sperry Corporation.

In 1974, during the Watergate investigation and scandal, John Ehrlichman, counselor to President Nixon, borrowed from Samuel Pepys, paraphrased and gave new meaning to the term that became part of the nation's political lexicon, when he advised Nixon to allow L. Patrick Gray III, then acting director of the FBI, to become the fall guy for Watergate, and to leave him "twisting slowly, slowly, in the wind."

It has been my deepest hope that when the dust has finally settled on this controversial issue, that John Mauchly, my friend and business collaborator, will finally be accorded his rightful place, as the generous original thinker he was, in the pantheon of individuals who enabled the rest of us to reap the enormous benefits of the Cyber Age.

Rectification of John Mauchly's reputation is important to all of us as a matter of justice. Moreover, it is vitally important to dreamers and would be inventors and innovators who stand as America's best hope to drive its economic engine to success in the global economy, to believe that proper recognition of the fruits of their labors and creative genius will not be usurped by others far less worthy of the accolades for their own purposes. It is disheartening to find that learned and dedicated men, scientists in their own self-image, will act like children seeking candy from others when it comes to credit for some invention or discovery. It is particularly appalling when the credit is underserved, stolen, or mistakenly attributed. Personally, I am disappointed that John Atanasoff did not voice dismay at the treatment accorded Eckert and Mauchly.

The credit for who was the first to build a counting circuit is somewhat murky. Certainly both men built such circuits at the same time. However, for whatever his reasons, Judge Larson did not understand this, nor did he take this into account whatsoever. He "rushed to judgment," ignoring facts, the Supreme Court, the law, and basic justice. He was out and out wrong. The invention of ENIAC could NOT have been derived from Atanasoff's ABC effort. Anyone knowledgeable in any way about computers and their design and manufacture knows that. A study of what Eckert said of the accomplishments of ENIAC – unchallenged in 1991 or since – justifies the accolade of ENIAC as the first truly general purpose electronic digital computer. Judge Larson agreed that Eckert and Mauchly invented ENIAC. His ruling that ENIAC derived from ABC is incomprehensible as there is no legal basis for it; and certainly no scientific or engineering basis.

John Mauchly and I spent considerable time working together. I respected him then, and now, as a brilliant man whose mind worked simultaneously in many channels. He was a dreamer and a doer. He could conceive of circuits, and then take a soldering iron and build it. He and I used to sing a ditty written by Tom Lehrer, a Harvard Mathematics Professor who was part-time entertainer who sang in bars and nightclubs. One of his favorite songs, and one which John admitted was his favorite, was one Lehrer called, "The Secret of Success – is plagiarism, plagiarism, plagiarism." The lyrics have been re-printed already in Chapter Four. John was always rueful, as was I, thinking of the occasions when he, and later I, had our ideas and work credited to others – often at their knowledgeable instigation. Foul!

My own opinion is based upon the following facts:

1. John Atanasoff never claimed that he had invented the computer, even at the trial. But he did afterwards.
2. Atanasoff and Mauchly were friends until after the trial.
3. ENIAC occupied a thousand square feet. It took a team of people three years to produce the operational machine which was demonstrated to the world on February 14, 1946. This machine continued to operate for 10 more years.
4. A patent was granted to Mauchly and Eckert on ENIAC. This patent met all the requirements as outlined by the Supreme Court and by the United States Patent and Trade Office (USPTO). It was not challenged until Honeywell decided it did not want to pay royalties. Honeywell offered to pay $3.5 million in royalties and drop the suit but Sperry Rand wanted $5 million and the suit continued. Judge Larson ruled to invalidate the patent, contrary to precedents established by the Supreme Court.
5. Honeywell was the largest employer in the state of Minnesota. The trial was held in Minneapolis.
6. John Atanasoff, together with graduate student Clifford Berry, built the ABC computer. This computer was partly mechanical. It was special purpose, not general purpose. It never completely worked. No patent application was ever created. It was abandoned.
7. Honeywell funded the rebuilding of the ABC in 1972 for the trial. The rebuilding process, of course, included all of the knowledge acquired over decades. The machine still did not work completely during the trial.
8. In 1945, Atanasoff was awarded a contract by the U.S. Navy. Mauchly was hired as an assistant. The testimony of those who worked there is that Atanasoff was never present and that Mauchly cleared up all of the problems and completed the NOL contract.
9. Mauchly left the University of Pennsylvania in 1946 and together with Pres Eckert founded the Eckert Mauchly Computer Corporation (EMMC)- which produced the BINAC and the UNIVAC. The UNIVAC became the first commercially available general purpose digital computer. EMMC became part of Remington Rand, then Sperry Rand, and then UNISYS. Hundreds of large scale computers were produced based on the designs of Eckert and Mauchly.
10. No computer was ever produced based on any design by Atanasoff.
11. In 1971 layman knew very little about computers and probably did not appreciate the difference between a general purpose computer and one that solved simultaneous equations. But the fact that the ABC was re-built and failed to work should have been the kiss of death to Honeywell's position.

Who Invented What?

My personal opinion is that Atanasoff was a brilliant man with ideas that he incorporated into his special purpose ABC computer design. The purpose of this machine was to solve simultaneous algebraic equations digitally. Eckert and Mauchly, on the other hand, set out to create a general purpose digital computer to tackle anything. In fact, it was used for calculations over a ten year period that included nuclear problems, aeronautical problems, electrical engineering problems, etc. It was the prototype for all of the electronic digital computers that followed, down to the cell phones today.

John Mauchly continued with his developmental work in computers as the godfather of the Critical Path Method, and actually produced a bird cage sized computer in 1960 to be used for planning and scheduling. He continued afterwards in the forefront of computer technology with Mauchly Associates. He also served as a founding member as well as president of the Association for Computing Machinery until his untimely death in 1980.

Eckert continued as the Vice President of Sperry Rand until his death in 1995.

John Atanasoff started the company Cybernetics in 1961 and operated it for twenty years. He passed away in 1995.

In summation, John Mauchly was not the person who would plagiarize anyone. He was always giving credit to those who developed a new idea. On the other hand, he was often plagiarized and much of his thought and work was claimed by others as theirs. I saw it happen. Mauchly and Eckert invented what we today call a computer.

As mentioned previously, a single idea is not an invention. Successfully turning that idea into a working entity constitutes an invention. Atanasoff was a brilliant man of ideas which he did not fully reduce to practice. John Mauchly and Pres Eckert turned their ideas into a working machine.

There is an ancient saying that goes, "Success has many fathers, but failure is an orphan." Atanasoff was an orphan until the trial.

This great passage by Herman Lukoff, author of *From Dits to Bits*, was printed posthumously in the Annals: vol 11 number 2, 1989, p 145:

"As to the derivation of work from Atanasoff, how this 300-tube, experimental, special-purpose machine, which had no input or output means, which used no flip-flop circuits, which could not multiply or divide, which was never intended to be programmable, and which, had it ever been completed, would have accomplished only one step at a time before requiring the reentry of information, can be thought of as an automatic electronic digital computer or in the same light as the ENIAC is beyond our comprehension."

That says it all. Larson was wrong! Larson's rulings must be considered to be in error. Larson was non-technical. There were thousands of briefs submitted. The Honeywell strategy was to paper over the entire case. It succeeded. The basic issues associated with the computer were clouded. Perhaps an analogy will clarify the issue. Both a jet engine and a piston engine have combustion chambers. Would Frank Whittle's patent on the jet engine be invalidated because of prior art with piston engines under combustion chambers? It seems to me the same situation occurred in this trial.

Who Invented the Computer?

This leads to the question: Who invented the computer? This answer depends on what you define as a computer. If you look to the grandfather of all modern computers, then Mauchly and Eckert were the originators. That distinction lies in the control circuit logic that made the machine function from a stored program without the entry of intermediate data as part of the process. That's what Eckert meant when he said:

"Mauchly's big idea, in my mind, was the sub-routine control concept.

My big idea was the idea of the stored-instruction sequence or program, using a single fast memory for both data and instruction, with no distinction between registers used for many purposes."

Who invented the computer? If this is a mechanical ability to produce answers, then probably Napier with the slide rule and Babbage with his calculating engine; if it is electric, then it is the myriad inventors of the rotary calculator; if it is special purpose, then the British with Colossus, V. Bush with the Differential Analyzer and perhaps Atanasoff with the ABC subject to the fact that ABC was never finished, and does not meet the conceptual and legal requirements of an invention; and if it is general purpose electronic digital computer, then Mauchly and Eckert with the ENIAC.

If it has to do with the computer as we know it today, then it all traces back to ENIAC and Mauchly and Eckert must be credited with being the inventors of the modern computer.

CHAPTER EIGHT

A BRIEF, PERSONAL HISTORY OF THE "PERSONALIZED" COMPUTER, AND OTHER REVOLUTIONARY TECHNOLOGIES

In this chapter, I offer my personal perspective on many of the most prominent of technologies and companies, from IBM's "mainframe" 360 to the personal computer. Three major forces—the PC, the Internet, and the cell phone-- propelled the vast expansion of computer use to the point that today, computers are used by over 20 percent of the world's population, and much higher in many countries (66% for U.S.); cell phone adoption is even more remarkable.

This chapter outlines the how and why of the expansion and provides sketches of the leading figures in the creation of the personal aspect of the Giant Brain. The computer, a laboratory curiosity of the late 1940s, is now ubiquitous, especially the hand-held instant communicator we know as the cell phone. This device is a more powerful computer in its own right than the multiplicity of the lumbering clanking monsters in use well into the 1960s.

Some Perspective on Change

Historian Arnold Toynbee[193] had a view of history that can be termed as challenge and response. Societies face periodic threats and crises which they must overcome to survive and to thrive. The historian's thesis seems to apply dead-on, if on a smaller scale, to the half-century-long computer industry. What is true of entire cultures can also be true for companies, and innovations. It has been my good fortune to have both studied under Toynbee and to have seen his view of history confirmed, by the rise and fall of major enterprises and technologies in the tumultuous computer industry.

The Information Revolution is rapidly replacing the Industrial Revolution. Fueled by the Internet, this transformation might be more appropriately called the Access Revolution. Its major tool, the computer, is the first and only machine invented that is an adjunct of the mind. Its impact is evident and omnipresent. Personal messages, streaming video and business transactions span the globe at electronic speed. Anyone can access anything from anywhere instantaneously -- whether the data's forms be social, educational, scientific, military, or commercial.

When the history of this age is written, it will be categorized as the birth of instantaneous, personal communications --for profit, power, education and pleasure.

Students of history well understand that nothing remains unchanged. And change is largely initiated because of need. It was the need to transport goods that led to the creation of the wheel. The need for simplification in accessing and sharing data led to the Internet. The need for universal computation power brought on the PC and laptop. The need for mobility in communication created the cell phone.

The wave of information technology has sundered many of the barriers to international trade and commerce and to global personal communication. This phenomenon is about 60 years old. Its movement took a big stride forward in the 1960s with IBM's shift to interchangeable components for the IBM 360. It intensified with advances in word processing in the 60s and 70s, burst forth with the PC in the 70s and 80s, and accelerated in the 80s and 90s with universal operating systems such as Windows, with electronic funds transfers, and with the cell phone. This revolution is now a raging torrent in the form of the mobile, multi-media cell phone.

All this spanned most of my professional lifetime. This period affords many interesting perspectives, and valuable lessons for the future, on the rise and fall of IT companies and products. I have closely observed – and have intimately worked on – many of these history-changing technologies, and I tell some of their stories below.

Smaller Is Better

We have seen how the big machines of IBM, its famous 700 series, overwhelmed the big UNIVAC machines of Remington Rand, and came to dominate the computing industry of the 1950s. Ironically, some of the first seeds of the trend toward miniaturization that was to transform the sector and society itself were sown by Big Blue during its time of mainframe preeminence.

During that period of the 1950s, in fact, IBM rolled out its IBM 650, a medium-size, punch-card-driven computer. Its sales were quite brisk: some two-thousand units. The 650 was a reliable machine, and its more limited capability made it easier to install and start up than the 700 series. Programmed in decimal instead of in binary, it was also easier to use. Its selling price was about $250,000, even though its manufacturing cost was an order of magnitude less – about $25,000. In the 1950's and '60s, IBM did not see smaller computers as the future. But it was happy to rake in the high profits from such a device, which was, in fact, the first computer to turn a significant profit for a company firm.

During this period, a company that was to have a very significant role in shrinking the computer arose. In fact, it was to create a new industry, the "minicomputer" sector that staked out a claim separate from IBM's large computers. The Digital Equipment

Corporation, or DEC, was formed in suburban Boston, in what would be later dubbed the Route 128 Technology Corridor. This university-rich region, as we will see, was to help spawn the personal computer, networking, and word processing. In 1964, DEC's chief officer, Ted Olson, an MIT-schooled engineer, rolled out the PDP-8 minicomputer. Compact enough to place on a 19-inch shelf, this "Peripheral Data Processor" sold for $16,000, and had many industrial applications. It was followed by the 16-bit, PDP-11 ("bit" refers to the number of alphanumeric characters the computer processes or "crunches" at a time). These minicomputers stored and accessed data quickly on disks, with magnetic tape for backup.

Ted Olson and DEC spun off several competitors in the Route 128 corridor, notably Wang Labs and Data General. DG's founder was a refugee from DEC, Edson deCastro, the PDP-8's chief engineer, and "Captain Eddie" to his DG employees. His firm's frenetic development of a 32-bit "superminicomputer" was chronicled in Tracy Kidder's Pulitzer Prize-winning popular science book, The Soul of a New Machine[194].

Toward the end of the 1960s, some computers got really small. The Datapoint 2200, released in 1970, was small enough to pick up and carry. I had one in my living room. Two of my sons would sit on my lap and play a computer game – featuring the Peanuts characters, Snoopy and Charlie Brown – on the Datapoint. Its market impact was limited, however. The screen was small, and it was not really a computer, but a computer terminal that one could program. One would load computer programs, like games, into it from cassette tapes. Still, the Datapoint helped inspire the Intel microprocessor, the workhorse of the PCs to come. It was another step forward in relentless trend toward miniaturization.

Intel, short for Integrated Electronics, had been founded in 1968 with Hall of Fame talent. It was the brainchild of Robert Noyce[195], the inventor of the integrated circuit, or computer chip. Noyce's collaborator was Gordon Moore[196], the author of "Moore's Law," the highly accurate 1965 thesis that the number of transistors placed on a chip would double every two years for the foreseeable future. Running the show was Andy Grove- the Hungarian-born András Gróf- the 1997 *Time* Man of the Year who, as Intel's top executive, made the company the leading manufacturer of PC chips.

Intel was to develop a whole series of miniaturized chips, including the wildly popular Pentium. It had great vision, with ability to scope out the future of the industry, and its place in it. Intel intended to use its chips as the central computing and control portion of computers. This would make it the generalized manufacturing arm of the host of smaller, more powerful computers it foresaw coming out through the 1970's and 1980's. Intel angled to become the sole source for the chips in PCs, and profited greatly when sales of PCs exploded in the 1980s. In the 2000's, Intel, although facing stiff competition, is still on top.

The World of Wang

While DEC started up the minicomputer industry, another of Route 128's powers, Wang Labs, sought to be the first to bring computer applications to masses of workers. The company's founder, An Wang[197], had emigrated from Shanghai in 1940, and worked with Howard Aiken at Harvard on a digital successor to the Mark I. Wang co-invented a "pulse transfer" device that enabled central processors to conduct read-write operations, the basis of magnetic core memory.

This was the kind of memory that computers employed before Intel came along with its silicon-based memory and logic chips. Wang Labs' first product, a sign of its future commercial niche, was an electronic phototypesetter. Then, in a throwback to the days before computers, the firm made highly regarded scientific calculators, priced around $5,000.

In the early 70s, An Wang introduced a machine for the then-novel commercial application of word processing.   Text was entered by a human operator via the computer screen and keyboard, as opposed to automated entry via magnetic tape, as IBM's machines had long done. The Wang word processors touched off a revolution in general publishing and technical publications; overnight, an industry that had still been very much rooted in the linotype and printing press, was transformed. Perhaps the most radical change was for writers and production workers, who could keep successive drafts of a text, and soon graphics, in the computer's memory instead of always starting "from scratch" on a typewriter or drawing board. The amount of time saved and the boost to productivity was immense.

In a parallel mode, as DEC rolled out mid-sized machines, An Wang labored to create a minicomputer of his own, the Wang 2200. These machines, with small, tubular screens, were aimed at small and mid-sized businesses, and had as a fundamental user interface, the BASIC computer language. BASIC had been invented in 1963 at Dartmouth College by Thomas Kurtz and John Kemeny[198]. Kemeny, a Hungarian émigré, had worked in the computer shop of the Manhattan Project under Richard Feynman[199], the godfather of "string theory" in physics, and was eventually made Dartmouth's president.

For many of those who had slogged through the complexities of FORTRAN or the rigid structure of COBOL, BASIC seemed a godsend. Its acronym stood for Beginner's All-purpose Symbolic Instruction Code. As that implied, it could be quickly learned. It also could immediately generate results from the instructions entered. Less intimidating than other languages, it was the software equivalent of
hardware that was increasingly more miniature and user-accessible. Those seeking a ready, simpler entry into programming swore by it.

The Wang computer had two versions of BASIC, the interpreter and the compiler. With the interpreter, the programmer typed in the instructions and ran the program, which "interpreted" or immediately produced and displayed the results on the screen. With the compiler, the machine would take the keyed-in instructions and produce code that was executed a little later. Its advantage was that compiled code ran between 5 and 15 times faster than interpreted code. If code needed to be run over and over, as was often done with a business program,
it was the way to go.

Wang's great success with word processors led, in 1978, to its VS or "virtual systems," clusters of networked minicomputers that could exchange libraries of documents. As customers grew enamored of smaller computers, and demanded more flexible machines, IBM rolled out its PC to much acclaim, and DEC its Rainbow personal computer, to lesser applause. In the spirit of the times, Wang developed a Wang PC, introduced in 1983. This was, in essence, a smaller version of the Wang 2200, and like the Datapoint, it could be carried about.

But Wang kicked the gift horse in its mouth. The company's sales force was more interested in its established, highly profitable application of word processing, not the newer, riskier proposition of personal computing. To be fair, at the time, many doubted whether the "average company" or "average person" would deem worthwhile the rather large expense of a PC. So, the thrust of Wang's marketing program stayed with its long-time market winner. In the history of the computer business, companies often err in following their marketing department instead of their technology group -- or their technology group instead of their marketing department! The industry is littered with the bones of CEOs who failed to correctly gauge which group was right.

The Roots of Redundancy

In a sense, the UNIVAC I, developed in 1950, was the first foolproof system. Pres Eckert's perfectionism had resulted in a machine with two sets of registers that performed the same functions and compared their results before moving on.

Redundant or shared systems, like our criss-cross machine, had their genesis in the late 1950's. The impetus was efficiency: a desire to make greater use of the processing power within a computer. Much of the machine's capability was wasted. Computers at that time were input/output bound, meaning they took much longer to get data into or out of the machine than they took to process the data once it got inside. The analogy often used here is that of water pipes, where the pipes leading to a destination are too narrow, or the water too slow-moving, and so the stream of water backs up. In the case of a computer, the "pipes" carrying the stream of data are too narrow, or the data flow is moving too slowly, to push the data into the processor fast enough. Another limiting factor was the "throughput," or speed at which the computer could process data in its interior central processing unit.

The invention of disk storage, and the rapid access of data on disk, helped with this problem, but only somewhat. In 1956, IBM rolled out its RAMAC, for Random Access Memory for Automatic Computers. RAMAC 305 was rather like a jukebox. This random access device would go up and down a storage drum, picking the data requested off of one of 50, stacked 24-inch disks. One did not have to drop in a quarter- however, just pay Big Blue an annual $35,000 fee. Engineers had realized by then that the alternatives to disk memory were pretty kludgey. Raytheon in 1957 installed its first Datamatic 1000, which was a very fast machine, practically too fast for its own good. In lieu of disk storage, Raytheon relied on tapes. The magnetic tapes of the time, to store the great amount of data, grew to monstrous size. Some were three inches wide. Some tapes weighed 25 pounds. In fact, the kiss of death for the D1000 occurred when a female programmer dropped a heavy tape on her foot, breaking it.

The RAMAC was a significant advance, although data storage has advanced remarkably since. In the early 1960s, I worked on a study for IBM of how we might create a big database of its international sales. We calculated we would need about 30 gigabytes of storage, or 30 billion bytes worth. The RAMAC only stored 4.4 megabytes, or millions of bytes.

Taking into account the giant storage devices of the day, we projected we would have to construct a whole new building at Yorktown Heights, New York, to store the data. In contrast, I recently spent just $200 for a 250-gigabyte disk drive for my little PC. For $300 more, I could have purchased a disk capable of holding a full terabyte, or a trillion bytes, an amount of data storage almost inconceivable in 1958.

Eventually, scientists tried another solution to the throughput and input-output dilemma. Instead of increasing the efficiency of a machine, went the reasoning, why not employ multiple machines? Surely two or more computers working on the same problem could, if they were coordinated effectively, solve it faster than one. Multiple brains are better than one.

Honeywell took this approach, and used the equivalent of multiple computers-registers actually. It placed eight sets of registers within a machine. These registers would retain the program step location of a program. As that step was executed, depending on what it did, control would move within the register to the next instruction, or shift to another register to work on another program. In this latter case, of course, the initial register would remain constant. The process would continue with control shifting among the registers to keep the machine busy while ostensibly performing multiple tasks, when in reality, it was merely rotating the use of the arithmetic, control, and input-output circuits.

Each of these would run a different program at the same time. Sophisticated hardware would control the programs, synchronizing them just so. Using this same approach, complex programs could be segmented as if they were different programs, and using multiple control registers would allow increased speed of throughput.

This strategy led in time to modern "parallel processing", where enormous speed and capability is created by latching together thousands of smaller-size machines. Still, another approach relied on the operating system instead of multiple registers. This was tried by IBM, in its 360 and 3000 series of computers, and by Remington Rand in its UNIVAC 1100 series. Using just one register, the operating system would split the processing of data. It input data in parallel paths, while at the same time running multiple programs. By cycling through program steps, the operating system would move the program to where it input data, and then it processed instructions and crunched data internally. Then it would input more data, and process more instructions internally, and on and on.

This sounds complicated, and it was. Parallel processing is much simpler than using an operating system to split up the processing.

Truly Personalized Computing

In the 1940s, IBM marketers were geared to its tried-and-true analog and mechanically oriented equipment, a reason the firm initially fell behind UNIVAC's digital machines. You will see that IBM made up for its mistake with a vengeance, and went on to dominate large-scale electronic computers. This, in turn, created a bias among its sales personnel for big machines, which caused the company for some time to miss the sales potential in minicomputers. Big Blue then atoned for this error by listening to its cutting-edge tech group, which argued
it could one-up the Wangs and the DECs with an even newer technology.

And in fact, the release in 1981 of the IBM PC legitimized the notion of a personal computer. IBM listened to its tech group and, just as importantly -- and unlike Wang and its PC -- it backed a general-purpose machine. Here, too, Wang's overemphasis on word processing helped trip it up. The Wang PC was a computer built around its word processing application. From today's perspective, when we are used to computer stores that feature hundreds of software packages, this seems odd. The IBM PC, in far-sighted contrast, was a non-specialized computer, geared to running many different applications. And it entered the market just as Bill Gates and Microsoft were readying to introduce multiple applications for a mass business audience.

The Brainiac behind the IBM PC was Philip "Don" Estridge, the tech group's leader. He had a penetrating vision of the future of both the hardware and software industries. Until Estridge, software was made by the maker of the computer itself. The same was true of the operating systems that controlled the workings of the machines. The operating systems for IBM's large computers, for instance, were synonymous with the computers themselves. When one said "OS," one meant an IBM machine with an IBM OS operating system.

Further, it was inconceivable that IBM would obtain the software for its machines from another vendor.

IBM's 360 series, which began development in 1961 and was released in 1964, epitomized this approach. Its chief engineer was Gene Amdahl, whose work on computers working in parallel later permitted the creation of supercomputers, the most powerful computing devices yet invented. IBM "bet the farm" on the project, pouring $5 billion into it, making it the 1960's second-most expensive technology initiative after the Apollo space program[200].

The 360 mainframe set the standard for creating software that would work with the various models of the machine, with little variation from machine to machine. Because almost every 360 model ran on the same instruction set, customers were able to buy in at the "low end," and then upgrade to more powerful machines as their businesses grew. The 360 was also "backwards compatible," meaning the programs from older versions ran on newer versions: customers did not have to buy new software every time they leased new hardware. These factors permitted many more organizations to afford computers.

IBM's 360 series were important for another reason, one integral to the thesis of this book. Anticipating the manufacturing process for today's Dell laptops and myriad of other devices, the manufacturing facilities for the 360 were established throughout the world. The production process for the 360 was so well worked out that it set the standard for the fast manufacture and assembly of the machines. The computer also had the now-ubiquitous "plug-to-plug compatibility" – it could be installed anywhere. With the 360, IBM had bet the future and the future worked. The 360 made our round planet quite a bit smaller.

Still, by the late 1970s, IBM's paradigm had broken down, and it had to reinvent itself once again. With the popularity of minicomputers and of networking, IBM's mainframes were seen as dinosaurs. The corporate sales force was addicted to the marketing of its large machines, whose market share was declining.

Fortunately for Big Blue, Estridge thought outside the box for his new box. He believed it vital that IBM develop a PC that would spur the most talented software developers from all over the world, not just employees of IBM, to write applications for it. He believed the quality of such applications would ignite an unquenchable demand for the PC.

Belying IBM's reputation as a slow-moving giant, Estridge's team produced the IBM PC in very rapid order, kicking off the project in 1980 and getting it on the market by 1981. In this, Estridge was greatly helped by his strategy of using an open architecture for the hardware and outsourcing the software. The software and operating systems were acquired instead of building them in-house from scratch. A host of software organizations would produce software for the IBM PC, after entering into joint venture agreements with the firm.

Estridge scoured the country to find an operating system for his PC. He settled on a little-known software firm called Microsoft. Its founder, Bill Gates[201], had already developed a BASIC compiler for the IBM PC, and promised Big Blue he would furnish it with a disk operating system. Gates knew that Gary Kildall, of Digital Research Corporation, had a program, called CP/M, or Command Program for Miniatures -- miniatures as in miniature or personal computing. Gates bought the rights for CP/M with $180,000, handing Kildall a $50,000 down payment. Gates renamed his new disk operating system DOS. An embittered Kildall died in 1994 after a being struck in a barroom fight.

Had Kildall held on to his invention, he might be the multi-billionaire today. However, I believe that unlikely. Kildall, like many brilliant people before and since, was focused on a technology. Whereas Gates, no technical slouch himself, was a genius of marketing. He recognized the futility of building something you cannot sell. And Gates really knew how to play his cards.

Under the contract that Gates signed with IBM, he retained all rights to DOS. IBM wanted to keep the rights, naturally, but Gates out-negotiated Big Blue in discussions at its headquarters. Gates was very determined, for he could afford to be -- he knew he had IBM over a barrel. IBM was rushing its PC to market; its announcements about its "next big thing" ready to hit the street. It certainly could not start a search for an alternative operating system at so late a date. It pretty much had to agree to Gates' terms. As a result, Bill Gates is now the richest man in the world, his former number two, Paul Allen, is the fourth richest, and Microsoft has the second biggest cash hoard, right behind Exxon, of any company on earth. Another sad side note: the IBM PC's designer, Don Estridge, and his wife were tragically killed in a 1985 Delta Airlines crash.

As a sidelight, in one of my work projects, I became quite familiar with Wang machines and with BASIC. I helped create a system called EasyWriter. It could be employed with Wang PCs using BASIC, which could be converted to other languages. The IBM PC had the same capability, which led to a dispute between Big Blue and the company for whom I had developed Easy Writer. IBM won that battle, but it lost a war of sorts, at least for a time.

As its name implies, Easy Writer, among its computer language features, enabled a user to do word processing. People forget that word processors did not derive from the publishing industry, as one might logically assume, but were originally an adjunct to computer programming. In Easy Writer BASIC, a user could press "control characters," for example, the Control key and then a letter key, to perform formatting functions such as arranging text in paragraphs. In fact, Bill Gates delivered a BASIC compiler of this type, one that could act as a word processor, to his very first client.

Easy Writer formed the basis of WordStar, the most popular word processing of the "floppy disk" era of PCs. WordStar was itself transformed into WordPerfect, a word processor popular in the 1980s and early 1990s. Writers and others using word processing as their stock-in-trade much preferred WordPerfect to Word, "by Microtrash," as they often termed it, frustrated by the latter's propensity to crash when handling large files and to baffle users with its Byzantine formatting styles. Eventually, WordPerfect's user friendliness was buried by Microsoft's marketing edge, and Word emerged as the dominant word processing package.

But Many That Are First Shall Be Last

Another important product around that time was technically superior to the IBM PC, but was relegated to second place. In 1977, Steve Jobs and Steve Wosniak introduced the Apple II computer, after the successful, hand-crafted production of 200 Apple I's in the garage of Jobs' parent's home. The Apple II was also a miniaturized machine, verging on a PC, although it was not a single box that you would carry but multiple boxes, including the characteristic, bulky "screen in a box". Although Apple played Avis to IBM's Hertz in terms of market share, its technology was first-rate, and its sales not inconsequential.

The Apple II, the Apple II-E, the Lisa, and the Mac that rolled out in succession were generally successful and always influential. Like WordPerfect, they captured a wide following from sophisticated users who looked at the application in terms of what it could do and not necessarily at market share or brute cost. Moreover, Apple's operating system, OS, was a harbinger of things to come. Microsoft borrowed its GUI, or graphical user interface, for the Windows family of the 1990s. A GUI is the use of graphical shortcuts like icons and menu lists that ease functionality.

It is often the case that he who is first is not necessarily the ultimate winner. Even in air carrier warfare, for example, the first wave of attackers is often shot down, while the follow-on waves gain the victory. This truism has applied to computers many times. The Apple preceded the IBM PC, and indeed the Xerox Palo Alto Research Center, and its Alto PC, preceded both. On the other end of the technical spectrum, perhaps, was the low-cost Radio Shack TRS-80, or "Trash 80," of 1977, which never cracked the market for corporate or sophisticated home users. Among the mainframes, UNIVAC was certainly the first wave, and like the Apple, was technically sweet, yet it fell to IBM's successive and relentless counterattacks. More guns and horses.

This lesson applies equally to software as it does to hardware. EasyWriter came before WordPerfect; WordPerfect beat Word to the punch, yet Word is today the unassailable champ. Then, there are electronic spreadsheets. The first successful one was VisiCalc. It was devised by Dan Bricklin after he observed a teacher tediously writing and rewriting calculations on a blackboard. The original "killer app." that every ambitious programmer dreams of, VisiCalc was a major selling point of the Apple II. Yet it was very rapidly supplanted by a major selling point of the IBM PC: Lotus 1-2-3. The latter spreadsheet was in turn supplanted by Microsoft, when it featured Excel on its Mac.

Along with the number of PCs, the sheer number of packaged software applications for PCs and other systems has been amazing. My office near Los Angeles was next to CSC, and its brilliant founder, Fletcher Johns. Fletch was really the father of software packages. Brilliant, dark-haired, tall, he resembled Gregory Peck in the movie *Keys of the Kingdom*. In fact, we referred to Fletch as "Gregory Peck with a Ph.D." In the mid-50s, he convinced Remington Rand to give him an 1100 series computer to develop an operating system for it. During that project, he worked out the concept we now take for granted – software packages, or applications that can run on different machines.

The modern approach is that the various software packages will work in different computers, independent of the hardware, and dependent only on the operating systems like Windows and Apple OS X. When you walk into a computer store today, you see packages of all kinds – Turbo Tax, video games, word processors, foreign language courses, and on and on. It was the genius of Bill Gates to put various standard office functions all together, namely, in Microsoft Office.

Whatever the company or application ruling the PC realm, the growth in the use and manufacture of PCs – from greater demand, ease of use, better technology, and lower cost -- is astonishing. In 1976, several hundred Apple computers existed. Today, according to the UN, the number of PCs world-wide is about one billion. Various organizations are planning a low-cost PC to reach another billion users in developing lands.

Given how much more powerful current PCs are, the growth of total computing power has been even more logarithmic. This 30-year rush to personalized computing is especially gratifying to me, who began my career working with machines that filled up whole computer centers.

At Your Service: Reframing the Mainframes

Even as the PC was gaining great success, IBM was facing a grave threat to its core business. In the early 1980s, the very trends toward computer networks, personal computers, minicomputers, and decentralization of computer power that allowed the IBM PC to flourish was undermining its traditional mainframe business. In place of a computer in a room, the zeitgeist called for a computer on every desktop. As in the early '50s, when it reoriented itself around electronic computing, Big Blue met the challenge of this changed environment by transforming its core business from the making of hardware to the provision of for-fee services.

Interestingly, some of the trends actually played to the advantage of powerful mainframes, if they could be adapted to meet the changes. This was so because the explosion in personal computers, and in time, other intelligent devices like the handheld computer, also meant an explosion in the kinds and amounts of data. Mainframes were suited to handling this mammoth task. Throughout the '80s, Oracle Corporation, under Larry Ellison, was penetrating corporate America with its database management systems. Meanwhile, new markets rose up for data warehousing, for the storage of vast amounts of data.

In the 1990s, the rise of the Internet and the search engine companies produced cascading demand for shared storage, to provide diverse services to a vast coterie of users accessing huge volumes of data from different machines. The savviest executives successfully made the shift from the older technologies to the new ones. For instance, John Chambers, the CEO of the 90s leading Internet hardware firm Cisco, jumped to Cisco from his post as Vice President of U.S. Operations for Wang.

Leading the renaissance at IBM was Louis Gerstner, who was named its chairman in 1993. Gerstner realized the company's revenues were dangerously dependent on the sale or leasing of large-scale machines, even as a major shift was continuing to small-scale devices. Over a decade earlier, in releasing its IBM PC, IBM had already been faced with this same dilemma of how to exploit the trend to miniaturization while retaining profitability. Gerstner's insight was that, although the traditional mainframe strategy was outmoded, a better, newer approach was staring IBM in the face. Stuck in its 1960s series 360 paradigm, his firm was giving away for free the valuable services of its army of technicians and developers.

Gerstner's book, Who Says Elephants Can't Dance?[202], recounts his redirection of IBM from a dependence on hardware alone to a diverse organization offering services for a price, as well as retooled mainframe offerings. Today, IBM's services account for about 50 percent of its revenues. The same sort of transformation occurred with other, smart mainframe companies- notably Unisys, a product of a merger between Burroughs and of Sperry, the latter a corporate descendant of Remington Rand. Unisys now derives fully 83 percent of its income from systems integration, consulting, infrastructure and other services.

In making this nimble shift, IBM and Unisys took a page from the book of Ross Perot. Exploiting the growing demand for computer services, Perot had turned Electronic Data Systems, EDS, into a giant contract house that would run the computer systems of the many organizations seeking to shed the pain of setting up and running their own IT shops.

The contracting organization called this outsourcing; that is, outsourcing its data management. The contractor dubbed it facilities management.

In a similar vein, Computer Sciences Corporation continued its rapid growth, despite the death of founder Fletcher Jones in a 1972 aircraft accident. At the same time, the major accounting firms, such as Arthur Andersen and Price Waterhouse, then known as two of the "Big 8" firms, were providing, through their management services arms, many consulting services associated with data processing. Further, consulting houses such as Booz Allen Hamilton, McKinsey and Company, and Planning Research Associates, were also gaining significant profits from computer services.

In the challenge-and-response world of computers, turns of fortune are frequent and often fast. In the late 80's, based on the success of its VAX line of minicomputers, DEC had a payroll of 100,000 employees and was knocking on IBM's door. Then, it got knocked on its back by the rise of the Intel-based PC. In response, it rolled out three PCs, and all were Edsels. Other, newer kids on the block -- the UNIX operating system, and new Internet standards -- also took away market share. DEC's machines had too many operating systems, too many different pieces -- many of which did not talk to each other. In 1998, after mammoth layoffs, it became a division of Compaq, before Compaq became part of Hewlett-Packard. Dog-eat-dog, and the little fishes are consumed by the leviathans.

The PC's Smaller and Smaller Footprints

The PC has continued to shrink, spewing out new devices. A logical development in the continuous miniaturization of electronic machines was the portable computer.

In 1981, the Osborne 1, the first true portable, was released. The company founder, Adam Osborne, was a devotee of ease of use. He ran a publishing business of easy-to-understand computer books, and dreamed of a computer small enough to carry like a luggage bag. The size of a large lunch box, the Osborne had slots for two floppy disks and a hinged screen that a user could pull down. For $1,795, a customer also got a suite of software: WordStar, BASIC, and SuperCalc. For its time, the Osborne was a remarkable feat. But it was hardly light: 26 pounds, and its tiny screen could only display 56 characters. The Osborne did not have the marketing heft of a major company, and bore fierce competition from its big-time rivals: Apple, IBM, and Compaq. The company went belly-up after two years.

It took the financial, marketing, and manufacturing strength of a Toshiba or a Hewlett-Packard to make a successful laptop. Among the first, so-called portables by a major manufacturer were the Hewlett Packard machines introduced in the '90s. But these were not really portable either: They weighed about 16 pounds, and would almost dislocate your arm when lugging them onto an aircraft. Its bulky box was about 15-inches long, 7-inches wide, and 12-inches deep. Later on, Toshiba, Compaq, Dell, and yes, HP, came out with real laptops, ones that would not crush your lap. The laptop's portability gave another push to the growth of the PC industry, and to the ongoing trends in miniaturization and distributed computer power.

The PC has transmogrified itself into a host of portable machines. The ongoing miniaturization of PCs and laptops naturally led to hand-helds and Personal Data Assistants, or PDAs. One of the first hand-helds produced by a major corporation was Apple's Newton, introduced in 1993, during the period when John Sculley had wrested control of Apple from Steve Jobs. (In a ferocious comeback typical of the rollercoaster computer field, Jobs returned to Apple in 1997, leading Apple to the spectacular successes in retail stores and the iPod.)

The Newton proved too far ahead of its time. Users objected to its $1,000 price tag, the difficulty of fitting it into shirt pockets, and to early problems with a key selling point -- its ability to read handwritten script. Still, it was a forerunner of more enduring PDAs like the Palm Pilot and the multi-tasking BlackBerry, the latter spawned from a two-way pager. Today's PDAs function as a pocket PC, possessing up to a gigabyte of memory and packing various operating systems like the Microsoft CE.

PDAs are turning the computer into a universal personal assistant that enables us as never before to control our lives – our schedules, our travel plans, our news of the world, and our communications with each other. I think "PC" will come to mean "personal control" as well as personal computer.

Currently, WIFI and WIMAX, the wireless technologies, are providing great impetus for the further development of personalized computing. WIFI offers relatively short-range wireless communications, up to 200-300 feet, while WIMAX systems, increasingly adopted by municipalities, have city-wide range. When combined with cell technology, wireless will fulfill the grand vision of communicating with any data source from any place at any time.

In 1998, I visited the Kurchatov Institute, the premier Russian science laboratory. Officials there talked of how they were going to provide cell capability throughout Siberia. Within the vast stretches of that 10 million-square-kilometer province, a fleet of barrage balloons was planned at altitudes ranging from 500 to 1,500 feet. The balloons would have transponders and responders to collect and broadcast all of Siberia's cellular signals. In 2006, given the widespread use of WIMAX, such a deployment might make great sense. WIMAX can readily distribute computing power across great geographic distances like those of Siberia. The notion of a fleet of low-Earth orbiting satellites – a failed, late '90s Motorola project launched 66 satellites for this purpose -- could provide the same capability.

Networking Considerations: The Path to the Future

As the all-conquering influence of the Internet shows, computer networks – along with miniaturization and explosion of applications – have fueled the computerization and globalization of the planet. The first networks were local area networks, typically limited to offices, which were succeeded by wide area networks that link together buildings, which were then superseded or complemented by wireless networks of varying extent. The World Wide Web links all such networks together in one vast communication hookup.

Increasingly, the small devices discussed above will plug into networks. I foresee a future where the networks will consist of a catholicity of devices used by a person anywhere in the word and all connected to a network of controllers and a network of databases.

In today's environment, we are moving rapidly towards ready access to such shared data and systems. These take the form of a grid. I believe that grid technology will be in the forefront of computing by the end of the first decade of this new century. With grid technology, networks will seamlessly link any database in any language to any device, individual, or group.

My Career as a Lesson for Our Future

In reviewing my half century in high-tech business, I am astounded by the extent of change in the sectors I have worked, by their exponential growth, and startling breadth of applications. This gives me hope for America, the land of pioneering change, which today faces stiff challenges in industries old and new from rising economic and technical rivals.

When I started out with Adalia in the early 1950s, management consulting was a still-new field, and IT consulting was just being invented. I knew the founder of the consulting firm Corporation Sciences Corporation, who was working out of a small office in suburban LA. Today, CSC has 80,000 employees, with offices worldwide, and several U.S. rivals like IBM and Booz Allen are comparable in size. America is today the management consultant to the world.

When I did my graduate work on orbital space flight, there was no space program. Today, we have gone to the moon, and are planning for an extended stay on Mars. Perhaps more importantly, in efforts that could open up outer space to all, entrepreneurs are vying to make orbital "vacations" routine, and young American researchers are starting to sketch out plans for a "space elevator". Such a device would render trivial the now-huge expense of moving materials into space.

When I started work with Remington Rand 's UNIVAC, computers were a billion-dollar industry; now they are a trillion-dollar industry, the world's largest next to travel, with both sectors indicators of just how fast-moving and globalized our economy has become.

When I worked with the computer's co-creator John Mauchly, the machine he and Pres Eckert spawned still filled up large rooms. Now, we all grasp in our hands tiny devices of far greater processing power that give us the ability to phone Nepal, dial up the British Museum, or send a friend the instantaneous video and audio of a concert.

I have been a pioneer in vital sectors that barely existed when I was doing my ground-breaking work. It is impossible today to imagine the publishing industry without word processors, but when I developed one of the first such programs in the '70s, tens of thousands of editors and typesetters still arduously retyped and re-set type and text for each print job. Now everyone – not just publishing professionals – publishes a highest-quality letter, term paper, or book with the wave of a finger. This revolutionary breakthrough was all invented and disseminated in America, by the likes of Microsoft, Wang Labs, and restless foes of the status quo like myself.

Just several decades ago, when I started out with XRT, the drudgery of manual labor also gripped the international banking world. In short order, another trillion-dollar business was birthed through the creation of electronic funds transfers.   The driving forces there included New York's banks and immigrant entrepreneurs like myself.

In surveying these tumultuous changes, it is critical to glean the right lessons for the challenges of the future.   It is vital for the United States -- from its founding, a leader of societal and technical change -- to keep reaping advantage of the overwhelming trends toward a globally oriented economy, and the application of revolutionary technologies -- instead of ignoring them.

A real challenge to our national security is the economic and technological competition from rising powers, in particular China. At current rates of growth, China's economy could exceed the United States, perhaps as soon as 2015. China and another emerging player, India, could soon surpass us in many aspects of scientific and technical excellence.

One sobering statistic involves the number of engineering students that foreign countries graduate. Twenty years ago, the United States and China graduated roughly the same number of engineers. Today, the U.S. graduates 60,000 engineers, while China graduates 200,000. India graduates 100,000, as does Japan, while tiny South Korea is close to the U.S. total. In a technology-driven world, these numbers are disconcerting.

The phenomenal growth of the Middle Kingdom and New Delhi has stemmed until now from very low labor costs that knock the legs out of U.S.-based manufacturers competing in the same fields. Although wages and thus labor costs in East and South Asia are rising, they are likely to be well below American standards for some time, and thus to continue to provide the likes of China a big edge. Such a reality necessitates that the United States enhance its own "economic edge" -- namely its ability to innovate.

Along with scientific talent, another arrow in the quiver of China's rising power is its far-sighted investment strategy. The Chinese government and Chinese industry are spending massively in the infrastructures, investments, and innovations of the twenty-first century. They are directing their resources to biotech and medical research, Internet networks, space travel, seaports, mathematics and science institutions, higher education generally, and other building blocks of the global, high-tech economy. They have eyed the future and are carefully mapping the fastest route to it. We must do the same, and do it better.

While we are all creatures of events, today we have the opportunity, in our lifetimes, to mold the world. As Winston Churchill once affirmed, circumstances provide the opening for individuals and nations to seize the moment and shake the tree of history.

In the not-distant past, measures of industrial capacity, such as tons of steel production and output of refrigerators, were used as the main indicators of national income. The rapid economic growth of China, India, Singapore, Taiwan, and Korea however, have created a new paradigm for measuring economic activity. Today, the number and use of computers, visualization techniques, communication systems, and personal electronic devices are the chief indices of a robust economy.

In past eras, many feared the death of the old-style industries, such as typeset printing, as word processing supplanted it, or the horse-and-buggy, before the automobile consigned it to history's dustbin. Yet whole new industries were created, and new job and wealth opportunities unfolded. The same is true today.

History is repeating itself.

I foresee that one such new opportunity -- distance learning -- will become readily available at negligible cost. It will enable for the poorest nations on earth to rapidly pull the educational level of its people into this millennium. And for more prosperous lands, a college education may become available for a fraction of the current cost.

With distance learning, interchange with instructors and fellow students is easy and flexible. Education can be conducted at the student's preferred pace. This technology, which is already growing exponentially, may radically transform our traditional notion of school; that is, of students gathered statically in a class or lecture room. It also may upend our notion of "student", for the very young or the elderly, traditionally kept outside the bounds of academe, can now readily gain access to it. In an information access era, distance learning could spur another trillion-dollar industry.

Another example of a far-ranging communications technology, one that may have the greatest impact on our prosperity and way of working, is teleworking. This application lets an individual participate in the full work of an office, class, or group without being physically present. As with distance learning, teleworking should put to good use the talents of hundreds of millions of the elderly and retired, often with long experience and still-excellent skills. Masses of people working from home will mean greatly reduced pollution, fewer traffic fatalities, more leisure, lower overheads, and vastly improved employee satisfaction. Further, teleworking, if widely adopted, could greatly cut our dependence on foreign oil.

Further, teleworking will provide a large capacity of well-trained, lower-cost workers to whom significant work can be "insourced". If we can outsource service work to Bangalore, India, then why can't we "homeshore" labor to American workers in Bowling Green, Indiana? What I propose with more teleworking is, in effect, *more*, not less, outsourcing.

Teleworking is but one example of new industries that will offer whole sets of devices and services to enhance commerce, individual freedom, and wealth creation on this planet. They will shatter barriers to distance, language, and information access.

At the same time, attitude is everything, and intangibles are key. In the "First", as well as the "Third" Worlds, we need, in addition to smart policies, spirit, drive, and the passion to succeed. Think of Thomas Edison, who forswore sleep, taking catnaps while inventing a new world of electricity. Steve Jobs and Steve Wozniak built the first three Apple machines in a garage. Bill Hewlett and David Packard devised a low-cost precision oscillator from a light bulb.

The United States became a superpower of global reach because it had passion, imagination, and innovative skills for the cutting-edge innovations of the time. The Henry Fords, Andrew Carnegies, David Packards, Bill Hewletts, Pres Eckerts, and John Mauchlys of the past created the dynamic economy that pushed the nation to the position of the world's superpower. These men, and others of the same bent, created the bedrock for the likes of Intel's Andy Grove, and network entrepreneur Frank Chambers, to move the economy from manufacturing to the Cyber Age. Likewise, the movements that propelled the Pacific Rim into dominance in electronic manufacturing and now toward the top of information technology had their roots in the innovative skills and visions of American entrepreneurs. That culture of entrepreneurship remains America's major heritage and strength.

So, as in the past half century, let us hope that innovation becomes the spirit of the day. Allow it to bridge the present to meet the needs and promise of our future.

CHAPTER NINE

THE CRYSTAL BALL

Globalization has already had a profound effect on personal and national economics and security. The effect has generally been positive with regard to national wealth, but muted if not negative for human factors of life. With increased affluence and the ability to have anything at any time has come dissatisfaction with tradition and the status quo. The gap between the haves and the have-nots is becoming larger. With everyone who enjoys instant information access on one side of the digital divide, the expectations for instant feedback or gratification have become more pronounced and may, in the long run, fall short of meeting those continuously expanding expectations. For those on the non-access side of the digital divide, the increasing awareness of being left behind is likewise, an unsatisfying reality in the near term. Human nature being what it is, the Flat World reality raises the bar for some and raises the barriers to a measure of economic success for those experiencing their personal emotional revolution of rising expectations.

During the first decade of the 21st Century, a new force has come to fruition- the force of social networking[203]. The tools have been in place for some time; the Internet since the DARPO creation in the 1960s. The communication capability with the Internet took almost forty years to be recognized for what it was-essentially an immediate two-way channel of communication. It was created to make research and the immediate exchange of documents possible. But coupled with hand-held devices, especially the Smart Phone, this capability morphed into the social networking phenomena, which can motivate and energize millions in short order. Social networking, in its infancy now, can topple governments as well as create instant billionaires.

    In this closing chapter, the crystal ball focuses on the future products and industries to be born. The chapter presents an optimistic, yet realistic, look. I consider the future of the West's economic confrontation with the East and the war on terrorism. I present concrete and specific approaches for success in these encounters. Chicken Little's warning is demolished, leaving challenges to be faced and success to be achieved, or not, by innovative thinking. The same spirit of innovation that began the computer genesis is needed now to reawaken the sleeping giant of American and Western ingenuity.

    The book closes by expressing the firm belief that the power of the computer can enable achievement of whatever goals the majority of people strive for. The author hopes and prays that leadership will emerge to lead humanity into a golden age – a new Renaissance. That is what we created the Flat World to be.

This is a great time in history to be alive. Opportunity lies all around us. History in the future will record our time as the dawn of the era of the mind and spirit instead of the back, of the birth of one world of co-operation in work and living.

Innovation has been a major force in bringing us to this day. Innovation is the accelerator to the future. Innovation is like a symphony, blending notes into a pleasing ensemble. So it can and must be to capture the tide of the future. The great composer Mozart spoke often of merely copying music from his mind to paper. So be it. Let innovation be the spirit of the day in bridging the present to meet the needs and promise of the future.

What is needed for the future? What targets can we project now for future invention and development? What does the future hold for the United States, for the world, and for the Church?

First, will Globalization fade or intensify? Despite doom and gloom naysayers, the indications from technology and international acceptance point to the intensification of Globalization. Throughout history, human development has moved on waves of opportunity and need. We can be assured that the technology of today will intensify the drive towards the Global Village of McLuhan rooted in communication, especially between cultures. The world today is becoming less symmetrical and more homogeneous. National boundaries, while intact and important, are giving way to groupings of common interest. The European Union, NAFTA, the WTO, UNESCO and even the United Nations point to increasing co-operative efforts in using the resources of each part of the world working together. This altruistic goal has not yet been achieved, nor might ever be achieved totally, but at least we are moving towards putting people and resources to work for individual gain while fulfilling greater needs on a wider basis.

For some, there is a dislocation as work, especially repetitive, manageable, and costly efforts that can be duplicated with lower costs elsewhere. This is especially so with tasks and skills that can be imparted easily. The application of distance learning techniques using modern technology with wireless inexpensive mobile devices will accelerate this trend. At the same time, whole new industries will be created, new job opportunities, and new wealth opportunities will unfold. Remember the buggy whip manufacturers went out of business as the motor industry was created, and the typewriter manufacturing jobs were replaced by infinitely more jobs in electronic word processing. Perhaps the most striking example of apparent dislocation that has led to vastly increased employment is the following: Consider the situation in the fifteenth century when books were hand-produced by scribes. How many books were there? How many people could read? How much did a book cost? Who had books?

Guttenberg's invention of the press in 1440 led to the first printing of the Bible in 1451. (It is significant that McLuhan called one of his early books <u>The Gutenberg Galaxy: the Making of Typographic Man</u>[204]). With the Gutenberg press, the world changed. This was the first step towards a "wheel" for knowledge. The invention of the linotype moved plentiful, inexpensive, books and newspapers closer to reality. The invention of word processing via computer and now by hand-held devices closed the loop. Books are plentiful, relatively inexpensive, and widely distributed. As each development increased productivity, lowered the cost, and created more opportunity for use, use increased dramatically. While some newspapers are losing subscriptions as people use the web, they are reaping greater profit as they market information and services. The cost of paper is saved, forests are preserved, profits rise, and even more people are working in the information supply business.

The same will be true of the future with new Gutenberg presses. These new innovations will create a vast number of new jobs because of the capability that will be available. Once again, for example, if distance learning becomes readily available at negligible cost for the poorest nations on earth, as for instance those in Africa, what will be the impact of a literate workforce of a billion or more? How many workers will be needed to train them? How many books will they need? How many inventions will they create? And how many dictators will survive if everyone can read and communicate outside their narrow environment with inexpensive wireless devices?

This is not altruistic. This is real. Electronic communication destroyed the Iron Curtain as much, or more, than all the policies of all the statesmen, including Pope John Paul II and President Reagan.   The electronic wave intensified and gave credibility to their message and efforts. So, too, will technology and globalization bring down all the iron curtains everywhere.

And how will the high-cost labor and well-educated nations compete with the low-cost labor market? The only way is to stay one step ahead. Progress can be made in a high-cost and well-educated environment by teaching new skills, providing better direction and management, by innovation – inventing new products, and by creating new industries. It has always been so. It can be a win-win situation.

The future demands new inventions, new development programs, and dynamically new leadership in diplomacy and politics.

First, the inventions.

There will be many new inventions as we move forward. The inventions needed are manifold. Those easily identified at this time, with great future consequence, lie in the area of communications. Currently, there is great ability to communicate easily with anyone, anywhere, at any time, at very low cost. Such communication can be visual as well as verbal and audio. Music, video, films, messages, video conferences, are all possible. These are all demonstrated by the spur of social networking sites, including Facebook and Twitter. But there is a need for:

- Participatory real-life video conferencing,
- Inclusion of the home as an information center,
- Communication without the boundaries of frequency, distance, or line of sight,
- Easy access and use of personal and public data grids and data warehouses.

Of particular significance will be inventions that permit everyone to be a participant in whatever action is unfolding to the degree possible. For example, currently video conferences can be staged with many participants. As a video broadcast, it is possible for the viewer to see and hear persons from many different places exchange views. An external editor selects the frames to display. The same is true of a football game, for example, with a producer selecting the images to be shown. What if the viewer becomes a participant and can be at a game, or in a conference, letting his or her eyes select what is to be seen. What if in a video conference, all the participants, no matter where, can feel they are in the same room, and are able to select what they are looking at?

Holographic imaging exists now to provide three-dimensional images. Its prospective benefits are now emerging with regard to telemedicine, which would be especially poignant with regard to brain surgery. Another step in this technology would be to connect these to multi-frame, multi-person, multi-location systems to present the virtual meeting for every participant. This is currently underway.

The ultimate, of course, is to provide this capability on wireless, on any frequency, with any bandwidth, at any distance, on a mobile device such as a cell phone.

Furthermore, commands will be by voice rather than by manipulation of miniscule keys or with a stylus.

The "cream" will be to project this image onto any wall or screen of any size in any light condition. The extensions and description can go on and on. That is a dynamic and dramatic extension of virtual reality to group participatory action. That will be a major wave of the future. That will expedite globalization dramatically.

The rush to Globalization is creating forces that will demand new products and services geared to on demand response no matter where or by whom. This will lead to more products and services associated with:

- Communication
- Entertainment
- Teleworking
- Communication including improved meeting arrangements
- Integration of home, family, and work activities
- Integration of disparate data in diverse locations organized in different fashions
- Notification of actions needed, especially in emergencies, independent of the characteristics of the transmitting devices; i.e., frequency independent receivers and broadcasters
- Change in the workplace from an office to which many go to a convenient work location closer, if not in, the home.

- Teleworking is a participatory endeavor with a group without being physically present with the group.
- Distance learning at minimal cost, with maximum effectiveness
- Improved monitoring of the ill
- Wireless communication without barriers of distance, line of sight, or obstructions
- The ability to beam messages as required for emergencies, education, training, or entertainment purposes. This would be especially important if the information matching a request pattern imitated by the receiving person or organization
- The ability to turn on a turned-off device, with the permission of the receiving person, or in an emergency of some kind.
- The ability to access up-to-date information, at all times.
- The use of personal robots to assist in both physical and psychological care
- The ability to use personalized medicine as both a preventative as well as curative means
- The ability to generate lighting at a significant price reduction which promotes a greener world
- The ability to communicate instantly

Participatory conferencing will provide the capability to provide all such capability and more.

To meet these demands, the following types of products will be necessary:

- Holographic conferences using imaging techniques that will create a sense of being in a room with a number of persons even though all are separated by distance, as described
- Projection within each hand-held device to create multiple images on a wall or screen
- Advances in the reduced size and cost of screen-based devices for wide distribution widely in homes and places that need to monitor, display results, and transmit such results for correlation and/or action
- Extension of the entertainment capability with music and video imaging to allow for participation by the viewer who can then become a participant
- Integration of signals no matter how received into coherent and useable data
- Education at a distance in any skill whatsoever can now become hands-on. Imagine the impact of providing such training to the have-nots of the world, providing the leaders will allow it. But then again, can they stop it? Could the Soviet stop the electronic signals beamed behind the Iron Curtain? They did not, and it is unlikely that dictators will be able to continue to isolate their subjugated people.
- Diagnostic systems in the home with personal robotic attendants
- Personalized medicine that can serve as preventions as well as possible cures
- LED lighting can reduce costs significantly while promoting an Earth-friendly approach
- The ability to instantly communicate with anyone, anywhere is now possible

Devices such as these will produce great convenience, significant commercial and personal benefit, and introduce a whole new set of dangers to freedom. There must be new international safeguards protecting the rights of individuals from government, corporate, or personal interference in their lives. This may become a problem, but the counter is that wider-range communication will permit the marshalling of public opinion much more readily in the event of attempts to dominate people through these newer technologies.

Such has always been the case throughout history, but at least the playing field will be infinitely more level.

These are but a few examples of a whole new set of devices and services that will enhance commerce, wealth creation, and life on this planet. The barriers to distance, language, and information will be shattered.

For example, using such capabilities as these will remove the problems with current video conferencing, providing a life-like reality more conducive to being involved in the meeting than just passively viewing it. In emergency situations, those affected can be directed to the nearest safe haven with directions that avoid difficulty. Home monitoring will dramatically improve a sense of family linkage, with greater control of the home environment.

Extended to the workplace, teleworking will become much more effective, the talents and skills of those retiring can be used, and energy consumption can be dramatically reduced. The end result will be to reduce pollution, increase free time, reduce the overhead of conducting business, and vastly improve productivity and employee job satisfaction.

That is the promise of globalization. That is the promise of the use of talents. Innovation once more will be the driving force to wealth creation. The sucking noise that Ross Perot promulgated will be a flow of income towards those who embrace the promise of globalization rather than stew over perils, real or imagined.

The book <u>All Quiet on the Western Front</u>[205] by the German writer Erich Maria Remarque created a sensation when it was published in 1929. The movie, released in 1930, continued the revulsion of people for war. One telling scene shows a French and German soldier, both wounded, both dying, in a shell hole between the lines, exchanging pictures of their families before dying. In the light of the Globalization movement today, the millions of lives lost during World War I seemed exceptionally and poignantly wasted. The same is equally true for all the lives lost in World War II and the Cold War and the "little" wars like Korea and Vietnam that continued afterwards.

In a globalized the environment, would World War II have happened? Would the Cold War have been possible, or lasted as long? Would we still be a captive of OPEC? Would the United States have the balance of payments deficit at the current level?

How do we recapture that growth cycle and use our culture of innovation to resurge in the market place? As a matter of fact, we are. Even in the midst of surging deficits in our current accounts, we are coming back. Our future lies in outing innovation as our number one product. The tools are at hand but not everyone believes that.

The catalyst for globalization is the computer and the accelerator is the ability to transmit electronic currency anywhere at any time. Technology has provided the tools. The leaders must provide direction.

That will be the greatest obstacle to achieving the future. Political leadership has been delinquent in many ways in failing to capture the promise of technology. That will provide significant challenge. The hope is that the globalization movement will provide vast improvements in the ability of everyone to understand what is happening, and to make choices, if they are allowed. We can hope that communication pressures will grant that capability. In any event, everyone is affected and must become involved as we move towards one world.

Technology miracles can belong to every nation. Progressive investment taxation policy is important. Tax credits for development and job creation are vital. Incentives are necessary to stimulate innovation. We need spirit, taxation policy, drive, and passion to succeed. Bill Gates slept in the kneehole of his desk as he was building Microsoft. Steve Jobs worked with Steve Wozniak building the first three Apple machines in his garage and getting to their first product show at dawn of show day. Bill Hewlett and David Packard built their devices in a garage. None of them had government grants. Consider how many jobs they created and their contribution to the GDP of the United Sates and of the world. The vital aspect is that bureaucracy, greed, incompetence, and sloth must not be allowed to stifle the promise of the future.

The Global Institution

The Church is universal – or Global. Its members represent all races and nations totaling over one billion people at this time. The leadership spans the globe in races and cultures. While Latin is used as a "common" language, every language in the world is used in one way or another at diverse locations. I have personally attended Mass in Tel Aviv where it was said in Italian, and in Italy where it was said in English, and at Lourdes where it was said in French with readings in German, Polish, and English. This is by way of illustrating the universal nature of the Church, and its global activities.

The Church is a living example of Globalization and has already been a great beneficiary of Globalization.

The future impact of the application of technology to further the global reach, activity, and influence of the Church is dazzling. I can epitomize the whole approach from a conversation with Pope John Paul II in October of 1995 in New York when the Internet potential was demonstrated to him at the United Nations Mission of the Church. Cardinal, then Archbishop, Renato Martino, 'Nuncio' to the United Nations, presented the Holy Father with a computer, and told him the machine, through the Internet, would be able to send his message anywhere he wanted.

The Pope asked, "Anywhere?"
The Archbishop answered "Yes, Holiness".
The Pope asked further, "Anytime?"
Again the Archbishop answered "Yes, Holiness."
Finally the Pope asked, "Anybody?"
The Archbishop smiled and said affirmatively. "Yes, Holiness."
The Pope beamed and said, "Good".

In summary:
The world is a small flat screen.
The world is made of silicon.
Globalization is a silicon screen.

The National Security Challenge: Fostering Economic Growth By Way Of Innovation

Eckert and Mauchly created a revolution that propelled this nation—and the world—forward over the past sixty-three years. We need more men and women like them to once again bring us out of the chaos into which our bureaucratic think –inside-the-box attitudes have led us.

But we also need a highly focused system of support that enables people of vision and drive to succeed. These people are America's best hope. To succeed, we must get back to the work of creating the proper support system for innovation, while we still have time.

We may or may not be at war with an evil empire like we confronted in 1942, but we certainly are in the midst of a war on terrorism. In fact, this war has introduced the concept of asymmetric combat- conflict without a pattern and without the normal concept of armies contending against each other. With the war on terrorism, military might is not as important as proper intelligence.

Intelligence has always been an important factor in warfare. The computer was certainly important in the Second World War when the British developed special purpose machines, labeled Colossus, and built one of them headquartered at Bletchley Park for the purpose of decoding the messages of the German communications. The Enigma Machine, which the British had captured from a sinking German U-Boat (submarine), was used to decode the messages of the Luftwaffe- the German Air Force. In the United States, the coded messages of the Japanese were regularly being decoded through the use of coding machines captured by the American Forces.

The National Security Agency- NSA- utilizes massive computer power to monitor communication traffic. This is augmented by recorded communication transmission with air crafted flight close to restricted borders, with tapping underwater cables using submarines, and with tunnels built close to communication exchanges. Furthermore, overhead satellites are also used for surveillance.

The gathering of intelligence has become very technology intensive, where all of this technology has the basic concept of a computer at its core. Hence, asymmetric warfare in the future, whether against terrorists or against a specific nation or group of nations, will depend heavily upon the intelligence gathered using technology. Such intelligence gathering capability will be increasingly augmented by a wide variety of new techniques and devices that will be used to expand human intelligence and analysis.

Historically, spying has been referred to as the Fifth Column. The concept of the Fifth Column originated during the Spanish Civil War (1936-39) with Nationalist General Emilio Mola who spoke of the Fifth Column- the spying- as being absolutely vital in assisting his Four Columns of fighting forces to conquer the enemy.

We are now confronted with a Sixth Column. The Sixth Column is Cyber Warfare. In popular fancy, this conjures visions of a "geek"- an introverted computer guru who spends his or her life at a computer terminal trying to penetrate the security wall of someone's system or database. Not quite true today! Now it is national teams of geeks.

The first elements of what we now call Cyber Warfare certainly existed when spies used induction coils in the '50s to steal the signals moving from a computer to a printer in order to penetrate military security. In the modern concept, nation states are engaged in concentrated and dedicated efforts to penetrate all aspects of life, and its support, in the infrastructure of a labeled "enemy". If the water supplies can be determined, if air traffic control can be disrupted, if none of the subways and trains can run, and if the financial institutions have their databases totally destroyed, then such a target can be controlled beyond the limits of what historically has been possible with troops. The concept of Cyber Warfare is to utilize the operational and informational networks of another nation in order to bring that nation to its knees in its ability to counterattack. Victory can be achieved, through this Sixth Column, without a single weapon being used, other than the weapon of electronics and software systems to penetrate and control other software systems.

Cyber Warfare can also be launched at the hardware interface. If a single nation can achieve domination of the making of chips, then it would be a simple matter for that nation to introduce a back door into such components that would allow it, when desired, to take over the electronic devices that control all manner of systems and machines in enemy locations. This could include military vehicles, aircraft, manufacturing facilities, finance, and also of a systems of everyday life now heavily dependent upon computer and computer-controlled devices.

The Sixth Column will spawn a significant industry globally in the development of techniques, systems, and hardware dedicated to the electronic control of other nations. An equal catalyst will be associated with developing the counter measures. That will be a significant arms race for the 21st Century.

There is no doubt that warfare henceforth will be asymmetric and will be heavily dependent upon cyber technology for both the offense and the defense. It is linked essentially for an increasing need for innovation and economic strength. In the future, the United States cannot afford to lose its leadership in all aspects of innovation, especially in the areas of software and hardware developments in Cybernetics. Furthermore, it is absolutely essential that the United States recapture its ascendency in the manufacture of chips, components, and devices utilized for its economic strength and security protection.

As a nation we are at a crossroads. Our economy, and that of the entire world, is in a shambles. People are comparing today's world to that of the Great Depression of the 1930s. That is one view. Another view, the one I personally prefer, is to compare ourselves to the world that existed after the Second World War, when many world economies were destroyed or non-existent, and untold cities lay in ruins.

In the 1930s we attempted to spend our way out of trouble. Stimulus packages were devised to put people back to work on government works programs. Bureaucracies were created that knew better than others how to solve the problem. The result was a continuing depression that lasted until the Second World War. While the message and rhetoric of the Roosevelt years were beacons of hope for the people, in reality the tax, spend, and protect policies of the administration did not completely succeed in restoring economic growth to the country. Initiative was stifled, and innovation was certainly not funded. The economy languished.

World War II is distinct from our own situation. Victory at any cost was the primary motivation. It was NOT billions in set-asides on an 825 billion dollar stimulus package. If you're going to stimulate the economy, then you cannot stifle it with pay-back and pork barrel politics. Tax and spend does not create success. The needs of warfare in 1941 swept away much of the stultifying impact of the blanket of bureaucracy created during the thirties. Innovation was sought, encouraged, and followed. True stimulus programs were enacted; lend-lease during the war, for example, and the Marshal Plan afterwards. The United States became the arsenal of democracy, with entirely new concepts of engineering and manufacturing replacing inefficient methods in shipbuilding, aircraft production, and research and development. The concepts of operations research came to the fore – the idea that a team of people with different disciplines could tackle problems – and solve them. Radar, jets, antibiotics, and atomic energy were born of this drive for innovation, investment, and the solution of problems by dedicated teams of people without bureaucratic blankets that may have protected but often smothered. This solution oriented approach led the United States Army Ballistics Research Laboratory to invest in a machine to calculate artillery trajectories. While this investment, of about $486,804 did not produce a solution during the war, it ushered in the innovation explosion that continued after that war, resulting in the greatest creation of wealth in history. That innovation was for the first general purpose electronic digital computer, the ENIAC – Electronic Numerical Integrator and Computer.

In World War Two, victory at any cost was the primary motivation. We need the same kind of approach now. Business as usual will take us further down the economic ladder.

Our current government must develop a conscious strategy to enable a Mauchly-type person to be able to achieve his dream - to predict the weather, even if it is supported by the need to calculate artillery trajectories. We have to get our minds outside the box.

I am reminded of the Chinese Proverb attributed to Lao Tzu :"Give a man a fish and you feed him for a day. Teach him how to fish and you feed him for a lifetime." Forty-five years ago, the US Peace Corps began sending mostly young idealistic Americans overseas with that concept in mind. In the super-competitive globalized world, the US must now apply such an approach to its own citizens if it hopes to succeed.

The financial meltdown of the present is a barometer what the future could bring. Success in countering this downturn can only come from creating jobs, igniting the spark of American ingenuity, and thinking outside the box. Social networking will certainly be a prime mover in such an endeavor. The last major worldwide economic meltdown was the Great Depression of the 1930s. despite all the government measures around the world, it was the Second World War from 1939-1945 that changed the economic climate. The impetus because of that war upon innovation led to the creation of the computer, jet travel, nuclear power, and all of the fallout from these tremendous inventions. It is from and with innovation that we can look to increase prosperity; and it is social networking to which we can look for the leadership in the implementation of the new inventions of the future. We can expect an economic renaissance- but only if we aim for it. There is an urgent need for a new ENIAC innovation. This, of course, will be centered as before around people, machines, and politics.

ENDNOTES

Foreword

[1] Santayana, George, (1863 – 1952), "Spanish-born US philosopher and poet, whose philosophical works include *The Life of Reason* (1905–6) and *The Realms of Being* (1927–40), which stresses the role of faith but asserts that scientific analysis should be the method of reasoning." The Canadian Oxford Dictionary. Oxford University Press, 2005.

[2] Smiley, Jane Graves (1949–), "U.S. writer. She wrote the award-winning novel *A Thousand Acres* (Pulitzer Prize, 1991), as well as *Moo* (1995), *The All-True Travels and Adventures of Lidie Newton* (1998), and *Horse Heaven* (2000)." The New Oxford American Dictionary, 2nd ed. Oxford University Press, 2005.

[3] Mauchly, John. See John Presper Eckert endnote below.

[4] Eckert, John Presper, Jr (1919 – 1995), "US electrical engineer, a pioneer in the development of the modern computer. Eckert was educated at the University of Pennsylvania, where in 1941 he joined the faculty. With the outbreak of World War II he was working on the calculation of ballistic tables for the US Army Ordnance Department. So complex and time-consuming were these calculations that Eckert and his colleague at Pennsylvania, J. W. Mauchly (1907 – 80), sought mechanical help. The result, completed in 1946 , was ENIAC (Electronic Numerical Integrator and Calculator), the world's first electronic computer. " Who's Who in the Twentieth Century. Oxford University Press, 1999.

[5] Atanasoff, John Vincent, (1904–1995), "American physicist and computer pioneer. Working with his assistant, Clifford Berry, Atanasoff built a prototype in 1939 of the suitably named ABC (Atanasoff-Berry Computer). Although the ABC was the first device to incorporate a number of key notions, it was unsatisfactory as a working machine. It was slow, could not be programmed, had to be controlled at all times, and suffered from a number of systematic errors." A Dictionary of Scientists. Oxford University Press, 1999.

[6] Turing, Alan Mathison, (1912–54), "English mathematician. He developed the concept of a theoretical computing machine, a key step in the development of the first computer, and carried out important code-breaking work in the Second World War. He also investigated

artificial intelligence." <u>The Oxford Dictionary of English, 2nd. ed. revised.</u> Oxford University Press, 2005.

[7] McLuhan, (Herbert) Marshall, (1911–80), "Canadian communications theorist. He is known for his theories on the role of the media and technology in society, claiming that the world had become a 'global village' in its electronic interdependence, and that 'the medium is the message', because it is the characteristics of a particular medium rather than the information it disseminates which influence and control society." The Canadian Oxford Dictionary.

Introductory

[8] "Morte d'Arthur." <u>English Poetry III: From Tennyson to Whitman.</u> 2008. <http://bartleby.com >.

[9] Greenspan, Alan. <u>The Age of Turbulence.</u> Penguin Press, 2007.

[10] Friedman, Thomas L. <u>The World Is Flat: A Brief History of the Twenty-first Century</u>. Farrar, Straus and Giroux, 2005.

[11] Berkeley, E.C. *Giant Brains or Machines That Think.* John Wiley & Sons, 1949.

[12] Press Release, War Department, Bureau of Public Relations. For Radio Broadcast. University of Pennsylvania Archives, February 15, 1946; Neukom, Hans, "The Second Life of ENIAC." *Annals of the History of Computing,* April-June (2006): 4.

[13] Toynbee, Arnold. <u>A Study of History.</u> 1934-61.

[14] Gargan, Edward T. "Toynbee Revisited: The Intent of Toynbee's History." <u>TIME</u> 12 May 1961.

[15] Taylor, Edmund, *Fall of the Dynasties: The Collapse of the Old Order 1905-1922* edited by John Gunther. London: Weidenfeld & Nicholson, 1963.

[16] McLuhan, Marshall H., *Understanding Media, the extensions of man*, critical edition, edited by W. Terrence Gordon. Gingko Press, 1964.

[17] See Einstein, Alfred, and Leopold Infeld. *The Evolution of Physics, From Early concepts to Relativity and Quanta.* New York: Simon and Shuster, 1967.

[18] Williams, Michael R. "FERUT Machine," *IEEE Annals of the History of Computing* Vol. 16 Issue 2 (1994): 12.

[19] McLuhan, Marshall H., <u>The Gutenberg Galaxy, The Making of Typographic Man.</u> 1962.

[20] Prestowitz, Clyde. <u>Three Billion New Capitalists: The Great Shift of Wealth and Power to the East</u>. Basic Books, 2005.

[21] Zakaria, Fareed. "How Long Will America Lead the World?." <u>Newsweek</u> 12 Jun 2006.

[22] <u>The Oxford Dictionary of Modern Quotations</u>. Oxford University Press, 2007.

[23] "Apple chief to grads: Glad I dropped out." <u>MSNBC: Technology and Science.</u> 13 Jun 2005. <http://msnbc.msn.com>.

[24] Stanford Report, "Steve Jobs' Stanford University Commencement Address." June 12, 2005.

[25] Kellogg, Steven. <u>Chicken Little.</u> Harper Trophy, 1987.

Chapter 1

[26] Galilei, Galileo, (1564 – 1642), "Italian astronomer and physicist. He discovered the constancy of a pendulum's swing, formulated the law of uniform acceleration of falling bodies, and described the parabolic trajectory of projectiles. He applied the telescope." <u>The Oxford Dictionary of English, 2nd. ed. revised</u>. Oxford University Press, 2005.

[27] Lister, Joseph, 1st Baron, (1827 – 1912), "English surgeon, inventor of antiseptic techniques in surgery. He realized the significance of Louis Pasteur's germ theory in connection with sepsis and in 1865 he used carbolic acid dressings on patients who had undergone surgery." <u>The Oxford Dictionary of English, 2nd. ed. revised</u>. Oxford University Press, 2005.

[28] Weik, Martin. "The ENIAC Story." <u>O R D N A N C E: The Journal of the American Ordnance Association</u> (1961).

[29] Mauchly, Kathleen R. <u>John Mauchly's Early Years</u>. American Federation of information Processing Societies, Inc., 1984.

[30] Weik, Martin. "The ENIAC Story." <u>O R D N A N C E: The Journal of the American Ordnance Association</u> (1961).

[31] ARPANET- "a network of computers, organized in 1960 s by the Department of Defense that linked U.S. scientific and academic researchers. It was the forerunner of today's Internet." <u>The Oxford Essential Dictionary of the U.S. Military.</u> Oxford University Press.

[32] The Revolution of Rising Expectations- "phrase coined, 1950; Arthur Schlesinger *A Thousand Days* (1965) ch. 16." <u>The Concise Oxford Dictionary of Quotations.</u>

[33] Toffler, Alvin, and Heidi Toffler. <u>Revolutionary Wealth: How it will be created and how it will change our lives</u>. New York: Alfred A. Knopf, Inc, 2007.

[34] Moore's Law- "an observation and prediction originally made in 1965 by Gordon Earle *Moore* (1929–), US microchip manufacturer, stating that a new type of microprocessor chip is released every 12 to 24 months, with each new version having approximately twice as many logical elements as its predecessor, and that this trend is likely to continue." The Oxford Dictionary of Phrase and Fable. Oxford University Press, 2006.

[35] Cyber Age- "relating to or characteristic of the culture of computers, information technology, and virtual reality." <u>The Oxford Dictionary of English, 2nd. ed. revised</u>.

[36] Santayana, George, (1863 – 1952), "Spanish-born US philosopher and poet, whose philosophical works include *The Life of Reason* (1905–6) and *The Realms of Being* (1927–40), which stresses the role of faith but asserts that scientific analysis should be the method of reasoning." The Canadian Oxford Dictionary. Oxford University Press, 2005.

[37] Crosland, Alan. <u>The Jazz Singer.</u> Warner Brothers. , 1929.

[38] Goldstine, Herman H. <u>The Computer from Pascal to von Neumann, Princeton.</u> Princeton: Princeton University Press, 1972.

[39] Augarten, Stan. <u>Bit by Bit An Illustrated history of Computers</u>. New York: Houghton Mifflin, 1984.

[40] Machiavelli, Nicolo. <u>The Prince</u>. 1515.

[41] Cyberspace- "An informal word first thought to have been used by the novelist William Gibson to refer to the total data on all the computers on all the networks in the world. The word has passed into common use as a way of referring to any large collection of network-accessible computer-based data." <u>A Dictionary of the Internet.</u> Oxford University Press. 2003.

[42] Nano- "(symbol: n) A prefix to a unit, indicating a sub multiple of one billionth, 10^{-9}, of that unit, as in nanosecond." <u>Dictionary of Computing, John Daintith ed.</u> Oxford University Press. 2004.

[43] "Are Government Bailouts Bad Business?" <u>Knowledge at Wharton.</u> 10 Oct 2001. University of Pennsylvania.

[44] Bennett, Dr. William J. <u>The Book of Virtues.</u> New York: Simon and Shuster, 1996.

[45] Bennett, Dr. William J. <u>The Death of Outrage: Bill Clinton and the Assault on American Ideals</u>. New York: Simon and Shuster, 1998.

[46] Shakespeare, William. <u>Julius Caesar.</u> 1599.

[47] Anaximander, (*c.*610–*c.*545 BC), "Greek scientist, who lived at Miletus. He believed the earth to be cylindrical and poised in space, and is reputed to have taught that life began in water and that humans originated from fish." The Oxford Dictionary of English, 2nd. ed. revised. Oxford University Press, 2005.

[48] Archimedes, (*c.*287–212 BC), "Greek mathematician, and inventor from Syracuse. He discovered the ratio of the radius of a circle to its circumference, and formulas for the surface area and volume of a sphere and of a cylinder." The Oxford Dictionary of English, 2nd. ed. Revised. Oxford University Press, 2005.

[49] Abacus- "a simple device for calculating, consisting of a frame with rows of wires or grooves along which beads are slid." The Oxford Dictionary of English, 2nd. ed. revised. Oxford University Press, 2005.

[50] Napier, John, (1550–1617), "Mathematician. Napier invented logarithms, greatly simplifying
calculations involving multiplying and dividing. As Kepler put it, he doubled the life of astronomers (by halving the time they took number☐crunching). Educated in France and then at St Andrews, he published his *Mirifici logarithmorum canonis descriptio* in 1614, with tables and explanations. In 1617, he published *Rabdologia*, describing 'Napier's bones', or rods calibrated logarithmically; as developed into the slide rule." A Dictionary of British History, John Cannon, ed. Oxford University Press. 2001.

[51] Oughtred, William, (1575–1660), "English mathematician. A number of mathematical symbols that are still used were first introduced by Oughtred. Among these were the sign '×' for multiplication, and the 'sin' and 'cos' notation for trigonometrical functions. Oughtred also invented the earliest form of the slide rule in 1622 but only published this discovery in 1632." A Dictionary of Scientists. Oxford University Press. 1999.

[52] von Leibniz, Gottfried Wilhelm, (1646–1716), "German rationalist philosopher, mathematician, and logician. He argued that the world is composed of single units (monads), each of which is self-contained but acts in harmony with every other, as ordained by God, and so this world is the best of all possible worlds. Leibniz also made the important distinction between necessary and contingent truths and devised a method of calculus independently of Newton." The Oxford Dictionary of English, 2nd. ed. revised.

[53] Babbage, Charles, (1791–1871), "English mathematician, inventor, and pioneer of machine computing. He designed a mechanical computer with Ada Lovelace but was unable to complete it in his lifetime." The Oxford Dictionary of English, 2nd. ed. revised. Oxford University Press, 2005.

[54] Jacquard's Punch Card- "A rectangular paper card into which data could be encoded by punching patterns of holes. The holes were then sensed by a *punched card reader*, which converted the punched patterns into binary code. Punched cards were used extensively for input, output, and file storage of data on early computer systems but are now obsolete. Stout

cards with holes punched in them were used by Jacquard to control the weaving of patterns on a loom in about 1800." <u>A Dictionary of Computing.</u> Oxford University Press. 2004.

[55] Lovelace, Ada, (1815–52), "English mathematician. The daughter of Lord Byron, she became assistant to Charles Babbage and worked with him on his mechanical computer." <u>The Oxford Dictionary of English, 2nd. ed. revised.</u> Oxford University Press, 2005.

[56] Bernoulli numbers- "Title used for the 'law of large numbers' in probability theory, proved by Jakob Bernoulli (1654–1705). The theorem provides the best-known link between probability and the frequency of occurrence of events in a sequence of trials. It is thus fundamental to the epistemology of probability." <u>The Oxford Dictionary of Philosophy.</u> Oxford University Press, 1996.

[57] Encryption- "converts (information or data) into a code, especially to prevent unauthorized access." <u>The Oxford Dictionary of English, 2nd. ed. revised.</u>

[58] Analog- "A computer that performs computations (such as summation, multiplication, integration, and other operations) by manipulating continuous physical variables that are analogs of the quantities being subjected to computation. The most commonly used physical variables are voltage and time. Some analog computers use mechanical components: the physical variables become, for example, angular rotations and linear displacements." <u>A Dictionary of Computing.</u> Oxford University Press. 2004.

[59] Ritchie, David. <u>The Computer Pioneers.</u> New York: Simon and Shuster, 1986.

[60] Bush, Dr. Vannevar, (1890–1974), "science administrator and engineer, born in Everett, Massachusetts. Bush was the chair of the National Research Council's Division of Engineering and Industrial Research (1936–40) and the chief adviser to President Franklin D. Roosevelt on military technology. As the director of the Office of Scientific Research and Development, Bush coordinated civilian research on military projects and oversaw the Manhattan Project and the development of many kinds of military technology, including radar and the proximity fuse." <u>The Oxford Essential Dictionary of the U.S. Military.</u>

[61] Electronic- "(as opposed to *electric*). Originally, concerned with the movement of electrons in free space, i.e. in vacuum tubes (UK: valves). Then, by extension, concerned with the movement of charges in semiconductors. Now, by extension, concerned with the representation, storage, and transmission of information by electrical means. That is now what distinguishes electronic engineering from electrical engineering, the latter dealing with energy rather than with information. A further distinguishing feature is that electronic engineering mainly deals with low power levels and frequencies of anywhere between zero and microwaves, while electrical engineering tends to focus on low frequency (50–60 Hz) high power (kilowatts to megawatts). Clearly there will be a gray area where the disciplines overlap." <u>A Dictionary of Computing.</u> Oxford University Press. 2004.

[62] Binary Code- "A code whose alphabet is restricted to {0, 1}." <u>A Dictionary of Computing.</u> Oxford University Press. 2004.

Chapter 2

[63] Global village- "the world considered as a single community linked by telecommunications." The Oxford Dictionary of English, 2nd. ed. Revised. Oxford University Press, 2005.

[64] Bletchley Park- "Victorian mansion situated 80 km. (50 mi.) north-west of London. Known as Station X, from 1939 it was the site of the British Government Code and Cypher School (Government Communications HQ from 1942). This had been formed in 1919, from the cryptanalytical sections of the Admiralty (Room 40 O.B.) and the War Office, 'to advise as to the security of codes and cyphers used by all Government departments and to assist in their provision', but it was also secretly ordered to 'study the methods of cypher communications used by foreign powers'. This meant that its staff worked to break those ciphers and it was, in fact, not a school at all but a highly secret organization which came under the aegis of the head of MI6." The Oxford Companion to World War II. Oxford University Press, 2001.

[65] Jonas Salk: Developer of first successful vaccine against poliomyelitis. Salk, Darrell. Jonas Salk Center. 2005. 3 Dec. 2009. http://www.jonas-salk.org

[66] Charles Lindberg: American Aviator, made first solo non-stop flight across Atlantic Ocean in 1927. Charles Lindbergh. 2007. The Spirit of St. Louis Project. 3 Dec. 2009. http://www.charleslindbergh.com/history/index.asp.

[67] David Sarnoff: Radio and Television Pioneer, head of RCA. The Museum of Broadcast Communications. 2008. 3 Dec. 2009. http://www.museum.tv/eo.tvsection.php?entrrycode=sarnoffdavi.

[68] Venter, Craig, "a specialist in gene sequencing at NIH. Profit-making competition entered genomics in 1992 when Craig Venter, a specialist in gene sequencing at NIH, left to head a new private center called The Institute for Genomic Research (TIGR). Although TIGR would be nonprofit, it was funded by a venture capital group that established Human Genome Sciences Inc. to develop and market products resulting from TIGR's research. Venter predicted that TIGR would track down one thousand genes daily and would identify the majority of human genes within three to five years. In 1998, Venter moved to a new, for-profit company called Celera that aimed to sequence the entire human genome by 2001 using rapid new automated machines supplied by its principal owner, the Perkins-Elmer Corporation. Goaded by Celera, the NIH genome center picked up its sequencing pace. In June 2000, at a White House ceremony presided over by President Bill Clinton, Venter and Francis Collins, the head of the NIH project, announced that they had both completed a full draft of the human genome." The Oxford Companion to the History of Modern Science.

[69] McLuhan, (Herbert) Marshall, (1911–80), "Canadian communications theorist. He is known for his theories on the role of the media and technology in society, claiming that the world had become a 'global village' in its electronic interdependence, and that 'the medium is the message', because it is the characteristics of a particular medium rather than the information it disseminates which influence and control society." The Canadian Oxford Dictionary.

[70] Atanasoff, John Vincent, (1904–1995), "American physicist and computer pioneer. Working with his assistant, Clifford Berry, Atanasoff built a prototype in 1939 of the suitably named ABC (Atanasoff-Berry Computer). Although the ABC was the first device to incorporate a number of key notions, it was unsatisfactory as a working machine. It was slow, could not be programmed, had to be controlled at all times, and suffered from a number of systematic errors." A Dictionary of Scientists. Oxford University Press, 1999.

[71] Prototype- "a first or preliminary version of a device or vehicle from which other forms are developed." The Oxford Dictionary of English, 2nd. ed. revised. Oxford University Press, 2005.

[72] Newton, Sir Isaac, (1642–1727), "English mathematician and physicist, considered the greatest single influence on theoretical physics until Einstein. (In his Principia Mathematical (1687), Newton gave a mathematical description of the laws of mechanics and gravitation, and applied these to planetary motion. Opticks (1704) records his optical experiments and theories, including the discovery that white light is made up of a mixture of colors. His work in mathematics included the binomial theorem and differential calculus.)" The Oxford Dictionary of English, 2nd. ed. Revised. Oxford University Press, 2005.

[73] Ohio History Central. 2009 Ohio Historical Society.
<http://www.ohiohistorycentral.org/entry.php?rec=2657>

[74] Martino, Rocco. "John William Mauchly—The Brain Behind the Giant Brain: Part 1". The Bulletin. 24 Mar. 2009: Page 2.

[75] Augarten, Stan. Bit by Bit an Illustrate History of Computers. New York: Stan Augarten, 1984.

[76] Albert Einstein, "After a certain high level of technical skill is achieved, science and art tend to coalesce in esthetics, plasticity, and form. The greatest scientists are artists as well." Johnstone, Gary. "The Producer's Story: Why Einstein was like Picasso". Einstein's Big Idea. June 2005. PBS Online. 7 Sept. 2009.
<http://www.pbs.org/wgbh/nova/einstein/producer.html>

[77] Mauchly, Kathleen R. John Mauchly's Early Years. American Federation of information Processing Societies, Inc., 1984.

[78] Copeland, BJ. "The Modern History of Computing". Stanford Encyclopedia of Philosophy. (2006).

[79] McCartney, Scott. ENIAC The Triumphs and Tragedies of the World's First Computer. New York: Walker Publishing Company, 1999.

[80] Young, Jeffery. Forbes Greatest Technology Stories: Inspiring Tales of the Entrepreneurs and Inventors Who Revolutionized Modern Business. New York: John Wiley & Sons, 1998.

[81] McCartney, Scott. ENIAC The Triumphs and Tragedies of the World's First Computer. New York: Walker Publishing Company, 1999.

[82] Meyerson, Martin. Gladly Learn and Gladly Teach. Camden, NJ: University of Pennsylvania Press, 1978.

[83] McCartney, Scott. ENIAC The Triumphs and Tragedies of the World's First Computer. New York: Walker Publishing Company, 1999.

[84] McCartney, Scott. ENIAC The Triumphs and Tragedies of the World's First Computer. New York: Walker Publishing Company, 1999.

[85] Allison, David. "Transcript of an Interview with J. Presper Eckert, Chief Engineer, ENIAC Computer." Smithsonian Institution Archives. 1988.

[86] McCartney, Scott. ENIAC The Triumphs and Tragedies of the World's First Computer. New York: Walker Publishing Company, 1999.

[87] Augarten, Stan. Bit by Bit an Illustrate History of Computers. New York: Stan Augarten, 1984.

[88] McCartney, Scott. ENIAC The Triumphs and Tragedies of the World's First Computer. New York: Walker Publishing Company, 1999.

[89] Keiger, Dale. "The Story that Doesn't Compute". Johns Hopkins Magazine. Nov 1999.

[90] Keiger, Dale. "The Story That Doesn't Compute." Johns Hopkins Magazine Nov 1999.

[91] Goldstine, Herman H. The Computer from Pascal to von Neumann. Princeton: Princeton University Press, 1972.

[92] Riley, Norton H. The von Neumann Architecture of Computer Systems. CA: California State Polytechnic University, 2005.

[93] Turing, Alan Mathison, (1912–54), "English mathematician. He developed the concept of a theoretical computing machine, a key step in the development of the first computer, and carried out important code-breaking work in the Second World War. He also investigated artificial intelligence." The Oxford Dictionary of English, 2nd. ed. revised. Oxford University Press, 2005.

94 Colossus- "An electronic special-purpose digital "computer" that was built in great secrecy by the Post Office Research Station in London and began useful work at the government establishment at Bletchley Park, Buckinghamshire, in late 1943. It contained 1500 vacuum tubes (valves) and could operate at high speed. The strategy or "program" was controlled from patchboards and switches. The faster Mark II machines, operating by mid-1944, contained 2500 tubes. Both versions were used for code-breaking purposes during World War II." A Dictionary of Computing. Oxford University Press, 2004.

95 Fritz, Barkley W. ENIAC-A Problem Solver. Virginia Tech: Blackbird, 1994.

96 Fritz, Barkley W. ENIAC-A Problem Solver. Virginia Tech: Blackbird, 1994.

97 Weik, Martin. "The ENIAC Story." O R D N A N C E: The Journal of the American Ordnance Association (1961).

98 Transcript 5, Rocco Leonard Martino Interview with Jean Jennings Bartik, Chestnut Hill College, 2005, p.16-17.

99 Transcript 5, Rocco Leonard Martino Interview with Jean Jennings Bartik, Chestnut Hill College, 2005, p.11.

100 Infield, Tom. "Faster Than a Speeding Bullet." Philadelphia Inquirer 1996.

101 McCartney, Scott. ENIAC the Triumphs and Tragedies of the World's First Computer. New York: Walker Publishing Company, 1999.

102 Neumann, John von, (1903–57), "Hungarian-born American mathematician and computer pioneer. His contributions ranged from pure logic and set theory to the most practical areas of application. He analyzed the mathematics of quantum mechanics, founding a new area of mathematical research (algebras of operators in Hilbert space), and also established the mathematical theory of games. Neumann also helped to develop the US hydrogen bomb, but perhaps his most influential contribution was in the design and operation of electronic computers." The New Zealand Oxford Dictionary.

103 Neumann, John von. "First Draft of a Report on the EDVAC." IEEE Annals of the History of Computing 15(1993): 27-43.

104 McCartney, Scott. ENIAC the Triumphs and Tragedies of the World's First Computer. New York: Walker Publishing Company, 1999.

105 McCartney, Scott. ENIAC the Triumphs and Tragedies of the World's First Computer. New York: Walker Publishing Company, 1999.

106 McCartney, Scott. ENIAC: The Triumphs and Tragedies of the World's First Computer. New York: Walker & Company, 1999.

[107] McCartney, Scott. ENIAC the Triumphs and Tragedies of the World's First Computer. New York: Walker Publishing Company, 1999.

[108] McCartney, Scott. ENIAC the Triumphs and Tragedies of the World's First Computer. New York: Walker Publishing Company, 1999.

[109] Guide to the ENIAC Trial Exhibits Master Collection. PA: University Archives and Records Center. University of Pennsylvania, 1864-1973.

[110] Rheingold, Howard. Tools for Thought. 1985.

[111] "Society for Industrial and Applied Mathematics." SIAM NEWS 38 (1999): 4.

[112] "Society for Industrial and Applied Mathematics." SIAM NEWS 38 (1999): 4.

[113] Ritchie, David. The Computer Pioneers: The Making of the Modern Computer. New York: Simon & Schuster, 1986.

[114] Ritchie, David. The Computer Pioneers: The Making of the Modern Computer. New York: Simon & Schuster, 1986.

[115] Fritz, Barkley W. ENIAC-A Problem Solver. Virginia Tech: Blackbird, 1994.

[116] EDVAC- "Acronym for *Electronic Discrete Variable Automatic Computer*. An early stored-program electronic digital computer, originally commissioned from the University of Pennsylvania's Moore School by the US Army in 1944 while the ENIAC was still under construction, but not operational until 1952. In 1945 John von Neumann prepared a proposal for the EDVAC that described the logical design of a computer with a "stored program", where the instructions to the machine would be stored in substantially the same fashion as the data. Although there is some disagreement as to whether von Neumann or the team of Mauchly and Eckert originated the stored-program concept, this was its first written documentation. Regardless of its origin, the stored-program model that formed the basis of the EDVAC design motivated all subsequent machine designs." A Dictionary of Computing. Oxford University Press. 2004.

UNIVAC- "Short *for Universal Automatic Computer* The US's first commercially available computer system, delivered in 1951 slightly later than the Ferranti Mark I. Its memory was in the form of mercury delay lines. It was the product of the Eckert–Mauchly Computer Corporation, formed in 1948 by the designers of ENIAC. From 1951 through the mid-1950s over 40 machines were produced. The company was acquired by Remington–Rand Inc., which merged with Sperry Corporation in 1955 to form Sperry Rand Corp. Sperry later merged with Burroughs Corp. to form Unisys." A Dictionary of Computing. Oxford University Press, 2004.

[117] Fritz, Barkley W. ENIAC-A Problem Solver. Virginia Tech: Blackbird, 1994.

[118] Goldstine, Herman H. <u>The Computer from Pascal to von Neumann.</u> Princeton: Princeton University Press, 1972.

[119] Goldstine, Herman H. <u>The Computer from Pascal to von Neumann.</u> Princeton: Princeton University Press, 1972.

[120] Goldstine, Herman H. <u>The Computer from Pascal to von Neumann.</u> Princeton: Princeton University Press, 1972.

[121] McCartney, Scott. <u>ENIAC the Triumphs and Tragedies of the World's First Computer.</u> New York: Walker Publishing Company, 1999.

[122] Goldstine, Herman H. <u>The Computer from Pascal to von Neumann,</u> Princeton: Princeton University Press, 1972.

[123] McCartney, Scott. <u>ENIAC the Triumphs and Tragedies of the World's First Computer.</u> New York: Walker Publishing Company, 1999.

[124] Goldstine, Herman H. <u>The Computer from Pascal to von Neumann.</u> Princeton: Princeton University Press, 1972.

[125] Goldstine, Herman H. <u>The Computer from Pascal to von Neumann.</u> Princeton: Princeton University Press, 1972.

[126] Transcript, Rocco Leonard Martino Interview with Kay Mauchly Antonelli, Chestnut Hill College, 2005.

[127] Ritchie, David. <u>The Computer Pioneers.</u> New York: Simon and Shuster, 1986.

[128] Transcript, Rocco Leonard Martino Interview with Kay Mauchly Antonelli, Chestnut Hill College, 2005.

[129] Ames Laboratory, <u>The Trial: Atanasoff-Berry Computer.</u> Scalable Computing Laboratory, 2005.

[130] "10th Anniversary of the Eckert Research International Corporation (ERIC)." <u>Presper Eckert's Speech</u> (April 15, 1991).

[131] Riley, Norton H. <u>The von Neumann Architecture of Computer Systems.</u> CA: California State Polytechnic University, 2005.

[132] Cortada, James W. "The ENIAC's Influence on Business Computing, 1940s—1950s." <u>IEEE Annals of the History of Computing</u> 28(2006): 26-29.

Chapter 3

[133] Troop, Henry S. "Grace Murray Hopper". <u>Encyclopedia of Computer Science. 4th Edition. 2003.</u>

[134] Troop, Henry S. "Grace Murray Hopper". Encyclopedia of Computer Science, 4th Edition. 2003.

[135] Rajaraman, V. "Grace Murray Hopper—Programming Pioneer". <u>Resonance Journal.</u> 6, 2 (2001): 2-3

[136] Transcode: The process of converting from one format to another, "Transcode" <u>PCMag.com Encyclopedia.</u> 1981-2009.

[137] Gates, Bill. "A Robot in Every Home". <u>Scientific American Magazine.</u> January 2007.

[138] Transcript, Rocco Leonard Martino Interview with Kay Mauchly Antonelli, Chestnut Hill College, 2005.

[139] <u>The Computers: The Untold Story of the Remarkable Women Who Programmed the ENIAC.</u> 2001.

[140] Differential Analyzer: A mechanical analog computer. It was crafted to solve differential equations. The Bush Differential Analyzer was developed in 1927 at MIT by Vannevar Bush. It was the first practical version constructed of the original. Holst PA (Oct-Dec1996). "Svein Rosseland and the Oslo Analyzer" <u>IEEE Annals of Computing.</u> 18 (4): 16026.

[141] Transcript, Rocco Leonard Martino Interview with Kay Mauchly Antonelli, Chestnut Hill College, 2005.

[142] Martin, Dr. C. Dianne. "ENIAC: Press Conference That Shook the World". <u>IEEE Technology and Society Magazine. Dec. 1995.</u>

[143] Michael, Katina. "The Automatic Identification Trajectory." <u>Faculty of Informatics-Papers.</u> (2003).

[144] C-10 Instruction code allowed the new UNIVAC machine to be controlled by keyboard commands instead of dials and switches which were the status quo of the time. Gurer, Denise. "Women in Computing History". <u>ACM SIGCSE Bulletin.</u> 34, 2 (June 2002): 116-120.

[145] As found in the New York Times obituary of Betty Holberten. Lohr, Steve. "Frances E. Holberten, 84, Early Computer Programmer." <u>New York Times.</u> 17 Dec. 2001: F5

Chapter 4

[146] "10th Anniversary of the Eckert Research International Corporation (ERIC)." <u>Presper Eckert's Speech</u> (April 15, 1991).

[147] See Chapter Five for a listing of those who attended the Moore School Lectures.

[148] Fritz, Barkley W. <u>ENIAC-A Problem Solver.</u> Virginia Tech: Blackbird, 1994.

[149] Fritz, Barkley W. <u>ENIAC-A Problem Solver.</u> Virginia Tech: Blackbird, 1994.

[150] Hans Neukom. "The Second Life of ENIAC." <u>IEEE Annals of the History of Computing</u> <u>28</u> (2006):
4-16.

[151] Goldstine, Herman H. <u>The Computer from Pascal to von Neumann.</u> Princeton: Princeton University Press, 1972.

[152] Augarten, Stan. <u>Bit by Bit an Illustrate History of Computers</u>. New York: Stan Augarten, 1984.

[153] Augarten, Stan. <u>Bit by Bit an Illustrate History of Computers</u>. New York: Stan Augarten, 1984.

[154] Augarten, Stan. <u>Bit by Bit an Illustrate History of Computers</u>. New York: Stan Augarten, 1984.

[155] Stern, Nancy. "The BINAC: A Case Study in the History of Computing." <u>IEEE Annals of the History of Computing</u> 1 (1979): 14-15.

[156] Stern, Nancy. "The BINAC: A Case Study in the History of Computing." <u>IEEE Annals of the History of Computing</u> 1 (1979): 14-15.

[157] Augarten, Stan. <u>Bit by Bit an Illustrate History of Computers</u>. New York: Stan Augarten, 1984.

Chapter 5

[158] Napper, Brian. "Introduction to the Mark 1." <u>Mark I Story.</u> Nov 2003. The University of Manchester. <http://www.computer50.org>.

[159] Napper, Brian. "Ferranti Mark I." <u>Mark I Story.</u> Nov 2003. The University of Manchester. <http://www.computer50.org>.

[160] Napper, Brian. "The Baby." <u>Mark I Story.</u> Apr 1999. The University of Manchester. <http://www.computer50.org>.

[161] Goldstine, Herman H. <u>The Computer from Pascal to von Neumann.</u> Princeton: Princeton University Press, 1972.

[162] Goldstine, Herman H. <u>The Computer from Pascal to von Neumann.</u> Princeton: Princeton University Press, 1972.

Chapter 6

[163] Battle of Britain; "a series of air battles fought over Britain during August–October 1940, in which the RAF successfully resisted raids by the numerically superior German air force. This led Hitler to abandon plans to invade Britain, although the Germans continued to bomb British cities by night for several months afterwards." <u>The Oxford Dictionary of English, 2nd. ed. revised.</u> Oxford University Press, 2005.

[164] Axel Wennergren- a Swedish industrialist who supported Hitler during the Second World War.

[165] John Diebold- inventor of the fax machine. He wrote a book entitled "Automation" which described the automatic production cycles in the automotive industry. Diebold, J. (1952). *Automation.* New York: American Management Association.

[166] Fletcher Jones- Found a Computer Sciences Corp (CSC) in Redondo Beach, California in the 1950s. He obtained a Ph.D. and was often referred to as "Gregory Peck with a Ph.D."

[167] Peck, (Eldred) Gregory, (1916–2003), "American actor. His many films range from the thriller *Spellbound* (1945) to the western *The Big Country* (1958); he won an Oscar for his role in *To Kill a Mockingbird* (1962)." <u>The Oxford Dictionary of English, 2nd. ed. revised</u>. Oxford University Press, 2005.

[168] BMEWS- " *abbr.* Ballistic Missile Early Warning System, the first operational missile detection radar system, designed to provide immediate, long-range warning of a missile attack over the polar region, established in the late 1950s. Part of the North American Aerospace Defense Command (NORAD) created in 1957 and 1958, BMEWS sites were established at Thule Air Base, Greenland, and Clear Air Force Station, Alaska, and in 1958 and 1960 at the Royal Air Force Station at Fylingdales-Moor in the United Kingdom." <u>The Oxford Essential Dictionary of the U.S. Military.</u> Oxford University Press.

[169] Gyrocompass- "*noun:* a non-magnetic compass in which the direction of true north is maintained by a continuously driven gyroscope whose axis is parallel to the earth's axis of rotation." <u>The Oxford Dictionary of English, 2nd. ed. revised</u>. Oxford University Press, 2005.

[170] Parallel processing- "A term applied rather loosely to a number of rather similar concepts but with important detailed differences. The essence of parallel processing is that more than one particular <u>process</u> is active at any given instant; however the term is often applied to a situation in which a large number of processes are potentially active but at any one instant

only one is active. Strictly speaking the term parallel processing should only be applied where more than one processor is active among a group of processes at any one instant. In practice it is seldom used with this accurate connotation." A Dictionary of Computing. Oxford University Press, 2004.

[171] PERT-"Abbrev. *For performance evaluation and review techniques.* Management techniques for planning, scheduling, and controlling projects. Dependencies are drawn as directed graphs to show the logical sequence of activities that must occur before a project can be completed." A Dictionary of Computing. Oxford University Press, 2004.

[172] Gantt chart- "*noun*: a chart in which a series of horizontal lines shows the amount of work done or production completed in certain periods of time in relation to the amount planned for those periods." The Oxford Dictionary of English, 2nd. ed. revised. Oxford University Press, 2005.

[173] Automatic programming- "the use of a high-level programming language." A Dictionary of Computing. Oxford University Press.

[174] Hally, Mike. Electronic Brains. Granta Books, 2005.

[175] Hally, Mike. Electronic Brains. Granta Books, 2005.

[176] Sherman Anti-Trust Act- "a product of countervailing market and political pressures. Section 1 of the Sherman Act banned "[e]very contract, combination or conspiracy" that restrained interstate or foreign trade of commerce; Section 2 prohibited individual firms from monopolization and attempted monopolization. The act's enforcement relied upon the state and federal courts. Federal or state prosecutors, as well as private litigants, could win treble damages by proving violations of the law." The Oxford Companion to United States History. Oxford University Press, 2001.

[177] Black, Edwin. IBM and the Holocaust: The Strategic Alliance Between Nazi Germany and America's Most Powerful Corporation. Three Rivers Press, 2002.

[178] Hally, Mike. Electronic Brains. Granta Books, 2005.

[179] Although this is a rumor, there was continual monitoring of the account by IBM executives since this was the standard practice on all IBM accounts to maintain close relationships and close control of all activity in those accounts.

Chapter 7

[180] Guide to the ENIAC Trial Exhibits Master Collection. PA: University Archives and Records Center. University of Pennsylvania, 1864-1973.

[181] Those 11 witnesses were Coleman, Legvold, Buchanan, Atanasoff, Murphy, Carr, Lura Atanasoff, Albert Davis, Richards, Rose, and Winsor.

[182] Moores, Calvin N. "Atanasoff at the Naval Ordnance Laboratory." IEEE Annals of The History of Computing 12(1993).

[183] Moores, Calvin N. "Atanasoff at the Naval Ordnance Laboratory." IEEE Annals of The History of Computing 12(1993).

[184] Burks, Alice Rowe. Who Invented the Computer? The Legal Battle That Changed Computing History. Prometheus Books, 2003.

[185] Rosen, Sauil. The Origins of Modern Computing. Indiana: Purdue University Press, 1990.

[186] Burks, Alice Rowe. Who Invented the Computer? The Legal Battle That Changed Computing History. Prometheus Books, 2003.

[187] Moores, Calvin N. "Atanasoff at the Naval Ordnance Laboratory." IEEE Annals of The History of Computing 12(1993).

[188] "10th Anniversary of the Eckert Research International Corporation (ERIC)." Presper Eckert's Speech (April 15, 1991).

[189] Rocco Leonard Martino Phone Conversation with Stanley Green, December 18, 2007. Noon.

[190] Minneapolis Star Tribune 08 Nov 2007.

[191] Rocco Leonard Martino Phone Conversation with Stanley Green, December 18, 2007. Noon.

[192] McCartney, Scott. ENIAC the Triumphs and Tragedies of the World's First Computer. New York: Walker Publishing Company, 1999.

Chapter 8

[193] Toynbee, Arnold (Joseph), (1889–1975), "English historian. He is best known for his twelve-volume *Study of History* (1934–61), in which he traced the pattern of growth, maturity, and decay of different civilizations." The Oxford Dictionary of English, 2nd. ed. revised. Oxford University Press, 2005.

[194] Kidder, Tracy. The Soul of a New Machine. Back Bay Books, 2000.

[195] Noyce, Robert Norton, (1927–1990), "American physicist. The first major success was the integrated circuit, the foundation of the modern electronics industry. Noyce filed his patent in April 1959, some six weeks after a similar patent had been filed by Jack Kilby at

Texas Instruments. Whereas Kilby's circuit had used the silicon mesa transistor, Noyce opted for a planar model. Unlike the mesa, Noyce's model had no raised parts to attract contaminants and was more easily protected by a layer of silicon dioxide. Parts were no longer connected by wires but by evaporating the aluminum wires onto the insulating surface. As an extra bonus it also proved much easier to mass-produce planar transistors." A Dictionary of Scientists. Oxford University Press. 1999.

[196] Moore, Gordon Earle, (1929–), "US microchip manufacturer, stating that a new type of microprocessor chip is released every 12 to 24 months, with each new version having approximately twice as many logical elements as its predecessor, and that this trend is likely to continue." The Oxford Dictionary of Phrase and Fable. Oxford University Press, 2006.

[197] Wang, An, (1920–90), "U.S. computer engineer; born in China. In 1948, he invented a magnetic core memory for computers. The founder of Wang Laboratories in 1951, he held 40 patents." The New Oxford American Dictionary. Oxford University Press, 2005.

[198] Kemeny, John George, (1926–1992), "Hungarian–American mathematician. Between 1963 and 1964 Kemeny, working with a Dartmouth colleague, Thomas Kurtz, developed BASIC (Beginner's All Purpose Symbolic Instruction Code), probably the best known of all computer languages. Previously the large computers could only be approached through specialized computer programmers. BASIC was conceived initially as something for Dartmouth students to use on Dartmouth computers. With a few simple self-evident commands and an equally simple syntax and vocabulary, it proved remarkably easy to use." A Dictionary of Scientists. Oxford University Press. 1999.

[199] Feynman, Richard Phillips, (1918–88), "American theoretical physicist, noted for his work on quantum electrodynamics. Nobel Prize for Physics (1965)." The Oxford Dictionary of English, 2nd. ed. revised. Oxford University Press, 2005.

[200] Apollo program- "US space exploration project to land men on the Moon. Initiated in May 1961 by President John Kennedy, it achieved its objective on July 20, 1969, when Neil Armstrong set foot on the Moon. The project terminated with the successful Apollo-Soyuz linkup in space during July 1975. It placed more than 30 astronauts in space and 12 on the Moon." World Encyclopedia. Oxford University Press.

[201] Gates, Bill, (b.1955), "American computer entrepreneur; full name William Henry Gates. He co-founded the computer software company Microsoft and became the youngest multi-billionaire in American history." The Oxford Dictionary of English, 2nd. ed. revised. Oxford University Press, 2005.

[202] Gerstner, Louis V. Who Says Elephants Can't Dance?. Collins Business, 2003.

[203] Social networking- "the use of dedicated websites and applications to communicate with other users, or to find people with similar interests to one's own." The Oxford Dictionary of English.Oxford University Press, 2010.

Chapter 9

[204] McLean, Marshall. <u>The Gutenberg Galaxy: The Making of Typographic Man.</u> University of Toronto Press, 1962.

[205] Remarque, Erich Maria. <u>All Quiet on the Western Front.</u> Little Brown & Company, 1929.

BIBLIOGRAPHY

Augarten, Stan. Bit by Bit an Illustrated History of Computers. New York: Houghton Mifflin, 1984.

Bennett, Dr. William J. The Book of Virtues. New York: Simon and Shuster, 1996.

Bennett, Dr. William J. The Death of Outrage: Bill Clinton and the Assault on American Ideals. New York: Simon and Shuster, 1998.

Black, Edwin. IBM and the Holocaust: The Strategic Alliance Between Nazi Germanyand America's Most Powerful Corporation. Three Rivers Press, 2002.

Burks, Alice R.; Arthur W. Burks (October 1981). "The ENIAC: First General-Purpose Electronic Computer". Annals of the History of Computing 3 (4): 310–399, 1981.

Burks, Alice R.; Arthur W. Burks. The First Electronic Computer: The Atanasoff Story. Ann Arbor, Michigan: The University of Michigan Press. 1988.

Burks, Alice. Who Invented the Computer? The Legal Battle That ChangedComputing History. Prometheus Books, 2003

Fraser, Stephen. The Bell Curve wars – Race, Intelligence and the Future of America.New York: Basic Books, 1995.

Friedman, Thomas L. The World Is Flat: A Brief History of the Twenty-first Century.Farrar, Straus and Giroux, 2005.

Fritz, Barkley W. ENIAC-A Problem Solver. Virginia Tech: Blackbird, 1994.

Gerstner, Louis V. Who Says Elephants Can't Dance? Inside IBM's Historic Turnaround. Collins Business, 2003.

Goldstine, Herman H. The Computer from Pascal to von Neumann. Princeton: Princeton University Press, 1972.

Greenspan, Alan. The Age of Turbulence: Adventures in a New World. Penguin Press, 2007.

Hally, Mike. Electronic Brains: Stories from the Dawn of the Computer Age. Granta Books, 2005.

Hofstadter, Douglas. Fluid Concepts & Creative Analogies: Computer Models of the Fundamental Mechanisms of Thought. New York: Basic Books, 1995.

Kellogg, Steven. Chicken Little. Harper Trophy, 1987.

Kidder, Tracy. The Soul of a New Machine. Back Bay Books, 2000.

Machiavelli, Nicolo. The Prince. 1515.

Mauchly, Kathleen R. John Mauchly's Early Years. American Federation of information Processing Societies, Inc., 1984.

McCartney, Scott. ENIAC: The Triumphs and Tragedies of the World's First Computer. New York: Walker Publishing Company, 1999.

McGraw-Hill. Information management: The dynamics of MIS. MDI Publications, 1968.

McGraw-Hill. Integrated Manufacturing Systems. McGraw-Hill, 1972.

McGraw-Hill. MIS Methodology. McGraw Hill, 1969

McLuhan, Marshall. The Gutenberg Galaxy: The Making of Typographic Man University of Toronto Press, 1962

Meyerson, Martin. Gladly Learn and Gladly Teach: Franklin and His Heirs at the University of Pennsylvania, 1740-1976. Camden, NJ: University of Pennsylvania Press, 1978.

Mollenhoff, Clark R. Atanasoff: Forgotten Father of the Computer. Iowa: Iowa State Press, 1988.

Morgenstern, Oskar, and John Von Neumann. Theory of Games and Economic Behavior. Princeton: Princeton University Press, 1949.

Penrose, Roger. The Emperor's New Mind: Concerning Computers, Minds, and the Laws of Physics. Penguin, 1991.

Perkins, David. Outsmarting IQ - The Emerging Science of Learnable Intelligence. New York: Free Press, 1995.

Prestowitz, Clyde. <u>Three Billion New Capitalists: The Great Shift of Wealth and Power to the East</u>. Basic Books, 2005.

Remarque, Erich Maria. <u>All Quiet on the Western Front.</u> Little Brown & Company, 1929.

Rheingold, Howard. <u>Tools for Thought: The History and Future of Mind-Expanding Technology</u>. 1985

Riley, Norton H. <u>The von Neumann Architecture of Computer Systems</u>. CA: CaliforniaState Polytechnic University, 2005.

Ritchie, David. <u>The Computer Pioneers: The Making of the Modern Computer</u>. New York: Simon & Schuster, 1986.

Rosen, Saul. <u>The Origins of Modern Computing</u>. *Computing Reviews*, Vol. 31, Number 9, September 1990.

Rosenberg, Jerry. <u>The Death of Privacy.</u> Random House, 1969.

Smiley, Jane. <u>The Man Who Invente the Computer: The Biography of John Atanasoff, Digital.</u> New York: Knopf Doubleday Publishing, 2010

Taylor, Edmond. <u>Fall of the Dynasties: Collapse of the Old Order 1905-1922.</u> Ed. John Gunther. London: Doubleday Co, 1963.

Toffler, Alvin, and Heidi Toffler. <u>Revolutionary Wealth: How It Will Be Created and How it Will Change Our Lives</u>. New York: Alfred A. Knopf, Inc, 2007.

Toynbee, Arnold. <u>A Study of History</u>. 1934-61.

ADDITIONAL READING

Copeland, Jack. <u>Colossus: The First Electronic Computer.</u> New York: Oxford University
    Press, 2006.

Hodges, Andrew and Douglas Hofstadter. <u>Alan Turing: The Enigma.</u> Walker Company, 2000.

Kennaley, Blair. <u>The Attack of ENIAC.</u> Booksurge Publishing, 2009.

Leavitt, David. <u>The Man Who Knew Too Much: Alan Turing and The Invention of the
    Computer.</u> New York: Atlas Books, 2006.

Lundstrom, David E. <u>A Few Good Men From UNIVAC (History of Computing).</u> The MIT
    Press, 1990.

Manes, Stephen. <u>Gates: How Microsoft's Mogul Reinvented an Industry and Made Himself
    the Richest Man in America.</u> New York: Touchstone, 2002.

Ornstein, Severo. <u>Computing in the Middle Ages: A View From the Trenches 1955-1983.</u>
    Authorhouse, 2002.

Petzold, Charles. <u>The Annotated Turing: A Guided Tour Through Alan Turing's Historic
    Paper on Computability and the Turing Machine.</u> Indianapolis: Wiley Publishers,
    2008.

Stern, Nancy B. <u>From ENIAC to UNIVAC: Appraisal of the Eckert-Mauchly
    Computers.</u> Digital Press, 1981.

About Dr. Rocco Leonard Martino

Dr. Rocco Leonard Martino himself was a contributor to many of the leading innovations that led
to the Cyber Age. An international authority on information systems, especially as directed to Global Finance, Dr. Martino has made contributions to space travel, artificial intelligence, electronic currency, network planning, cell phones, and the Internet. In his early career he worked with Sir Robert Watson Watt, the inventor of Radar, with Dr. Grace Murray Hopper, a leading figure in computer languages, and with Dr. John Mauchly, the co-inventor with J. Presper Eckert of ENIAC and of electronic computers. He was founder and CEO of XRT, the company that created global financial systems for many of the largest companies in the world. He served as Professor of Mathematics and of Systems Engineering at the University of Waterloo, and at New York University. The author of twenty published books, Dr. Martino holds many patents for telecommunications in the United States and abroad. He is currently the founder and CEO of CyberFone Technologies, and a Senior Fellow of the Foreign Policy Research Institute.

Further information may be found on Dr. Martino's website:

www.roccoleonardmartino.com

004 Mar   9-12
Martino, Rocco Leonard
People, machines and
politics of the cyber age
creation

WITHDRAWN

SIC

CPSIA information can be obtained at www.ICGtesting.com

265014BV00002B/1-50/P